RETAINING AFRICAN AMERICANS
IN HIGHER EDUCATION

RETAINING AFRICAN AMERICANS IN HIGHER EDUCATION

Challenging Paradigms for Retaining Students, Faculty and Administrators

Edited by Lee Jones

STERLING, VIRGINIA

Published in 2001 by

Stylus Publishing, LLC
22883 Quicksilver Drive
Sterling, Virginia 20166

Library of Congress Cataloging-in-Publication Data

Retaining African Americans in higher education : challenging paradigms for retaining students, faculty and administrators / edited by Lee Jones.—1st ed.
   p. cm.
  Includes bibliographical references and index.
  ISBN 1-57922-041-X (alk. paper)—
  ISBN 1-57922-042-8 (pbk. : alk. paper)
   1. Afro-American college students. 2. College attendance—
  United States. 3. College dropouts—United States—
  Prevention. I. Jones, Lee, 1965–

LC148.2 .R48 2001
378.1'982996073—dc21   00-067027

First edition, 2001
ISBN: hardcover 1-57922-041-X
ISBN: paperback 1-57922-042-8

Printed in the United States of America

All first editions printed on acid-free paper

10 9 8 7 6 5 4 3 2 1

CONTENTS

CONCLUSION

> The Hottest Places in Hell are Reserved for Those who, In Times of
> Great Moral Crisis, Maintain Their Neutrality.
> —Dante (1265–1321)

In a world preoccupied with outer appearances and organized hypocrisy, it is
truly no surprise that we have seen the demise of affirmative action in higher
education. I am not surprised, nor am I shocked over the Hopwood decision
in Texas, Proposition 209 in California, Proposition 200 in the state of Washington, and now the One Florida Initiative. Not only are attempts made to
ensure that affirmative action becomes a thing of the past, but America has
once again turned its back on the number one issue affecting this place we call
the home of the free—Equality! My question is free from what? Free from
whom? It is no secret that many in the academy truly believe that we have
reached a point of equity, equality, and justice in our hiring practices and
admission selections. As educational leaders, we are still forced to spend
countless hours debating the legitimacy of affirmative action programs.

The Challenges . . .

Recent attacks on affirmative action programs across the country have caused
many institutions in the academy to pause and ponder just how far they are
willing to stand up for equality in the workplace. Some institutions have completely eliminated plans to diversify the student body and the work environment, while others have waffled and become baffled about just what to do. Still
others have successfully involved themselves in what I call "Image Management"—strategically manipulating the image of the institutions to avoid public
criticism. Despite the fact that many reports and empirical studies have shown

that underrepresented communities have not been the major benefactors of affirmative action, there are those who occupy the walls of ivy who still believe that affirmative action is about quotas and hiring unqualified people and admitting students who should retain themselves. This cannot be further from the truth.

There have been many heated debates and much political fallout about what some consider separatist programs for students of color in higher education. Some of these debates have proven to be educationally and intellectually stimulating, whereas others have proven to be a mindless game of persistent ignorance and vicious politics aimed at maintaining the status quo.

Although affirmative action and ethnic and racial diversity are closely related, we need to understand that maintaining access for underrepresented communities is a prerequisite for addressing and ensuring a climate that is inviting and livable for all who have to coexist. There is no doubt that these are very delicate and sometimes dreaded issues to discuss. As a society, and certainly as educational enterprises, we must at least talk openly and freely about the reality of the changing demographics we are experiencing in this country. If there were ever a time to address these issues, the time is now and the place is in the academy.

As our nation grapples with the reality of the demographic shifts of its citizenry, we in higher education must be willing to take the lead to challenge overt and disguised attempts to take away the one thing that aims to provide ethnic diversity in our institutions. I would like to think that we were at a point in history where we can rely on the good will and ensure the consistency of Americans to make fair and equitable hiring and admissions decisions. We simply are not there.

The Choices

It is no longer acceptable for policy makers in higher education to pay lip service to the development of strong recruitment initiatives for underrepresented populations coupled with a strong campus climate where all students can matriculate and ultimately graduate. University recruitment and retention programs for underrepresented populations must have the unequivocal support of all policy makers if we hope to reap positive results. When racial and ethnic communities have to constantly fight over a small piece of the pie, and when we have to constantly debate over the need for strong recruitment and retention programs, we all lose. We can pay now or pay later! If the academy is to demonstrate its greatness, it must (we must) not participate in situational commitment! There is tremendous strength in achieving racial and ethnic diversity on our campuses. Maintaining complacency with minor adjustments in enrollments is dangerous. Hence, an image without substance is counterfeit. There are several choices higher education can make relative to the affirmative action attack:

- We can continue to breed mediocrity and wallow in chaos relative to these issues.

- We can separate the rhetoric from reality and accept that people come to universities with different hues, languages, and, yes, perhaps a non-European way of viewing the world.

- We can take bold nonpolitically correct steps to constantly challenge the status quo to ensure an environment for all people without asking them to check their ethnicity at the door.

The Solutions

As for the academy, we have many challenges and choices that confront us as they relate to retaining underrepresented students, faculty, and staff of color. The moral and ethical mandate for all of us, certainly for policy makers, is to manifest our commitment to justice, equity, and equality. We must first invest in educating ourselves to better understand racial and ethnic diversity beyond the rhetoric. We must allow ourselves to move to a point where we are willing to be personally challenged and to challenge systems designed to maintain the status quo. Simply put, universities must make difficult decisions during a time of racial polarization.

These decisions will serve to provide access to higher education for underrepresented students, become more intentional in diversifying every facet of the academy, and make personal choices to provide a climate that humanizes the environment. Achieving diversity is our greatest resource, and if we fail to recognize this we have all failed no matter what our individual successes. I know the capacity lies within each of us. Your (our) choice is to take the personal lead to make it happen. The goal of this book is to talk openly and candidly about some of the issues surrounding the retention of African Americans in higher education. The book also proposes to open dialogue by challenging traditional paradigms for retaining African-American students, administrators, and faculty at predominately whites colleges and universities. Finally, and perhaps most importantly, we seek to offer recommendations and strategies that will assist universities in their retention initiatives. In no way do we suggest that this book is inclusive of all of the traditional literature on retention.

The significance of this particular book, however, is that it is written about African Americans by African Americans.

The Content

The book is divided into three sections: Retaining African-American Students, Retaining African-American Administrators, and Retaining African-American Faculty. Part One addresses the issues confronting African-American students. Chapter 1 provides a broad overview and comparison of the enrollment and persistence rates of underrepresented students as compared to African-American students. The chapter also explores the major issues that affect African-American retention in higher education. The chapter concludes with some recommendations universities might pursue as they attempt to better retain African-American students on their campuses. Chapter 2 by Jason DeSousa provides a more detailed account of the educational pipeline. The chapter offers a fresh perspective on the participation and edge attainment levels of African-American students. Paul E. Green challenges us in Chapter 3 to review the policies and politics of retention and access for African-American students. He purports that universities must understand the larger issues affecting retention at the national, regional, state, and local levels. The challenge in retaining African-American students is to refrain from attempting to "fix the student." Rather universities must constantly examine issues for higher education as institutional commitment, review curriculum, support services, power relationships, and so forth. In Chapter 4 Eugene L. Anderson reviews the alternatives to race-based admission as he examines the X-percent plans in California, Texas, Washington, and Florida. He uses the theory of problem definition to show how the opponents of affirmative action gained a significant political advantage by defining the problem and its alternatives and how those who support diversity must define a new problem. Chapter 5 concludes Part One with concrete recommendations on developing African-American students into academic warriors. James L. Moore III postulates that there are factors to academic achievement that go beyond traditional predictive measures (e.g., high school grade point average, SAT scores, class rank, student commitment and persistence, etc). Moore provides concrete recommendations to assist administrators, faculty, and parents to empower African-American students to take responsibility for their own academic performance.

Part Two of this book focuses on strategies for retaining African-American administrators at predominately white universities. In Chapter 6 Jerlando F. L. Jackson starts with a review of literature on retaining African-American administrators. He develops a conceptual model for retention and provides a working definition of what it means to retain African-American administrators. In Chapter 7 Raphael M. Guillory provides strategies for overcoming the barriers of being an African-American administrator on a predominately white university campus. The barriers addressed are intended to assist administrators in overcoming and dealing with the crippling effects of institutional discrimination, organizational politics, limited access to upper management positions. J. W. Wiley focuses Chapter 8 on examining the miscommunication and mixed messages many African Americans receive from their employers. He strategically addresses the marginalization of administrators, why it happens, and how to prevent it from occurring. We conclude Part Two with reflective narratives written by Kipchoge N. Kirkland and Eddie Moore, Jr. Kirkland's narrative provides the reader with creative insights about what it means to be an African American in higher education who seeks to maintain the central importance of one's historical, contemporary, individual, and collective sense within a social academic setting. Eddie Moore's narrative provides a case study and records his personal experiences as an African-American administrator in a small white liberal arts college in Iowa.

Part Three speaks to the retention of African-American faculty. André J. Branch walks us through the ways to retain African-American faculty during a time of challenge for higher education. He includes strategies universities may employ to meet the challenges of retaining African-American faculty. Derrick P. Alridge in Chapter 10 takes on the task of addressing the positionality of the African-American academician in conducting and disseminating research on the black experience. He argues that the academy has traditionally set the parameters by which African Americans conduct research on the black experience. Shuaib Meacham continues in Chapter 11 by exploring academic environments that promote retention of African-American scholars in the academy. He purports that the logic that informs this chapter suggests that an environment that retains African-American faculty must support the cultural structure underlying its presence within the academy. Leon D. Caldwell coauthors with James B. Stewart a very informative chapter on "Rethinking W. E. B. DuBois' Double Consciousness: Implications for Retention and Self-preservation in the Academy." The chapter provides readers with a basic understanding of DuBois' perspectives on double consciousness. The authors discuss the implications of identity dynamics on retention and self-preservation for students, faculty, and administrators. The premise of Chapter 12 is that retaining African Americans is jeopardized when African Americans either enter the campus or conform to the institutional standard of disengaging from African culture. In Chapter 13 Lemuel W. Watson addresses the dreaded issues surrounding tenure for African-American faculty in higher education. He talks candidly about the politics of tenure and the promotion of African-American faculty.

Finally, the book concludes with the editor's chapter on preparing the university to achieve success for recruiting and retaining African Americans in higher education. The goal of this final chapter is to include concrete and tangible ideas that universities might consider as they prepare for retaining underrepresented students.

Acknowledgments

I give all Honor and Praise to God who is the ruler of the universe and the head of my life. We give full homage to our ancestors who, through their commitment to equality, have allowed us to stand proudly on the soils of America. To my mom and dad, thank you for continuing to teach through your spirits. I owe the positive substance of my life to you! To my family, mentors, friends, and colleagues I send a special thank you for putting up with me. I sincerely appreciate you and will continue to welcome your constant feedback as we all strive to bring out the best in our human potential.

Words will never be able to express my sincere gratitude to my graduate assistants, Ingee Lee, Issac Albert, and Wendy Wang, who have endured my requests during the process of developing this book. Their hard work, dedication, and enthusiasm added a great deal to the substance of this book. To Vontrell Randall, I am forever indebted to you for giving so much of your time while completing your degree. You will be an *excellent* teacher! The students with whom I interact at Florida State University give me constant reminders of why I decided to become a university professor and administrator. Please know that students help tremendously with retaining African-American faculty. I am very appreciative of the feedback and support from: Anna Green, Lekita Scott, Xavier Allen, Tony Anderson, Michael Coleman, Amanda Turner, Kamau Siwatu, Tom Hollins, Charles Osiris, John Wright, Lavon McNeal, James Dabney, Patrick Lee, Will Guzman, Phylissa Smith, Jamel Hodges, Michael Coleman, James Jackson, and countless others. I appreciate the intellectual capital of people such as Brenda Jarmon, Sandra Rackley, Dean Melvin Stith, Na'im Akbar, Freddie Grooms, Captain Scott, Brian Williams, Billy Close, Bill Jones, Dean Penny Ralston, Joy Bowen and other colleagues at FSU who continue to support my scholarship and my professional goals. I am very grateful for mentors such as James Scott King, Irving P. McPhail, Frank Hale, Jr., Jack Miller, Nancy Zimpher, Louis Castenell, Bill Harvey, Cheryl Fields, Adam Herbert, Joyce Breasure, Cynthia Dillard, and so many others. My administrative assistant Yvonne Weems and secretary Charlene Meeks played a significant role in keeping this project on task from start to finish. Without their meticulous work, we would not have completed this project. I send a sincere thank you to my administrative staff: Ken Tellis, Bruce Daniels, Edward Vertuno, Gwen Johnson, Stephen Mosier, Dannette Green, Alex Cohen, Sandra Martindale, Raishell Adams, and Pat Kitchens for holding everything together when things got a little busy. I appreciate each of you.

To all the brothers and sisters of the academy, thank you for lending us your ears and eyes. Each of you has made an indelible impact on higher education despite the many obstacles that confront us.

I appreciate the hard and diligent work of Jason DeSousa, Paul E. Green, Eugene L. Anderson, James L. Moore III, Jerlando F. L. Jackson, Raphael M. Guillory, J. W. Wiley, Kipchoge N. Kirkland, Eddie Moore, Jr., André J. Branch, Derrick P. Alridge, Shuaib Meacham, Leon D. Caldwell and James B. Stewart, and Lemuel W. Watson for making valuable contributions to this book. Without your chapters, this book simply would not be possible. It was a pleasure working with such thorough colleagues.

Thomas Rasheed, I send a personal thank you to you for taking the time from your *very busy* schedule to design the cover. The visual representation of the book's cover design has captured the reality of the revolving door for many African-American students, administrators, and faculty in higher education. Your work is as powerful as the written word. To Alexander Astin, Rick Turner, Mimi Wolverton, Barbara Mann, George Kuh, and Daryl Smith, thank you for meeting me half way and lending us your incredible reputations by endorsing this book. Your work on retention and higher education issues will continue to be the benchmark for many who study retention.

What can I say to John von Knorring, owner and publisher of Stylus Publishing? You have been a living example of what powerful things can happen when we allow other paradigms to coexist in the academy. Your support of this project began with the release of the other two books: *Brothers of the Academy* and *Sisters of the Academy*. Your commitment to other views, your genuine spirit, and your willingness to stand firm on your beliefs that all voices deserve a seat at the intellectual table made this book possible. I am very fortunate to work with a man of your caliber. I look forward to many more projects down the road.

Finally, to all who will read this important and timely book, I pray that the substance revealed throughout the pages will open your minds to yet another way of looking at how to retain African Americans in higher education. Additionally, I hope this book personally challenges you to become an integral part of the solution to what ails America: Race Relations! Remember that the bottom line is results and anything else is rhetoric! *Asante Sana* (Thank You)!

Lee Jones

PART ONE

RETAINING AFRICAN-
AMERICAN STUDENTS

I

CREATING AN AFFIRMING CULTURE TO RETAIN AFRICAN-AMERICAN STUDENTS DURING THE POSTAFFIRMATIVE ACTION ERA IN HIGHER EDUCATION

Lee Jones

The 1999-2000 seventeenth Annual Status Report on Minorities in Higher Education, released by the Office of Minorities in Higher Education of the American Council on Education (ACE), summarizes the most recent data available on key indicators of progress in American higher education. The report touches on a number of areas such as trends in high school, degrees conferred, and so forth, but for our scope of interest we reflect on college participation and educational attainment, college enrollment, and college graduation rates.

College Participation and Educational Attainment

The number of 18 to 24 year olds currently enrolled in colleges decreased during the 1980s but remained relatively unchanged at approximately 25 million during the 1990s. Since 1990, the number of white college-age youths has fluctuated slightly around 20 million, while the number of African American college-age youths increased by nearly 8 percent between 1977 and 1997 and

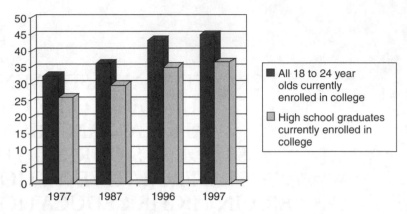

FIGURE 1.1   College participation rates of 18 to 24 year olds by high school completion status, 1977, 1987, 1996, and 1997.

by 3.7 percent in 1990. The Hispanic college population more than doubled during the past 20 years, in addition to a 31 percent increase during 1990. High school graduates ages 18 to 24 increased in 1997 as shown in Figure 1.1.

College participation rates for whites in 1997 had increased by more than 13 percentage points, whereas the African Americans' rates dropped during the 1980s with an increase of 10 percentage points during the past 10 years. Hispanics' 1997 college participation rate is significantly higher as indicated during the late 1970s and 1980s.

The number of African-American females registered at colleges varied from 36.4 percent in 1996 to 43.6 percent in 1997. The latter rate is the highest ever recorded by African-American women. Meanwhile, the participation rate of male African-American high school graduates remained constant between 1996 and 1997 at roughly 35 percent. It is worth mentioning that African Americans maintained the highest gender gap in college participation in 1997 in comparison with Hispanics and Native Americans.

Nationally, the proportion of adults, ages 25 to 29, who had completed four or more years of high school education was fairly constant during the past two decades. In 1997 more than 87 percent in this group had graduated from high school, which shows an increase of less than 2 percentage points over the 1988 rate of 85.7 percent (Figure 1.2). The percentage of African Americans and Hispanics with four or more years of high school was up slightly for 1997, while the corresponding percentage of whites remained constant.

Although African-American men in this group, ages 25 to 29, with four or more years of high school education decreased from 87.2 percent in 1996 to

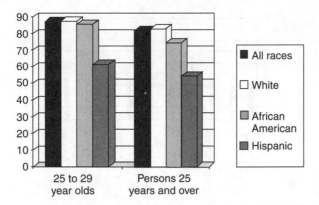

FIGURE 1.2   High school completion rates for 25
to 29 year olds and persons 25 years and over by
race and ethnicity, 1997.

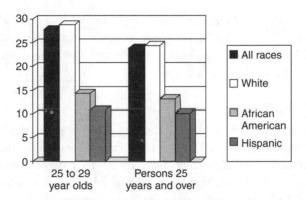

FIGURE 1.3   College completion rates for 25 to
29 year olds and persons 25 years and over by
race and ethnicity, 1997.

85.2 percent in 1997, there was an increase of nearly 4 percentage points since
1990. African-American women in this category increased by nearly 3 percentage points from 1996 to 1997 to 87.1—an increase of more than 5 percentage points since 1990.

According the Current Population Reports (CPS) of the U.S. Department
of Commerce, 27.8 percent of all young adults ages 25 to 29 held a bachelor's
degree or higher as of 1997. Approximately 29 percent of whites in this age
group held at least a baccalaureate degree in 1997, compared with 14.4 percent of African Americans and only 11 percent of Hispanics (Figure 1.3). The

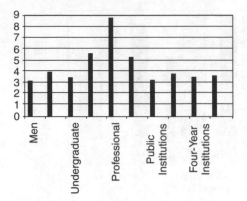

FIGURE 1.4   Changes in minority
enrollments by gender, degree level,
and type of institution, 1996 to 1997.

proportion of African-American men with at least a bachelor's degree
decreased slightly in 1997 to 12.1 percent, while the rate for women remained
unchanged at 16.4 percent. Consequently, African-American women indicated
a higher completion rate than men.

College Enrollment

Since the late 1980s, African Americans have shown great strides in college
attendance (Figure 1.4). From 1988 to 1997 their overall enrollment in higher
education increased to 57.2 percent, including a 16.1 percent increase during
the past five years. Conversely, the number of white student enrollments has
decreased by 3.1 percent, while total enrollment has increased by only 1.4 percent. Women of color increased by 4 percent from 1996 to 1997, while men
of color showed a 3.3 percent increase from 1996 to 1997.

Despite the enrollment gains at independent colleges and universities,
lower-cost public institutions enrolled the vast majority of African-American
students. Furthermore, African-American enrollment at historically black colleges and universities (HBCUs) continues to decrease compared with other
types of institutions. HBCUs enrolled 14.4 percent of all African Americans
attending U.S colleges and universities, down from 15 percent in 1996 and 17
percent in 1988 (Figure 1.5). Hispanic enrollment in higher education increased
79.2 percent from 1988 to 1997, which was the highest among the four major
ethnic groups. Asian-American enrollment increased 73 percent from 1988 to
1997, and American Indians achieved a 54 percent increase in college enrollment during the past decade, including a 3.6 gain from 1996 to 1997.

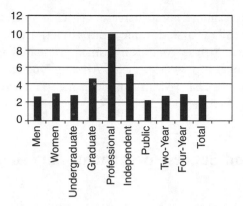

FIGURE 1.5   Changes in African-American enrollments by gender, degree level, and type of institution, 1996 to 1997.

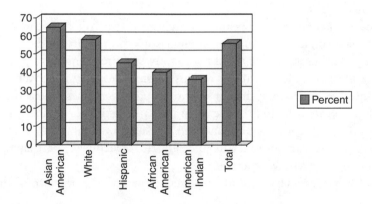

FIGURE 1.6   National Collegiate Athletic Association Division 1 Graduation Rates Report, 1998: Six-year graduation rates by race and ethnicity, 1997.

College Graduation Rates

Figure 1.6 shows that 65 percent of Asian-American students completing college had the highest graduation rate of all racial and ethnic groups. White students are second with 58 percent, trailed by Hispanics, African Americans, and American Indians. The six-year graduation rates for African Americans at Division I institutions increased from 38 percent in 1966 to 40 percent in

1997. With a 6 percentage point increase, African Americans exhibited the greatest progress of all racial and ethnic groups in terms of increasing their college graduation rate. African-American women graduated at a rate of 45 percent in 1997, compared to 34 percent for African-American men. The gap in college completion rates of African-American men and women is the largest among all racial and ethnic groups.

Persistence and Success of African-American Students: Critical Issues

A review of the literature is needed to determine critical issues affecting performance, persistence, and graduation rates of African-American students attending postsecondary institutions. The literature suggests that students' likelihood of remaining through graduation depends on the level of social and academic integration into college life. Social and academic integration depends on a number of cognitive and noncognitive factors shared by many African-American students.

A caveat is in order. For years, researchers have studied African-American students as a single entity, making comparisons to majority students as a single group. The more recent trend is to study specific ethnic groups and subgroups and then compare various groups to the majority group. Acknowledging the need to understand the expectations and experiences of specific groups and subgroups in order to propose programmatic institutional changes to meet their unique needs, we suggest that there are factors common to various ethnic groups across campus that can guide efforts to encourage participation and success in the university experience.

Student issues relevant to institutional climate that emerge from the literature are:

1. *The need to adjust to a new environment, a different value system and an intensified awareness of one's own ethnic minority status.*
   As underscored by recent research, college for most majority students is a continuation—the next logical, expected step in an established set of family and sociocultural values and traditions. For most African-American students, attending college represents disjunction—not a rite of passage into one's cultural traditions, but often a breaking away from family and cultural heritage. Research has only begun to examine the subtle effects of disjunction on the success of multicultural students as they separate from yet try to maintain connection with their cultural heritage and identity.

African-American students often bring to college a lack of understanding of the expected conventions of academic culture. Students are concerned about their academic preparation, yet they are often unaware of the skills needed to balance the multiple demands of the academic, social, cultural, and personal dimensions of their lives. In addition, conventional behavioral expectations of college classes (assertion, competition, and individualism) often conflict with the students' cultural norms and values. Self-doubt combined with issues of alienation enhances their sense of disjuncture, thus inhibiting the potential for success. Living on a predominantly white campus intensifies awareness of one's own ethnic difference. Differences in speech patterns, dress codes, and behavioral norms underscore the need to adopt to the novel—and sometimes bewildering—world of academe.

2. *The need to receive adequate financial aid.* The contribution to the successful persistence and graduation of African-American students of adequate amounts and types of financial aid cannot be overly stressed. Financial aid is often the primary consideration in making the decision to continue or leave. Students consider not only the amount awarded, but also the proportion of grant to loan aid. Burdensome loan debt creates stress that affects student success and satisfaction with the college experience. Anxiety as a result of financial stress becomes even more pronounced when added to the student's general feeling of alienation and dissatisfaction.

3. *The need to perceive the social and academic climate as inclusive and affirming.* The influence of the campus climate on the persistence of multicultural students at predominantly white institutions is replete in the literature. The research is consistent in pointing out that, for example, African-American students attending predominantly white campuses experience more stress, racism, and isolation and are less likely to persist than their counterparts at historically black colleges. Students' interaction with faculty, staff, majority peers, and the social environment of the campus affects attitude, behavior, and perceptions, thus enhancing or diminishing satisfaction, academic achievement, and persistence. Being a "Guest in Someone Else's House" (Sotello Viemes Turner, 1994) means being always on your best behavior and under scrutiny, having little or no history in the house—feeling that you do not belong. Feeling apart from the academic and social campus life is one of the main reasons multicultural students drop out.

In the classroom, students may find themselves isolated and ignored—except as examples of stereotypes from often well-intentioned faculty. Large classrooms are perceived as impersonal and intimidating. Students encounter curricula designed with a monocultural perspective and faculty who discount their cultural views as irrelevant and their ways of learning as inappropriate. Eurocentric curricula and traditional methods of teaching and testing imply one fixed truth and deny plurality of shifting interpretations based on different experiences. Classroom conversations dominated by majority students remind multicultural students of their guest status. If students do not succeed they are misunderstood as underprepared and unmotivated (Adams, 1992). Students know in which classes they will find a supportive atmosphere, a respect for cultural difference, high expectations, and positive role models.

The research also points to the positive influence of informal faculty-student interaction on the success of African-American students. With few African-American faculty as role models and mentors, multicultural students tend to have little interaction with faculty, reporting reticence toward approaching majority faculty.

Outside the classroom, African-American students note the proportion of faculty, administrators, and staff who are persons of color. They are keenly aware of whether enough African-American students are recruited to create a community to which they can belong, and whether there are accessible programs and services that support but do not stigmatize. They are sensitive to the climate in their classes, in the residence halls, as they walk down the mall, gather informally in the student union, and interact with their peers whether majority students or multicultural students.

African-American students' interactions with majority peers are often fraught with tension. A lack of familiarity with the background and expectations of African-American students account for infrequent socialization among students. Although the official message from the institution may be "yes, we want you as part of our academic community," the community of majority peers can appear unsupportive, placing the psychological well-being of the multicultural student in jeopardy (Wright, 1987).

4. *The need to establish long term goals, short term objectives, and a commitment to both.* Adjustment for success requires congruencies

between one's career plans, a selected academic program, and a realistic appraisal of one's own interests, strengths, and weaknesses. African-American students often share with majority students incongruence in long- and short-term goals and the ability to achieve them. However, incongruence between goals and realistic self-appraisal is particularly critical for the multicultural student whose models of careers or educational opportunities may be limited.

5. *Students' personal characteristics.* Student background characteristics that were found to correlate with successful achievement include family income level, educational level of parents, and the student's academic preparation. Positive self-image, self-esteem, and internal locus of control also influence students' successful experiences.

The relationship between family income, the educational level of parents, and student persistence is clear. A parent who herself has attended college and who is able to share in the experiences of her son or daughter attending college can provide invaluable psychological support and encouragement, offer informal suggestions on how to "work" the system, and may be able to ease the student's financial anxieties. Although the student's socioeconomic background may aid in the transition and adjustment, a hostile and unsupportive campus climate may place the student in psychological jeopardy and at risk academically.

More so than the second-generation African-American college student, the first-generation college student feels at odds with the expected conventions of the academic culture and the institutional climate if it is perceived as intimidating and threatening. Parents unable to assist their son or daughter financially contribute to the student's sense of uncertainty and anxiety.

For some nontraditional students the personal and academic transition requires a redefinition of self and values. The importance of the role of self-perception in the transition process is significant. Institutional practices, academic regulations, and policies may contribute to undermining students' perception of self and sense of being in control. An inclusive climate, faculty involvement, positive interaction with peers, classroom practices, and curricula that validate differences combine with a student's positive self-image and sense of being in control.

Rowser (1997) conducted a study of African-American students at predominately white institutions and found that more than 90 percent of the students surveyed perceived their academic preparation for college as adequate. More than one-third of students in the study expected to earn a 3.0 or greater grade point average during their first year in college, while more than 90 percent of the students expected to graduate in five years or less (Rowser, 1997).

Despite the positive expectations of the African-American students in the study, Rowser found the expectations of these students disturbing. She pointed out that research indicated that: (1) African-American students earn fewer credits than white students in their first year; (2) African-American students have poorer grades than whites throughout the college experience; and (3) African-American students will flunk out at a significantly higher rate than white students, or will be more likely to drop out during their first two semesters than white students (Rowser, 1997).

As a result of these findings, Rowser (1997) determined that the African-American students' expectations were "unrealistic" because less than 70 percent of the students had a 3.0 or better grade point average on entering college, yet 90 percent of the students expected a 3.0 or better. In addition, since African-American students often begin college in remedial courses, where credits do not apply toward graduation or major requirements, it would be difficult to graduate in four years, as 50 percent of the students in the study expected. The gap between student expectations and their outcomes alludes to another misperception of African-American students, that some students perceive the college experience as an extension of high school (McNairy, 1996).

In the article "The Challenge for Higher Education: Retaining Students of Color," McNairy (1996) indicates that inadequate high school preparation and inadequate study habits contribute to student attrition. Citing Crosson (1988), McNairy (1996) further elaborates that this lack of student preparation is reflected in the students' standard measures of academic performance in college, their overall performance, and retention rates. One reason for the lack of student preparation and inadequate study habits can be attributed to some students having attended high schools that lacked resources to properly prepare students and, as a consequence, to develop adequate study habits (McNairy, 1996).

In *Leaving College: Rethinking the Causes and Cures of Student Attrition,* Tinto (1987) discussed the concept of commitment with regard to attrition, categorizing it into two types: student and institutional. Tinto indicates that the higher a student's goal (educational or occupational), the higher the chances that a student is willing to work to attain that goal. Given this position, it must be noted that the level (whether high or low) and the clarity of a student's goals can positively or negatively impact student attrition. McNairy (1996) indicates that most students of color tend to be first-generation college students and generally have a generic goal: to obtain a good job. These students usually lack the best academic background and information that would allow them to select a lucrative field or even work through the system to achieve their goals (McNairy, 1996; Obiakor and Harris-Obiakor, 1997). This concept has a substantial connection to Tinto's (1987) idea, which indicates that an extended period of uncertainty in the student's intentions contributes to student departure.

Thus far I have attempted to highlight key concepts of student attrition as it relates to the student (i.e., student preparation, study habits, intentions and commitment, and goal-setting patterns). Any reason or combination of the reasons mentioned can impact a student's stay in college. However, student attrition is not solely a student problem, nor is it solely caused by students. Institutional factors have a tremendous influence on student attrition, which is the next factor I examine.

Causes of Attrition: Institutional Factors

Institutional factors that impact student attrition can be viewed in two categories: organizational policies and institutional or campus climate. Organizational policies extend throughout an entire college/university system, from student services and student affairs to academic areas and majors. McNairy (1996) highlighted financial aid as a difficult area given the students' unfamiliarity with financial-aid applications; and erroneous assumptions made by white financial-aid staff members; and family emergencies that may affect the financial status of the student. Love (1993) had similar findings with regard to black students' lack of information on financial aid but notes cutbacks in funding, the shift from grant assistance to more loan assistance, and an assurance by the institution to the students for continuous financial support. In another study of black student attrition at a large predominately white northwestern university, Sailes (1993) found that 45 percent of the participants in the study indicated that they received inadequate financial aid, while another 35 percent reported that they received no aid. Although the delivery of financial aid relies on sophisticated federal and state methodologies, it is one area of a vast number of areas that is crucial in determining student persistence and should be explored by institutions.

Campus or institutional climate is another area (and what I believe is a major area) that impacts student attrition. Love (1993) discusses the climate of most predominately white institutions, indicating that they were established under the law and/or practice that excluded black students (and other minorities), which was built into the structure and fabric of the institution. She further notes that there has been little discussion about white racism on campus and even denial. Throughout time we have seen racism manifested in student-student interactions, staff-student interactions, and faculty-student interactions. It can be overt or subtle. For example, low expectations by white faculty based on presumptions of lack of preparation, lack of ability, and prior disadvantage can block communication with students of color (Love, 1993). In addition, the ignorance of the cultures and contributions, as well as the lack of professional role models for students of color, all impact student retention (McNairy, 1996). This supports Tinto's (1987) theory that the lack of academic integration whether formal or informal can influence student departure.

As described in the causes of student attrition, both students and institutions are very much involved in the process. Students of color are completely responsible for their performance in school. However if they are placed in environments that are not welcoming (via organizational policies or the formal and informal interactions with other students, staff, and faculty), chances of these students feeling alienated can increase, consequently increasing student attrition rates.

The next section explores characteristics of effective retention models, and is followed by a discussion on quality in higher education, and how these strategies combined can positively influence student retention in the next millenium.

Characteristics of an Effective Retention Model

There are many strategies that can be incorporated to develop an effective retention model. Of these strategies, models should: (1) have the support of administration, by incorporating retention/diversity into the strategic plan of the university; (2) recruit faculty for participation; (3) provide motivational lectures; (4) provide proactive financial aid counseling; (5) get students involved with programming activities; (6) maintain up-to-date knowledge on retention issues; (7) regularly assess program effectiveness; (8) incorporate early assessment and intervention; (9) develop faculty mentoring; (10) develop leadership seminars; and (11) develop and maintain a caring and competent staff (Carreathers et al., 1996). Carreathers et al. (1996) highlight some or all of these characteristics in Texas A&M's Department of Multicultural Services, the University of Louisville's Center for Academic Achievement's Thriving and Surviving program, and the University of Texas at Austin's Preview Program. These three models were initiated and are supported by the leadership of their respective universities and/or governing bodies. Texas A&M's Department of Multicultural Services was initiated by the institution's Division of Student Services. The University of Louisville's Thriving and Surviving Program was mandated by the U.S. Office of Civil Rights. Lastly, the Preview Program at the University of Texas at Austin is a part of the Office of the Dean of Students. Parker (1997) and Madison (1993) both indicate the crucial need for an institutional leader to support such efforts.

Suggestions for retention models are infinite. However, other notable strategies include mentoring, peer advising, student leadership conferences, student skills workshops, and cultural events (Carreathers et al., 1996). Mallinckrodt and Sedlacek (1987) suggest policies to maximize use of athletic facilities and campus gyms; more union programming for specific groups; and use of areas such as libraries and career and counseling centers to also help retention. Lastly, Parker (1997) and Tinto (1987) provide suggestions that discuss retention from a systems perspective. Parker suggests: (1) the creation of positions dedicated to handling retention activities; (2) the recognition of the need for additional funding sources; (3) the establishment of mentoring programs for minority students—programs that help minorities to see successful staff and students who can show them a path to success and that give them the confidence and support they need; (4) the reorganization of faculty/staff duties and responsibilities to assist in retention activities, especially for institutions with limited resources; (5) the development of a reporting system for identification and tracking so that institutions can have accurate data and data-processing capabilities on the different facets of their programs; and (6) the development of faculty/staff training to better understand minority populations (Parker, 1997, p.120). Tinto (1987) indicates that: (1) institutions should ensure that the new students enter with or have the opportunity to acquire skills needed for academic success; (2) institutions should reach out to become more personal with students beyond the formal domain of academic life; (3) institutional retention actions should be systematic in character; (4) institutions should start as early as possible to retain students; (5) the primary commitment of institutions should be to their students; and (6) education not retention should be the goal of institutional retention programs.

A review of the characteristics of effective retention models demonstrates that there is no shortage in concepts or ideas to assist universities in retaining African-American students. However, even with the implementation of these models, African-American students continue to leave higher education without accomplishing degrees, which is cause for concern by the higher education community. The advent of the new millenium presents many new challenges for the higher education enterprise, particularly with regard to issues such as diversity, quality, accountability, and productivity. Minority populations continue to increase, while calls for accountability and productivity and the need to do more with less continue to haunt institutions. Because of these pressing issues, it is imperative that institutions consider new, or maybe not so much new, alternatives to address these concerns.

The next section examines two approaches that can, if properly applied to retention, improve retention, as well as improve quality in higher education.

Reframing African-American Student Retention with Total Quality Management (TQM) and the Learning Paradigm

Over the past decade, two trends have gained the attention of the higher education community: Total Quality Management (TQM) and the Learning Paradigm. Bryan (1996, p. 5) defines TQM as:

> A comprehensive philosophy of operation in which community members (1) are committed to CQI [Continuous Quality Improvement] and to a common campus vision, set of values, attitudes, and principles; (2) understand that campus processes need constant review to improve services to customers; (3) believe the work of each community member is vital to customer satisfaction; and (4) value input from customers.

Two key elements of TQM are improvement and customer orientation (Melan, 1993). Along with these elements, establishing a mission and vision are significant to TQM, as well as systematic analysis or assessment, participation, and viewing the university as a system (Lozier, 1993). TQM's focus on processes, improvement, and saving costs is what attracts higher education particularly when legislators, trustees, and industry demand accountability and productivity (McDaniel, 1994). While TQM has experienced some success in student affairs administration, it has yet to be accepted in the academic arena. However, the Learning Paradigm offers a transformation in pedagogy, with hints of quality and TQM.

The Learning Paradigm offers a complete change in teaching as we know it. Barr and Tagg (1995) note a change in instruction that will create environments and experiences that allow students to discover and construct knowledge for themselves. As opposed to teachers simply providing lectures, professors will now coach, counsel, and collaborate with students during the learning process (McDaniel, 1994; Barr & Tagg, 1995). Because funding for the Learning Paradigm will be outcome-based, Barr & Tagg (1995) indicate that it will save money. At the same time they purport that the Learning Paradigm will promote success for diverse students as opposed to simply access. Overall, the learning paradigm presents several similarities to TQM because of continuous improvement through teaching methods, student roles changing to that of a teammate in the learning process, and the quality and accountability aspects since students will be responsible for their own learning.

In its application to the retention of African-American students, TQM and the Learning Paradigm appear to offer bright prospects. TQM examines entire processes and how they relate to one another; therefore, it would view retention models as a system within the university, as Tinto (1987) suggested in one of his six principles. The assessment/systems analysis aspects of TQM would consider any deviations from that of the stated mission and goals and allow for continuous improvement. Another aspect that is appealing to retention of African-American students is the customer orientation of TQM. TQM allows for feedback from customers, thereby giving a voice to African-American students in colleges and universities. In addition, if universities view African-American students as customers, an inherent reliance on these students intellectually, culturally, and financially by colleges and universities will develop as a means for survival. In its application to retention models, the primary benefit of the Learning Paradigm is the increased interaction between the student and the teacher. The fact that students and teachers will collaborate in the learning process will allow students to establish a rapport with faculty who would otherwise not have interacted with them as much. According to Tinto (1987), academic integration both formally and informally increases the likelihood that a student would remain in school. Of course, the collaboration of African-American students with white faculty does not remove any stereotypes, preconceived notions, or even racist acts by some faculty. However the clear and continuous statement of the institution's mission by leadership and a visible display of commitment to diversity could reshape the behavior, beliefs, and culture of some racist faculty and staff in institutions.

Recommendations for Improved Retention Programs

In order to improve African-American student retention in higher education, it is apparent that institutions must do more. Not only does retention require the design of elaborate models that include mentoring, financial incentives, and other support services for students, but also leadership and faculty must become and remain involved beyond what they have been in the past. Some recommendations that leaders in higher education institutions should follow in order to achieve improvement in the retention of African-American students are:

- Leadership in both the academic and administrative realms must establish clear missions and strategic plans. They must also support diversity initiatives and make themselves visible in efforts to retain African-American students (Howard, 1996). Leaders must also know how to identify relevant research and data to implement change in processes as well as organizational culture (Kinnick & Ricks, 1993).

- Assessment must be used in administration and the classroom to continuously improve quality and initiate change (Gray, 1997).

- Faculty must be encouraged to participate in retention efforts, which include establishing formal and informal relationships with students. Nonblack faculty should also become involved in retention efforts such as mentoring (Kobrak, 1992).

- Administrative units such as student service areas and academic areas should implement quality improvement teams (Holmes, 1996).

- Students should be viewed as customers in both the classroom and student service areas.

- African-American and other diverse faculty and staff should be hired.

- Zero tolerance policies for racism should be established on college campuses (Madison, 1993).

- Faculty and staff should be continuously trained on multiculturalism and professional topics.

- African-American student involvement should be encouraged in campus activities and in the use of campus facilities and services.

- The institution should be viewed as an entire system by which everyone has a role in the education of students.

If institutions consider these concepts, improvement in not only the retention of African-American students can be achieved, but also the retention of other diverse groups.

Conclusion

Over the years African-American students have increasingly enrolled in predominantly white institutions. However, despite their growing numbers, African-American students have left predominantly white institutions without bachelor degrees in disproportionate numbers. Part of the reason for the early departures from school result from inadequate preparation by the students, inadequate study habits, poor goal setting, and a lack of commitment by the student. However, research indicates that a large part of these departures (which include the students' lack of commitment) is because of the poor institutional climates and instances of racism. Faculty plays a large role in the perpetuation of these environments, in addition to retention models, which have not been maximized in terms of their potential. TQM and the Learning Paradigm are the latest trends in higher education. They both focus on quality, continuous improvement and assessment, and teamwork. Other aspects of TQM include strategic planning, clear goals and mission, and accountability. Leadership plays an important role in implementing these models. If leadership were successful in implementing these models, along with demonstrating a strong commitment to diversity, institutions would improve retention for African-American students tremendously.

References

Adams, F. T. (1992). *Putting democracy to work: A practical guide for starting and managing worker-owned businesses.* San Francisco: Berrett-Koehler Publishers.

Barr, R. B., & Tagg, J. (1995). From teaching to learning: A new paradigm for undergraduate education. *Change* (November-December):13–25.

Bryan, W. A. (1996). What is quality management? *New Directions for Student Services* 76:3–15.

Carreathers, K. R., Beekmann, L., Coatie, R. M. & Nelson, W. L. (1996). Three exemplary retention programs. *New Directions for Student Services* 74:35–52.

Crosson, P. (1988). Four-year college and university environments for minority degree achievement. *Review of Higher Education* 11(4):365–382.

Gray, P. J. (1997). Viewing assessment as an innovation: Leadership and the change process. *New Directions for Higher Education* 100:5–15.

Holmes, A. B. (1996). *Ethics in higher education: Case studies for regents.* Norman: University of Oklahoma Press.

Howard, N. L. (1996). Pros and cons of TQM for student affairs. *New Directions for Student Services* 76:17–31.

Kinnick, M. K., & Ricks, M. F. (1993). Student retention: Moving from numbers to action. *Research in Higher Education* 34(1):55–69.

Kobrak, P. (1992). Black student retention in predominantly white regional universities: The politics of faculty involvement. *Journal of Negro Education* 61(4):509–530.

Love, B. J. (1993). Issues and problems in the retention of black students in predominantly white institutions of higher education. *Equity and Excellence in Education* 26(1):27–36.

Lozier, G. G. (1993). *Pursuit of quality in higher education: Case studies in total quality management.* San Francisco: Jossey-Bass Press.

Madison, E. (1993). Managing diversity: Strategies for change. *CUPA Journal* 44(4):23–27.

McDaniel, T. R. (1994). College classrooms of the future: Megatrends to paradigm shifts. *College Teaching* 42(1):27–31.

McNairy, F. G. (1996). The challenge for higher education: Retaining students of color. *New Directions for Student Services* 74:3–14.

Mallinckrodt, V., & Sedlacek, W. (1987). Student retention and the use of campus facilities by race. *NASPA Journal* 24(3):28–32.

Melan, E. H. (1993). Quality improvement in higher education: TQM in administrative functions. *CUPA Journal* 44:7–8, 10, 12, 14–18.

Obiakor, F. E., & Harris-Obiakor, P. (1997). *Retention models for minority college students.* (Report No. HE 030 081) Emporia, KS: Research and Creativity Forum. (ERIC Document Reproduction Service No. ED 406 907).

Parker, C. E. (1997, February 20). Making retention work. *Black Issues in Higher Education* 13(26):120.

Rowser, J. F. (1997). Do African American students' perceptions of their needs have implications for retention? *Journal of Black Studies* 27(5):718-726.

Sailes, G. A. (1993). An investigation of black student attrition at a large, predominately white, Midwestern university. *Western Journal of Black Studies* 17(4):179–182.

Tinto, V. (1987). *Leaving college: Rethinking the causes and cures of student attrition.* Chicago: University of Chicago Press.

Turner, C.S.V. (1994). Guest in someone else's house: Students of color. *Review of Higher Education* 16:355–370.

Wright, P. L. (1987). *Organization theory: Readings and cases.* Englewood Cliffs, N.J.: Prentice-Hall.

2

REEXAMINING THE EDUCATIONAL PIPELINE FOR AFRICAN-AMERICAN STUDENTS

Jason DeSousa

The complexion of American higher education is not what it once was. It has undergone profound demographic changes that have been influenced by dramatic shifts in the racial/ethnic, age, and socioeconomic composition of society. Historically, the earliest American institutions of higher education were established to educate civic and religious leaders (Brubacher, 1977; Cross, 1971; Godbold, 1944; Kuh, in press; Rudolph, 1962). Most of those collegians were the ages of today's high school students (Dannells, 1997). "For most of its history American higher education, despite its much vaunted land grant colleges, was not a very democratic enterprise. If [one] were poor, black, Spanish-speaking, native American Indian, female, or physically handicapped, [one's] chances of participating in it equally . . . were extremely limited" (Pifer, 1978, p. 2).

Today, colleges and universities are more racially/ethnically diverse than ever before, although nearly all institutions of higher education seek still greater levels of diversity. Changes in the composition of gender and older students have also changed the complexion of colleges and universities. More women than men are enrolled in colleges and universities in the United States, a trend that reversed itself between 1976 and 1986 (Kuh, 1990). In fact, women accounted for more than 75 percent of the 3.5 million new students during the 1970s (Mortenson, 1998, cited in Kuh, in press). Currently, because of the expanding ratio of women to men on college and university campuses, enrollment managers and other higher education officials are seeking ways to increase the college-going rate for men (Kuh, in press). Another noticeable change is the increased presence of adult learners. During American higher education's early history, the principle of *in loco parentis,* whereby institutional officials acted in place of students' parents, guided institutional practice. In short, parents sent their sons and daughters to colleges and universities under the surrogate watch of faculty and staff. Today, even if *in loco parentis* were practiced (which it is not), there is a greater likelihood than ever before that students will be enrolled alongside their parents. As Burr, Burr, & Novak (1999, p. 242) suggested, "One could argue that the traditional student profile is a slowly melting ice cube, gradually being replaced by an older student base, assuming that an institution views all of the population as a potential market rather than limiting itself to the eighteen to twenty-four age group."

Moreover, as a result of federal government intervention, several historic court decisions, and changing social values (in addition to the clandestine or sparsely funded educational institutions that African Americans had to create), access for African Americans and other minority groups to higher education improved dramatically. Although the typical college student tends to be white and from a relatively advantaged family background (Brown, 1996), higher education is indeed a more diverse enterprise, with a shift toward a growing presence of more minority students (Levine & Cureton, 1998). Never before have college students been able to benefit from the rich array that diversity brings to the educational experience. Despite the progress of access for most underrepresented groups, retaining students of color, particularly African Americans, remains a major challenge for American higher education. In essence, the educational pipeline is now far reaching, but it continues to have troublesome leaks for African-American students.

The Reach of the Educational Pipeline: The Level of Participation of African Americans in Higher Education

The Bureau of Census projects that between 1996 and 2020 the U.S. population will increase from about 265 million to approximately 325 million, a 2.5 million annual increase taking into account deaths and in-migration during this period (Burr, Burr, & Novak, 1999). Within this period, demographers and scholars anticipate that other demographic changes will occur (e.g., family income, median age of population, parents' educational background), shifts that will influence the workforce, education, and ultimately the economy. In terms of education, for example, a 10 percent increase in the number of new high school graduates is expected during the first decade of the 21st century (Kuh, in press). The growth in high school graduates will be largely attributable to increases in native-born and immigrant minority students entering the educational system (Burr, Burr, & Novak, 1999). Furthermore, in many states, the minority college-age population (i.e., 15–24 year olds) is projected to increase. For instance, in Maryland a 39 percent increase is expected in the minority college-age population between 1995 and 2010 (Maryland Southern Education Foundation Leadership Group, 1999).

At the present time, the U.S. Census Bureau estimates that African Americans, Hispanics, American Indians, and Alaska Natives comprise about 28.5 percent of the U.S. population. By 2020, these minority groups will constitute one-third of the U.S. population (Marshall & Glover, 1996). Looking beyond this period, Marshall and Glover (1996) suggest that by approximately 2080, these groups could possibly no longer be referred to as minority, as their collective growth will surpass that of the non-Hispanic white population. There is already evidence that this is occurring rapidly in certain U.S. geographic locations.

Participation Levels

Unlike the 1970s and 1980s, the 1990s were a period of dramatic growth in the number of African Americans participating in higher education. According to the National Center for Education Statistics (1999), between 1991 and 1997, the number of African Americans enrolled in higher education increased from 1.3 million to 1.5 million, a gain of 16.2 percent. Other underrepresented racial/ethnic groups in higher education (i.e., Asian Americans, Hispanics, Native Americans) experienced gains during the same time period. In fact, gains made by these groups were more dramatic than they were for African Americans (see Table 2.1). In particular, between 1991 and 1997, the participation rates of Hispanic students were the largest of all racial/ethnic groups (40.5%), followed by Asian Americans (34.8%), and American Indians (24.5%). During the same period, whites experienced a 6.5 percent decrease in their level of participation in higher education.

Gender Differences   African-American women have outpaced their male counterparts in the level of participation in American higher education. As Table 2.2 shows, between 1991 and 1997, the number of African-American

Table 2.1 Total Enrollment in Higher Education by Race/Ethnicity, 1991 to 1997

Race/Ethnicity	1991	1992	1993	1994	1995	1996	1997	Change (%)
				(Numbers in Thousands)				
Whites	10,990	10,875	10,600	10,427	10,311	10,264	10,266	-6.5
African Americans	1,335	1,393	1,413	1,449	1,474	1,506	1,551	16.2
Hispanics	867	955	989	1,046	1,093	1,166	1,218	40.5
Asian Americans	637	697	724	774	797	828	859	34.8
American Indians	114	119	122	127	131	138	142	24.6
Nonresident Aliens	416	448	457	457	454	466	465	11.8
Total	14,359	14,487	14,305	14,280	14,260	14,368	14,501	1.0

Source: Adapted from the National Center for Education Statistics, U.S. Department of Education. (1999). Enrollment in Higher Education. Washington, D.C. as cited in D. J. Wilds (2000). *Minorities in Higher Education, 1999–2000: Seventeenth Annual Status Report,* Washington, D.C.: American Council on Education.

Note: 1990 data were excluded from the Seventeenth Annual Status Report; therefore, such data are not presented in this table.

women participating in college increased by 18.7 percent. This compared to a 12.2 percent increase for African-American men during the same period.

Participation Levels at Public and Independent Institutions   There are striking differences between the number of African-American students participating in public and independent institutions, with such students being enrolled in the former type of colleges and universities in greater levels. As shown in Table 2.2, slightly more than one million African Americans have been enrolled in public institutions in each year from 1991 to 1997, with a record high 1.2 million in 1997. In comparison, African-American students have an average participation level of 309,000 in independent colleges and universities during the same period. However, during this seven-year period, the number of African Americans participating in independent institutions increased by 22.7, as compared to a 14.4 percent increase at public institutions of higher education.

Two-Year Versus Four-Year Institutions   During the past few decades, African Americans have been purported to be disproportionately enrolled in community colleges (Justiz, 1994; King, 1999; Wilson, 1994). The most recent data from the National Center for Education Statistics (1999) reveal otherwise. African-American student enrollment in four-year institutions is at a peak, with almost 900,000 African-American students enrolled in such colleges and universities (see Table 2.2). Furthermore, between 1991 and 1997, the number of African Americans enrolled in four-year institutions increased from approximately 758,000 to 896,000, a gain of 18.2 percent. Conversely, while enrollment among African Americans in two-year institutions increased from approximately 577,000 to 655,000 (a 13.5% gain), at no time between 1991 and 1997 were more African Americans enrolled in two-year than in four-year institutions. For comparison purposes, between 1991 and 1997, the level of participation in four-year institutions of higher education of American Indians, Asian Americans, and Hispanics also increased (41.2%, 38.4%, and 36.2%, respectively). Whites, however, experienced a 4.34 percent decrease during the same period. With regard to two-year institutions, a similar pattern emerged. The number of American Indians, Asian Americans, and Hispanics participating in two-year institutions increased (12.7%, 33.2%, and 42.3%, respectively), whereas the number of whites enrolling in such institutions decreased by 10.2 percent.

There appears to be a little known caveat about participation levels of African Americans in two-year versus four-year institutions. As shown in Table 2.3, when comparing their enrollment levels in historically black institutions (HBIs), predominantly white institutions (PWIs), and community

Table 2.2 Participation Levels of African Americans in Higher Education by Gender, Institutional Control, and Institutional Type, 1991–1997

	1991	1992	1993	1994	1995	1996	1997	Change (%)
				(Numbers in Thousands)				
Gender								
Men	517	537	540	550	556	564	580	12.2
Women	818	856	873	899	918	942	971	18.7
Total	1,335	1,393	1,413	1,449	1,474	1,506	1,551	
Institutional Control								
Public	1,053	1,101	1,114	1,145	1,161	1,178	1,205	14.4
Independent	282	292	299	304	313	328	346	22.7
Total	1,335	1,393	1,413	1,449	1,474	1,506	1,551	
Institutional Type								
Four-Year	758	791	814	834	852	870	896	18.2
Two-Year	577	602	599	615	622	636	655	13.5
Total	1,335	1,393	1,413	1,449	1,474	1,506	1,551	

Source: Adapted from National Center for Education Statistics, U. S. Department of Education. (1999). Enrollment in Higher Education. Washington, D.C. as cited in D. J. Wilds (2000). *Minorities in Higher Education, 1999–2000: Seventeenth Annual Status Report.* Washington, D.C.: American Council on Education.
Note: 1990 data were excluded from the Seventeenth Annual Status Report; therefore, such data are not presented in this table.

Table 2.3 Participation Levels of African Americans in Higher Education by Institutional Type, 1991–1997

Institution Type	1991	1992	1993	1994	1995	1996	1997
HBIs	213,904	224,946	230,078	229,046	230,279	225,886	223,898
PWIs	543,096	566,054	583,922	604,954	622,721	644,114	672,106
Community Colleges	578,000	602,000	599,000	615,000	621,000	636,000	655,000
Total	1,335,000	1,393,000	1,413,000	1,449,000	1,474,000	1,506,000	1,551,004

Source: Adapted from National Center for Education Statistics, U. S. Department of Education. (1999). Enrollment in Higher Education. Washington, D.C. as cited in D. J. Wilds (2000). Minorities in Higher Education, 1999–2000: Seventeenth Annual Status Report. Washington, D.C.: American Council on Education.

Note: 1990 data were excluded from the Seventeenth Annual Status Report; therefore, such data are not presented in this table.

colleges, the latter has tended to be the type of institution where African Americans had slightly higher participation levels from 1991 to 1994. This trend changed in 1995, when there were more African Americans enrolled in PWIs (622,721) than in two-year (621,000) and in HBIs (230,279). The same trend continued for 1996 and 1997. Recall, however, that when HBIs and PWIs are combined to form four-year institutions, the vast majority of African Americans are enrolled in four-year colleges and universities rather than in two-year institutions.

Enrollment by States   In their *Fall Enrollment Survey* 1997 report, the National Center for Education Statistics (NCES), Integrated Postsecondary Education Data System (1997) provides insight into enrollment by states. These data, however, do not take into account the overall racial/ethnic composition of each state. Although it is beyond the scope of this chapter to examine whether or not the participation levels of African-American students lag behind or exceed their population within each state, comparing state ethnic composition to college and university enrollment is insightful. For example, in South Carolina African Americans represented 36.1 percent of the 18- to 24-year-old population but less than 20.2 percent of first-time, full-time freshmen enrolled in the state's institutions of higher education (Southern Education Foundation, 1999).

As Figure 2.1 illustrates, California, New York, and Texas enrolled the largest numbers of African-American students in "all degree-granting" institutions, which includes both two- and four-year colleges and universities. In descending order, this pattern is followed by Illinois, Florida, and Georgia. The states with the fewest number of African Americans in degree-granting institutions in 1997 were Montana (158), South Dakota (275), Wyoming (275), North Dakota (340), Idaho (406), and Vermont (413). (These states are not depicted on any of the figures.)

By comparison, enrollment in degree-granting, public four-year institutions provides a different picture of the states in which African-American students are enrolled in large numbers (see Figure 2.1). California no longer ranks among the top three; instead, Louisiana joins New York and Texas as the three states in particular that enroll a large number of African-American students in public, four-year institutions. In descending order, this pattern is followed by Georgia, California, and North Carolina. With regard to degree-granting, public two-year institutions, New York, California, and Texas enrolled the largest numbers of African-American students, with New York enrolling the lion's share of these students (see Figure 2.2). This group is followed by Illinois, Florida, and North Carolina.

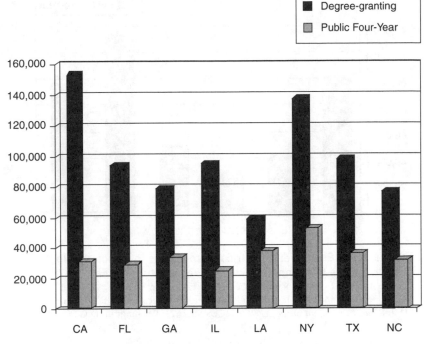

FIGURE 2.1   Enrollment of African Americans in Title IV-eligible all-
degree granting and degree-granting public four-year institutions by
selected states, Fall 1997.
Source: Adapted from the National Center for Education Statistics, U.S. Department of
Education, Integrated Postsecondary Education Data System. (1997). *Fall Enrollment
Survey, 1997* (NCES 99-162). Washington, D.C.: GPO.

There are few differences in enrollment by state among other racial/ethnic
groups in "all degree-granting" institutions. California's colleges and universities enrolled the highest number of all racial/ethnic groups. New York and
Texas ranked second and third, respectively, among all racial/ethnic groups
with the exception of Hispanics. For Hispanics, Texas ranked number two and
New York three in 1997 in the proportion of such students enrolled in degree-
granting institutions.

Historically Black Institutions   In general, the 1990s were a decade of
growth in student enrollment at HBIs. As Table 2.4 reveals, between 1991 and
1997, total student enrollment at HBIs increased from 257,006 to 273,752, a
6.5 percent increase. During this period, the most noticeable increases in
enrollment were not among African Americans, but were among Asian Americans and American Indians, though their actual numbers are small and they

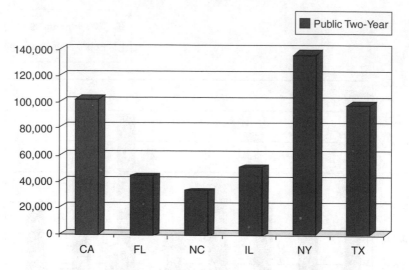

FIGURE 2.2   Enrollment of African Americans in selected Title IV-eligible degree-granting, public two-year institutions, Fall 1997.
Source: Adapted from the National Center for Education Statistics, U.S. Department of Education, Integrated Postsecondary Education Data System. (1997). *Fall Enrollment Survey, 1997* (NCES 99-162). Washington, D.C.: GPO.

are dispersed among the nation's 105 historically black colleges and universities, which may make it difficult to notice their increasing presence. These groups are followed by Hispanic and white students. There was a substantial decrease (22.6%) among nonresident aliens enrolled in HBIs during the same 1991 to 1997 period.

Perhaps more interesting are the changes that occurred from 1995 to 1997: While the participation levels for African-American (and white) students decreased, there were increases among American Indians and Asian Americans, with the latter ethnic group doubling their level of participation during this period. The Hispanic and nonresident alien student participation levels also increased in 1996, but decreased the following year.

With regard to gender differences among African Americans at HBIs between 1991 and 1997, the number of women participating in college was higher than it was for men. In fact, while African-American men made steady increases in their participation levels in HBIs from 1991 to 1993, from 1994 to 1997 the level decreased by 5 percent. The decrease for women (0.4%) was not as sharp as it was for men.

Finally, the comparison in growth rates between public and independent HBIs is striking. While African-American students participate in public HBIs in large numbers, larger growth rates have been occurring at independent

Table 2.4 Participation Levels in Historically Black Institutions by Race/Ethnicity, 1991–1997

Race/Ethnicity	1991	1992	1993	1994	1995	1996	1997	Change (%)
African American	213,904	224,946	230,078	229,046	230,279	225,886	223,898	54.7
American Indian	388	447	518	586	598	622	748	92.8
Asian American	2,009	2,151	2,357	2,374	2,251	2,520	5,671	182.3
Hispanic	2,131	4,755	5,021	5,186	5,105	5,593	2,421	13.6
Nonresident Alien	7,489	7,360	6,757	6,262	5,985	6,340	5,793	-22.6
White	31,085	36,203	37,375	36,045	38,936	37,013	35,224	13.3
Total	257,006	275,862	282,106	279,499	283,154	277,974	273,752	6.5

Source: Adapted from the National Center for Education Statistics, U.S. Department of Education. (1999). Enrollment in Higher Education. Washington, D.C. as cited in D. J. Wilds (2000). *Minorities in Higher Education, 1999–2000: Seventeenth Annual Status Report,* Washington, D.C.: American Council on Education.

Note: 1990 data were excluded from the Seventeenth Annual Status Report; therefore, such data are not presented in this table.

HBIs. As presented in Table 2.5, between 1991 and 1997 public HBIs experienced a 1.1 percent increase in the participation levels of African Americans. In comparison, independent HBIs enjoyed a 13.2 percent increase in the participation levels of such students.

Cracks in the Pipeline: Graduation Levels for African Americans

The data that has emerged from the 1990s demonstrate that African-American students have made much-needed progress in their participation in higher education, although much more progress is needed. Moreover, important demographic data (e.g., increases in the U.S. population and in high school graduation and college-going rates) offers tremendous promise for the educational plight of African Americans. That said, the next challenge for college and university officials and others is to better improve the degree attainment or graduation rates of African-American students. While some evidence suggests that improvements have been made in this regard, more must be done to address the disparate persistence levels between African Americans and other racial/ethnic groups.

Degree Attainment Levels

Two recent, major studies shed new insights on graduation levels for African Americans in particular and for students generally. Firstly, the National Collegiate Athletic Association's *Division I Graduation Rates Reports* (1999) is discussed. Secondly, a study by Astin, Tsui, & Avalos (1996) entitled *Degree Attainment Rates at American Colleges and Universities: Effects of Race, Gender, and Institutional Type* is examined briefly.

Six-Year Graduation Levels   To compare athlete students and nonathlete students, the National Collegiate Athletic Association (NCAA) collects and analyzes six-year college graduation levels. (It is beyond the scope of this chapter to make such comparisons between these student groups; therefore, graduation levels are examined broadly.) The study is limited in that it only samples NCAA Division I institutions, which ranged from 298 to 308 colleges and universities from 1992 to 1997, the reporting periods of the data.

In general, from 1992 to 1997, the six-year completion rate for African-American students increased (see Table 2.6). In particular, between 1992 and 1997, the graduation levels for African Americans increased from 34 percent to 40 percent, a 6 percent increase. Nevertheless, the fact that only 40 percent (which was the highest level in both 1995 and 1997) of African Americans graduated in six-years clearly demonstrates that the educational pipeline is in

Table 2.5 Participation Levels of African Americans in Historically Black Institutions by Gender and Institutional Control, 1991–1997

	1991	1992	1993	1994	1995	1996	1997	Change (%)
Gender								
Men	85,713	90,831	92,397	91,667	91,546	88,896	87,097	1.6%
Women	128,191	134,115	137,681	137,379	138,733	136,990	136,798	6.7%
Total	213,904	224,946	230,078	229,046	230,279	225,886	223,895	
Institutional Control								
Public	150,707	156,623	159,581	158,888	159,492	156,111	152,362	1.1%
Independent	63,197	68,323	70,497	70,158	70,787	69,775	71,533	13.2%
Total	213,904	224,946	230,078	229,046	230,279	225,886	223,895	

Source: Adapted from National Association for Equal Opportunity Research Institute. (1999). *Annual Fall Enrollment Surveys, 1987–1997*. Washington, D.C.: National Association for Equal Opportunity Research Institute.

Table 2.6 African-American Students' Six-Year Graduation Rates at NCAA Institutions, 1992–1997

	1992 (N=298) (%)	1993 (N=301) (%)	1994 (N=302) (%)	1995 (N=305) (%)	1996 (N=306) (%)	1997 (N=308) (%)	Change (%)
All Institutions	36	34	37	38	40	38	406
Gender							
Women	36	41	41	43	42	45	9
Men	30	33	34	35	33	34	4
Institutional Control							
Public	31	34	36	37	35	38	7
Independent	52	56	51	49	51	52	0

Source: Adapted from National Collegiate Athletic Association. (1999). *Division I Graduation Rates Reports, 1991–92, 1992–93,* and *1993* through *1997* as cited in D. J. Wilds (2000) *Minorities in Higher Education, 1999–2000: Seventeenth Annual Status Report,* Washington, D.C.: American Council on Education.

Note: The six-year graduation rates were based on the following freshman cohort: 1992, 1986–1987; 1993, 1987–1988; 1994, 1988–1989; 1995, 1989–1990; 1996, 1990–1991; 1997, 1991–1992. N represents the number of NCAA institutions.

need of dire fixing. Although it is not depicted on any table, with the exception of American Indians, African-American students lag behind all other racial/ethnic groups. (Differences by race/ethnic background are shown in Table 7 in the Astin, Tsui, & Avalos study.)

As shown on Table 2.6, African Americans have posted higher graduation levels at independent than at public colleges and universities. In general, half of all African-American students who entered an independent institution of higher education in each freshman cohort year starting in 1986 and ending in 1991 graduated in six years. There is an upward trend in the graduation levels for African Americans at public colleges and universities, but on average slightly more than one-third of these students have graduated in the same six-year period.

Four-, Six-, and Nine-Year Graduation Levels
The Astin, Tsui, & Avalos (1996) study compared degree attainment levels for several racial/ethnic groups (i.e., African Americans, American Indians, Asian Americans, Mexican Americans/Chicanos, Puerto Rican Americans, whites, and others) across four-, six-, and nine-year periods. The data were based on a national sample of the 1985 entering freshman cohort from 365 baccalaureate degree-granting institutions that participated in the Cooperative Institutional Research Program.

As shown in Table 2.7, for all three time intervals, the graduation levels for African-American students are troubling, with less than 20 percent of freshmen graduating in four years. The degree attainment level for African-American students improved somewhat during the six- and nine-year periods, though it does not exceed 35 percent in either of these intervals. With the exception of

Table 2.7   Four-, Six-, and Nine-Year Degree Attainment Rates by Racial/Ethnic Group

Race/Ethnicity	4 Years (%)	6 Years (%)		9 Years (%)
African American	19.4	31	.2	33.9
American Indian	22.9	30	.7	33.2
Asian American	50.2	56	.6	57.6
Mexican American/Chicano	30.5	38	.3	39.5
Puerto Rican American	26.8	34	.6	36.9
White	42.7	46	.8	47.3
Other	34.4	41	.3	43.7

Source: From A. W. Astin, L. Tsui, and J. Avalos. (1996). *Degree Attainment Rates at American Colleges and Universities: Effects of race, gender, and Institutional Type,* Los Angeles: Higher Education Research Institute, University of California, Los Angeles.
Note: Degree attainment rates were based on the fall 1985 entering freshman cohort.

Asian-American students, the graduation level for all other racial/ethnic groups is problematic, and represents a major leak in the educational pipeline for underrepresented students (Astin, Tsui, & Avalos, 1996).

Speculations About Graduation Levels at Historically Black
Institutions   A considerable body of research compares the educational experiences of black students enrolled in HBIs and PWIs (e.g., Allen, 1992; Allen, Epps, & Haniff, 1991; Cheatham, Slaney, & Coleman, 1990; DeSousa & Kuh, 1996; Fleming, 1984; Watson & Kuh, 1996). Most of these studies examined how the collegiate experience differs in various learning and social domains for African-American students at both types of institutions. In general, certain evidence suggests that African-American students perform and succeed better at HBIs (e.g., Allen, 1986; DeSousa & Kuh, 1996; Fleming, 1984; Thomas, 1986).

The literature that emerged during the 1970s and 1980s suggested that HBIs were more successful than PWIs in retaining and graduating African-American students. Whether in four-, six-, or nine-year periods, there is very little current research assessing the effect of HBIs on degree attainment levels of African-American students (Phillip, 1993; Stith & Russell, 1994). As discussed earlier, the studies conducted by the NCAA and Astin and his colleagues (1996) reported graduation levels at selected NCAA institutions and at baccalaureate degree-granting institutions, respectively. Although it is likely that HBIs were represented in both studies, the NCAA and Astin did not examine the graduation levels of African Americans at HBIs specifically. Thus, there remains a dearth of current research on this topic. Unequivocally, this area requires in-depth study.

Astin and his colleagues (1996), however, provide some current insight on the effects of HBIs on degree completion. Certain results challenge the body of literature showing that graduation and retention levels are better for African Americans at HBIs than at PWIs. In short, Astin, Tsui, & Avalos (1996, p. 28) found:

> The simple correlation between attending an [HBI] and degree completion was −.01, indicating that African-Americans who attended [HBIs] are slightly (but nonsignificantly; p>.05) less likely to complete their degrees in comparison to African-Americans who attend other types of institutions. However, when we control for the student's high school grades and SAT scores at the first two steps of the regression, the standardized Beta coefficient becomes positive (Beta = .07) and highly significant (p = .001). This Beta remains pretty much unchanged as all other input variables are controlled. What this means . . . is that African-Americans who attend [HBIs] are actually *more* likely to complete their degrees when they are compared with African Americans of *comparable academic preparation* who attend non-[HBIs].

The net benefit turns out to be a six percent absolute improvement in the student's chances of completing the bachelor's degree.

Inasmuch as these findings shed new light on helping to predict degree completion levels for African-American students, the Astin, Tsui, & Avalos (1996) findings on the effects of institutional size on degree attainment for African-American students provide more interesting results. When Astin and his colleagues controlled for institutional size (which had a negative affect on degree completion among African-American students), the positive effect of attending an HBI disappeared (for a greater narrative on the regression analysis see Astin, Tsui, & Avalos, 1996). According to Astin and his colleagues, "the positive effect of [HBIs] on degree completion can entirely be explained in terms of their relatively small size. In other words, it appears that there is nothing inherent in the [HBI's] environment that enhances degree completion rates among African-American students other than its small size" (1996, p. 29). So it appears as though African-American students at PWIs are not as disadvantaged as previously thought, although both types of institutions must redouble their efforts to improve the level of graduation for African-American students.

Although the data regarding degree completion rates expand our understanding of student persistence, current thinking suggests that caution should be taken in interpreting such data, particularly data related to student retention. Because most retention models do not take into account transfer-out behavior, student attrition rates could be inflated (Porter, 1999). According to Porter (1999), most retention models calculate student attrition based on initial registration and graduation data, leaving no separate calculation in the analysis for students who have transferred to another institution. As a result, a student who transfers from one four-year institution to another is often calculated as a stop-out student at the initial institution. (For an in-depth discussion of transfer-out behavior, see Porter, 1999). Very little is known about transfer-out behavior for African-American students. Thus, the attrition rate for African-American students may not be as profound as previously thought.

Some Implications of the Educational Pipeline of the 21st Century

The status of the educational pipeline of the 21st century has some important implications for access and diversity for African-American students and institutions of higher education. These implications are in the area of (1) legal and political developments; (2) access issues for late bloomers; and (3) issues related to diversity.

Legal and Political Developments

After decades of important legal and political victories, and even federal intervention, African Americans have gained better access to many institutions of higher education that previously denied them access based on race. The *Plessy v. Ferguson* (1896) decision, which affirmed that separate but equal facilities do not violate any provision of the Constitution, legally permitted segregated colleges and universities. However, cases such as *McLaurin v. Oklahoma State University Board of Regents* (1950), *Brown v. Board of Education of Topeka* (1954), and *Adams v. Richardson* (1973) helped to dismantle the dual system of American higher education.

Although these cases have had a discernable effect on improving access for African-American students, recent legal and political developments threaten the educational pipeline for minority students and could weaken diversity initiatives on college and university campuses. The *Hopwood v. State of Texas* (1996) case and California-initiated Proposition 209 of 1996 are two developments in particular that appear to have seriously hampered institutions of higher education from taking affirmative action initiatives designed to better increase the representation of African-American students and other minorities.

Specifically, both developments challenged colleges and universities in their respective jurisdictions from considering race in the admission of students. The action seems to have had an impact on enrollment within the province of Proposition 209's reach of authority, and it seems to have created ripple effects elsewhere. For instance, the plaintiffs in the *Johnson/Bogrow v. Board of Regents* (2000) case challenged the University of Georgia's use of race-based admissions' criteria. During the period directly after the passage of Proposition 209, two of California's flagship institutions experienced sharp declines in the number of African-American students admitted for enrollment. In particular, during the period directly after the passage of Proposition 209, African Americans admitted to the University of California, Los Angeles, and the University of California, Berkeley, dropped by 43 percent and 55 percent, respectively (Stecklow, 1998). Currently it is unclear how these and other legal and political developments related to affirmative action will unfold.

Access for Late Bloomers

Access to higher education will also be affected by the policies that colleges and universities and/or state systems of higher education implement regarding access for underprepared students, many of whom represent a large number of high school students from mostly all racial/ethnic groups. In essence, throughout the country higher education systems and institutions of higher education are raising performance expectations, which translate into higher admissions requirements for applicants (Southern Education Foundation, 1999). As the Southern Education Foundation (SEF) suggests, the implementation of new admissions standards have resulted in the phaseout of college-based remedial courses and programs at four-year institutions.

Focusing on African-American students, the Maryland Southern Education Foundation Leadership Group (1999) reported that Maryland's African-American college-bound seniors had taken fewer years of study in academic courses than their white college-bound counterparts. If this is indicative of other geographic locations, it could be difficult for many African-American college-bound students to gain access to colleges and universities that have eliminated remedial education programs. However, given the much larger number of white college-bound seniors who are late bloomers, institutions of higher education that have disbanded such college-based remedial education programs will be hard pressed to enroll these students too.

Understandably, critics of remedial education programs proffer that institutions spend an inordinate amount of money funding such programs at a time when state appropriations for higher education are decreasing and when state legislatures and accreditation bodies are placing increasingly greater accountability demands on colleges and universities. State policy makers and others expect colleges and universities to partner with K-12 schools on early intervention programs, yet many of the students participating in these intervention programs ultimately are denied access to these very same institutions. While many of these students eventually enroll in two-year institutions, few transfer to four-year, baccalaureate degree-granting institutions.

Issues Related to Diversity

As the projected demographic shifts come to fruition, institutions of higher education can expect to become increasingly diverse in their racial/ethnic mix of students, notwithstanding the impending legal and political developments. Given that 60 percent of students attend a college or university within 100 miles of their home (Bryant, 1999; Sax et al., 1999), institutions in states such as California, New York, Texas, and Florida, where there are large numbers of minority students, can expect an unusually high market share of these students. In other states, institutions that set the diversification of their campuses as a primary institutional goal have capitalized on these demographic shifts in their own locales.

Once (and not if) African Americans enroll in colleges and universities at higher levels throughout the country, the crucial next step is to keep them enrolled. Much is known about campus climate, such as that African-American and other students perceive that they are marginalized on campus. Influencing the persistence rates for African Americans remains an important goal for colleges and universities. With this as a backdrop, institutions that engage in intentional diversity practices create "staying environments" (Hossler, Bean, & associates, 1990) for these and other students, environments where students feel supported, comfortable, and connected to the institution.

Colleges and universities cannot take lightly the educational benefit diversity brings to students' collegiate experiences. In particular, it expands teaching and learning that occurs in formal and informal settings on campuses (Milem & Hukuta, 2000). In recognizing the benefit of diversity, two bellwether student affairs professional associations (i.e., Association of College Personnel Administrators and the National Association of Student Personnel Administrators) assert that "student learning occurs best in communities that value diversity, promote social responsibility, encourage discussion and debate, recognize accomplishments, and foster a sense of belonging among their members" (Association of College Personnel Administrators and the National Association of Student Personnel Administrators, 1997, p. 5).

To best achieve the benefits that diversity brings to the academy and its students, faculty, and staff, colleges and universities must better understand what the concept of diversity means, which groups it includes, and address cultural norms and practices that work against it. While diversity is a difficult concept to pin down, the process of attempting to reach a common understanding about it is an important task. Because there is divergence of opinion in many arenas over both the ends to be sought and the means by which to attain them, there will be no direct path. Still, the debates, if engaged diligently, will focus conversations about diversity, with its inevitable conflicts, on substantive issues. Nonetheless, diversity initiatives demand that colleges and universities press for "meaningful patterns of interaction" (Kuh, 1990, p. 86) and civil discourse on the cultural differences students bring to campus, differences from which all people, regardless of background, can benefit.

Diversity at Historically Black Institutions   As discussed previously, the levels of other-race students enrolling in HBIs has increased dramatically (see Table 2.4). And although HBIs continue to be predominantly African American, making the environment more inclusive and supportive for other-race students will be an important goal, especially as HBIs seek to increase their enrollments. To their credit, many HBIs have created offices designed to meet the needs of minority students, which in this sense of the word means non-African-American students. It is possible that there will be a greater emergence of such programs at HBIs, programs similar to those of the multicultural affairs and minority student services found at PWIs.

Creating a staying environment at HBIs also means addressing intrarace diversity or intrapersonal multiculturalism, which Cortes (2000, p. 6) describes as "the presence of multiple racial backgrounds in a person's heritage." In other words, the cultural background and differences of African Americans with ancestry from, let's say, Jamaica, Haiti, or Panama, must be considered when attempting to foster staying environments, as these students also bring unique cultural differences to campus. Respecting and embracing the culture of such student groups contribute to the creation of supportive and inclusive environments.

Conclusion

The latest data regarding the number of African Americans participating in higher education are encouraging. Yet given the slight decrease in 1997, as reported by the U.S. Department of Education, close attention should be given to how the participation levels unfold over the next several years. Of particular importance will be whether or not African-American men realize gains in their participation levels in institutions of higher education.

Although more must be done to address the participation levels of African Americans, it is also clear that greater emphasis must be placed on the retention of African-American students. In general, the graduation levels for African Americans lag behind all other racial/ethnic groups. Perhaps no subject during this century will be more important to the socioeconomic plight of African Americans than higher education. In other words, enrolling in a college or university and subsequently earning a college degree is not only a springboard to newly acquired knowledge and skills needed to succeed in a rapidly changing labor market, but also leads to substantially higher wages and salaries (Kuh, in press).

Why students decide to leave a college or university is difficult to understand precisely (Hossler, Bean & Associates, 1990). Nevertheless, colleges and universities must redouble their efforts to recruit African-American students and create campus conditions that ensure greater persistence to graduation, preferably within six years, for these students.

References

Adams v. Richardson, 480 F2d 1159 (D.C. Cir 1973).

Allen, W. (1986). *Gender and campus race differences in black student academic performance, racial attitudes and collegiate satisfaction*. Georgia: Southern Education Foundation.

Allen, W. (1992). The color of success: African-American college student outcomes at predominantly white and historically black public colleges and universities. *Harvard Education Review,* 62(1):26–44.

Allen, W., Epps, E. G., & Haniff, N. Z. (1991). *College in black and white: African American students in predominantly white and in historically black public universities.* New York: State University of New York Press.

American College Personnel Association and National Association of Student Personnel Administrators (1997). *Principles of good practice for student affairs.* Washington, D.C.: ACPA and NASPA.

Astin, A. W., Tsui, L., & Avalos, J. (1996). *Degree attainment rates at American colleges and universities: Effects of race, gender, and institutional type.* Los Angeles: Higher Education Research Institute, University of California at Los Angeles.

Brown v. Board of Education of Topeka, 347 US 483 (1954).

Brown, S. V. (1996). Responding to the new demographics in higher education. In *Educating a new majority: Transforming America's educational system for diversity,* L. I. Rendon, R. O. Hope & Associates (Eds.), pp. 71–96. San Francisco: Jossey-Bass.

Brubacher, J. S. (1977). *On the philosophy of higher education.* San Francisco: Jossey-Bass.

Bryant, P. S. (1999). *The must do enrollment strategies.* Paper presented at the National Conference on Student Retention, San Francisco, CA.

Burr, P. L., Burr, R. M., & Novak, L. F. (1999). Student retention is more complicated than merely keeping the students you have today: Toward a "seamless retention theory." *College Student Retention: Research, Theory & Practice* 1(3):239–253.

Cheatham, H. E., Slaney, R. B., & Coleman, N. C. (1990). Institutional effects on the psychosocial development of African-American college students. *Journal of Counseling Psychology* 37(4):453–458.

Cortez, C. E. (2000). The diversity within: Intermarriage, identity, and campus community. *About Campus* 5(1):5–10.

Cross, K. P. (1971). *Beyond the open door: New students in higher education.* San Francisco: Jossey-Bass.

Dannells, M. (1997). *From discipline to development: Rethinking student conduct in higher education.* ASHE-ERIC Higher Education Report Vol. 25, No. 2. Washington, D.C.. Graduate School of Education and Human Development, George Washington University.

DeSousa, D. J., & Kuh, G. D. (1996). Does institutional racial composition make a difference in what Black students gain from college? *Journal of College Student Development* 37:257–267.

Fleming, J. (1984). *Blacks in college.* San Francisco: Jossey-Bass.

Godbold, A. (1944). *The church college of the old south.* Durham, N.C.: Duke University Press.

Hopwood v. State of Texas, 518 US 1033 (1996).

Hossler, D., Bean, J. P., & Associates (1990). *The strategic management of college enrollments.* San Francisco: Jossey-Bass.

Justiz, M. (1994). Demographic trends and the challenges to American higher education. In *Minorities in higher education,* M. J. Justiz, R. Wilson, & L. G. Bjork (Eds.), pp. 1–21. Phoenix, AZ: Oryx Press.

King, J. E. (1999). *Money matters: The impact of race/ethnicity and gender on how students pay for college.* Washington, D.C.: American Council on Education.

Kuh, G. D. (1990). The demographic juggernaut. In *New futures for student affairs,* M. J. Barr, M. L. Upcraft, & Associates (Eds.), pp. 71–97. San Francisco: Jossey-Bass.

Kuh, G. D. (in press). College students today: Why we can't leave serendipity to chance. In *In defense of the American university,* P. Altbach, P. Gumport, & B. Johnstone (Eds.), Baltimore: Johns Hopkins Press.

Levine, A., & Cureton, J. S. (1998, May/June). Collegiate life: An obituary. *Change: The Magazine of Higher Learning,* pp. 12–17.

Marshall, R., & Glover, R. W. (1996). Education, the economy, and tomorrow's workforce. In *Educating a new majority: Transforming America's educational system for diversity,* L. I. Rendon, R. O. Hope & Associates (Eds.), pp. 35–50. San Francisco: Jossey-Bass.

Maryland Southern Education Foundation Leadership Group. (1999, January). *Miles to go in Maryland: Pursuing educational equality, ensuring economic growth.* Maryland: Maryland Southern Education Foundation Leadership Group.

McLaurin v. Oklahoma State Board of Regents, 339 US 637 (1950).

Milem, J. F., & Hakuta, K. (2000). In *Minorities in higher education, 1999–2000: Seventeenth annual status report,* D. J. Wilds (Ed.), pp. 39–67. Washington, D.C.: American Council on Education.

Mortenson, T. G. (1998). Men behaving badly . . . Where are the guys? *Postsecondary Education Opportunity* 76:1–8.

National Association for Equal Opportunity Research Institute (1999). *Annual fall enrollment surveys, 1987–1997.* Washington, D.C.: National Association for Equal Opportunity Research Institute.

National Center for Education Statistics, U.S. Department of Education. (1999). *Enrollment in higher education.* Washington, D.C.: U.S. Department of Education.

National Center for Education Statistics, U.S. Department of Education, Integrated Postsecondary Education Data System. (1997). *Fall enrollment survey, 1997.* (NCES 99-162). Washington, D.C.: GPO.

National Collegiate Athletic Association. (1999). *Division I graduation rates reports, 1997 and 1998.* Indianapolis, IN: NCAA.

Phillip, M. L. (1993). Too many institutions still taking a band-aid approach to minority student retention, experts say. *Black Issues in Higher Education* 9(24):24–26.

Pifer, A. (1978). Introduction: Some current issues. In *Systems of higher education: United States,* A. Pifer, J. Shea, D. Henry, & L. Glenny (Eds.), pp. 1–18. New York: Interbook.

Plessy v. Ferguson, 163 US 537 (1896).

Porter, S. R. (1999). *Including transfer-out behavior in retention models: Using the NSLC enrollment search data.* Paper presented at the annual conference of the North East Association of Institutional Research, Newport, RI.

Rudolph, F. (1962). *The American college and university.* New York: Vintage Books.

Sax, L. J., Astin, A. W., Korn, W. S., & Mahoney, K. M. (1999). *The American freshman: National norms for fall 1999.* Los Angeles: Higher Education Research Institute, University of California at Los Angeles.

Southern Education Foundation. (1999). *Miles to go: Executive summary.* Georgia: SEF.

Stecklow, S. (1998). Minorities fall at universities in California. *Wall Street Journal,* April 1998.

Stith, P. L., & Russell, F. (1994, May). *Faculty/student interaction: Impact of student retention.* Paper presented at the annual forum of the Association for Institutional Research, New Orleans, LA. (ERIC Document Reproduction Service No. ED 373 650)

Thomas, G. E. (1986). *Black students in U.S. graduate and professional schools in the 1980's: A national and institutional assessment.* Chicago: Spencer Foundation.

Watson, L. W., & Kuh, G. D. (1996). The influence of dominant race environments on students' involvement, perceptions, and educational gains: A look at historically black and predominantly white liberal arts institutions. *Journal of College Student Development* 37:415–424.

Wilds, D. J. (2000). *Minorities in higher education, 1999–2000: Seventeenth Annual Status Report.* Washington, D.C.: American Council on Education.

Wilson, R. (1994). The participation of African Americans in higher education. In *Minorities in higher education,* M. J. Justiz, R. Wilson, & L. G. Bjork (Eds.), pp. 195–209. Phoenix, AZ: Oryx Press.

3

THE POLICIES AND POLITICS OF RETENTION AND ACCESS OF AFRICAN AMERICAN STUDENTS IN PUBLIC WHITE INSTITUTIONS

Paul E. Green

The American higher education system, and the secondary education system as well, continue to face a crisis. That crisis is the increasing attrition rates of African-American students from colleges and universities before graduation and the decreasing numbers of African-American students enrolling in graduate and professional schools across the country. Clewell & Ficklsen (1986) and Allen, (1992) indicated that the attrition of students of color from postsecondary education is one of the major obstacles to the attainment of educational equity and is a serious threat to eroding the gains that have been made in enrolling students of color in postsecondary institutions over the past decade. Thus, as the gap widens between the proportions of students of color and whites receiving college degrees, it is logical that the gap between access to opportunities and career success between the two groups will also widen.

Over the past few years much debate has been raised about the increasing attrition rates of African Americans from postsecondary education and corollary problems of African-American student retention in institutions of higher education. This debate has focused on several critical areas that affect these problems: (1) the preparedness of the African-American student for matriculation in higher education; (2) the psychosocial and intellectual factors that affect African-American students' performance and success in college; (3) the institutional barriers to African-American student success or failure; and (4) the intrinsic social, economic, and political problems facing African-American students. Although these are neither mutually exclusive nor exhaustive of the issues that face African-American student retention and attrition, they are certainly among the most pertinent.

Identifying the Problem(s)

What role is higher education playing to reduce the endemic problems facing African Americans? What are the reasons for this situation? What can or needs to be accomplished to change these trends? What are the potential consequences if these trends are not changed? One of the more salient problems is assisting African-American youth in making the transition from high school to college. The problem addressed in this chapter, however, is moving African-American youths through college to graduation and into and graduated from graduate and professional schools. In order to address these pertinent questions, it is necessary to examine factors that are affecting opportunities for African-American students in higher education.

Recent research suggests that higher attrition rates of African-American students are largely attributable to their socioeconomic background and to the peculiar characteristics of higher education institutions. In fact, studies of African-American students attending predominantly white postsecondary institutions commonly report (1) their social and economic characteristics (Allen, 1986a, 1986b; Blackwell, 1982); (2) their levels of adjustment (Fleming, 1984; Webster, Sedlacek, & Miyares, 1979); and (3) their academic success and attrition rates, (Nettles et al., 1985).

The parents of African-American students are typically urban, have fewer years of education, earn less and work at lower-status jobs than parents of white students (Bayer, 1972; Blackwell, 1982; Boyd, 1974). Yet, it has also become clear that when socioeconomic factors are controlled, the attrition rate of African Americans after enrolling is not terribly different from that of whites. This implies the increasing significance of institutional factors on the attrition of African-American students after college enrollment.

Researchers (Astin, 1975, 1982; Christoffel, 1986; Elam, 1988; Niba and Norman, 1989; Allen, 1992; Obiakor & Barker, 1993; Cuyjet, 1997; Gaither, 1999) have identified critical junctures where significantly disproportionate numbers of students of color are misplaced in the educational process between completing high school and completing college or graduate and professional school. Those junctures are between high school and college, between two-year college and completing four-year college, between graduating from undergraduate college and entering graduate or professional school and graduation, and before obtaining an advanced degree. At each of these critical junctures, significant numbers of students of color, namely, African-American students, disappear from the educational system.

The research literature further provides specific factors that explain a disproportionately large share of the variance in attrition rates for African-American students. Those factors are the academic preparation of African-American students for higher education, the availability of family resources and access to institutional financial aid, and institutional barriers to access, enrollment, and retention (Lang, 1988; Obiakor & Lassiter, 1988; Obiakor, Steinmiller, & Barker, 1993; Cuyjet, 1997).

Institutional Access and Students of Color

Why does access to equal opportunity in higher education institutions continue as a problem for students of color? Why have the retention and graduation rates of African Americans declined while the rates of other groups of color improved? And, what options exist for improving the access and retention of students of color in institutions of higher learning?

The civil strife of the 1950s and 1960s was in part a struggle to gain equal access to and equal opportunity in the nation's institutions of higher learning. Yet, students of color are still underrepresented, both as students and as faculty and staff, at predominantly white colleges and universities across the country. The inequitable status of persons of color in higher education continues to be a major concern and has generated considerable scholarly debate over the last few years (Chang et al., 2000; The College Board, 1999).

As scholars debate issues of access to higher education, they do so without recognizing that equal access to educational opportunity as a matter of national policy is a new phenomenon for persons of color. In other words, some discussions are often ahistorical in that little attention is paid to the decades of social, economic, and political discrimination and exclusion from access and opportunity. Not until 1954, with the *Brown v. Board of Education* decision, did the U.S. Supreme Court make equal access the law of the land. It was even more recently in the 1960s and 1970s, after the passage of the Civil Rights Acts of 1964 and 1965 that de facto rights of admission were granted to persons of color at many institutions of higher education, especially predominately white institutions.

While the access of students of color to higher educational opportunities has improved in general, the access of African-American students specifically has not. What accounts for this lack of progress? Without question the progress of African Americans in gaining access has slowed considerably. The situation for Latino students has not been significantly better when we consider that their numbers were considerably lower as a matter of progress.

It was during the administration of President John Fitzgerald Kennedy that significant programs were initiated to provide federal financial aid for students of color to pursue postsecondary education. During the early 1960s the federal government instituted such programs as the National Defense Education Act (NDEA), the National Defense Student Loan program (NDSL), and other work-study programs that made it possible for students of color (especially African Americans) to have the financial support necessary to attend college for the first time. Other programs followed in the mid- and late 1960s, such as the Basic Equal Education Opportunity Grants program (BEOG) and the Equal Education Opportunity program (EEOP). Each of the programs provided direct loans or grants to low-income students and students of color who qualified for college admission and enrollment.

Because of these programs, low-income students and students of color began to enroll en masse at colleges and universities across the country. By the late 1970s the enrollment of African-American students had reached its historical peak. The predominately black colleges and universities received the initial effects and reaped the benefits of these programs. Moreover, by 1976, the enrollments of historically black colleges and universities (HBCUs) had increased dramatically, with an overwhelming majority of their students supported by some form of financial aid (Turner & Rosen, 1979).

Since the early 1990s, this situation has changed dramatically. Prior to the late 1970s many African-American college students were enrolled at HBCUs. By the late 1980s more African-American students were enrolling in predominately white institutions than in HBCUs, a dramatic change from the previous decade.

A great many of the institutional shifts by African-American students from predominately black to predominately white institutions occurred as a result of sweeping educational reforms in lower and postsecondary education. Reports and studies such as *A Nation at Risk* had widespread political implications (Cuban, 1990) influencing these enrollment shifts. These reports emphasized higher test scores and quality in education with less emphasis on equity and culturally sensitive approaches that work (Obiakor, 1990; 1991; 1992; 1993; Obiakor, Steinmiller & Barker, 1993; Gordon, 1995). Moreover, during the administrations of President Ronald Reagan and President George Bush, substantial reallocations were made in federal student aid programs, with a significant impact because most students of color in college depend on some form of financial aid.

The decrease in federal support for financial aid programs diminished access opportunities for students of color, but their poor socioeconomic status and lack of available family resources continue to be severe deterrents to higher education as well. For example, approximately 31 percent of African-American and non-Hispanic families in the United States live below the poverty line. Fifty-three percent of these families are female-headed households. Similarly, about 28 percent of Latino families live below the poverty line and 51 percent are female-headed households (The Office of Education Research and Improvement, 1999; National Center for Educational Statistics, 1999).

These statistics have serious implications for family resources available to support higher education. They also have serious implications for the preparedness of students of color to succeed in college once they are accepted. In truth, families of color in general earn substantially less than white families in the United States. Thus, fewer family resources are available to provide exposure to as many learning and enrichment experiences for students of color outside of the school environment. Considering the generally poorer quality of public secondary schools and programs in neighborhoods of color, these students are often inadequately prepared to score as high on college entrance tests as white students. Yet, scholars seldom consider this when they debate the lower level of performance by students of color on college entrance exams.

Compounding this dilemma, rapid increases in college and university tuition undoubtedly reduce the access of poorer students of color to college entrance. During the last decade, college tuition increases have outrun inflation rates almost every year (Carnoy, 1994; Hebel, 2000). Coupled with the demise of state and federal aid programs during the Reagan and Bush administrations more and more minority students are finding it extremely difficult, if not impossible, to afford college even if they are adequately prepared. Though the number of African-American students who enroll in college has increased over the past decade, the number who drop out before graduation because of financial reasons has almost doubled.

Nevertheless, sufficient data exist to show that when the college entrance test scores of African-American and white students of similar socioeconomic status and background are compared, their scores are relatively the same. This fact substantiates that the lack of institutional resources, family socioeconomic status, and other social, political, and economic factors contribute to the unpreparedness of some African-American students for college and university success.

Institutional Barriers to Educational Opportunity

In 1988, Orfield and Paul concluded that four major issues are clearly linked to the declining access and success of students of color to higher education:

1. Segregation in elementary and secondary schools

2. Increasing college costs

3. Inadequate assistance to unprepared students

4. Lack of commitment to equal opportunity by institutions of higher education

In a recent report, Underwood (1998) addresses larger social, economic, and political factors that underlie the comparatively low rate of African-American student eligibility for university admission. According to Underwood (1998, p. 2):

> The historical and social conditions that have shaped the structure of American society have significantly restricted the social mobility of a large proportion of the black population. A dual system of social status, in which birth ascribed status is reckoned along with achieved status has emerged. Discriminatory practices in a range of institutional domains—from housing and employment to education—have profoundly affected the structure of opportunity in American society. These practices have systematically excluded large numbers of black people from valued positions and placed severe limits on their ability to achieve economic security.

The report clearly suggests that eligibility for university admission is not simply a matter of what African-American students can or cannot accomplish in school. It is equally a question of institutional channels and structural forces that shape the school and determine the kind of contact that African-American students and their families have with the school and concomitantly the school with the community (Underwood, 1998).

Hence, continuing high levels of segregation in elementary and secondary schools that have large numbers of African-American students are reflected in poorer facilities, affecting every aspect of student preparedness. Orfield and Paul (1988; 1998) compared majority white schools to schools where more than five out of six students were students of color. In many cases, schools with predominately large numbers of African-American and Latino populations had more crowded classrooms, teachers with fewer advanced degrees and degrees from less prestigious or less selective colleges, less resources for counseling than those students who relied on counselors for course decisions and for making colleges choices, and wider differences in scores on achievement tests.

The growth of segregation in elementary and secondary schools, according to Orfield and Paul (1988, 1998), also translates into widening the gap between the learning experiences of students of color and their white counterparts with each additional year of schooling. This results from institutional policies and practices of academic tracking, less enriching curricula and academic programs, and ultimately diminished preparation and capability for college entry.

Scholars as well as municipal and civic leaders recognize the deteriorating conditions of inner-city communities (neighborhoods and schools) that many students of color attend. In spite of the conditions, an unspoken agreement exists among higher education institutions (especially white institutions) to ignore these structure factors when recruiting and evaluating these students for admission. The philosophy undergirding policies of admission of white institutions is to attract and admit the best prepared students they can find. Thus, they look on remediation and developmental programs that address the needs of underprepared students as lowering the standards, unqualified merit, undeserved opportunity, tarnishing the image, and damaging the image and reputation of the institution.

Community and two-year colleges are designed to address these needs. Yet, community colleges far too often lack the necessary resources and the staff to provide the educational and social development students from poorer backgrounds need. Consequently, few students of color who enroll in two-year community colleges successfully transfer to four-year institutions.

Awareness of Institutional Expectations

In keeping with institutional barriers, leaders in many colleges and universities have failed to understand that their programs do not reflect the thinking of an expanding and diverse community. African-American and Latino students are sometimes viewed as unqualified persons imposed on the college or university because of their race, color, ethnicity, gender, or national origin. This salient perception has led to bigotry and racism in many programs. As Banks (1977, p. 32) suggested some years ago:

> We live in a world society beset with momentous social and human problems, many of which are related to ethnic hostility and conflict. Effective solutions to these critical problems can be found only by active sound decisions that will benefit our technically diverse world community.

Remedying the Problem(s)

It appears that little is likely to change regarding the access and retention of students of color in higher education until pervasive attitudes of the systems and decisions that guide and control higher education access and opportunity change. Part of the problem derives from the fact that those leaders and governing bodies that are responsible for instituting change are in some part responsible for creating the problems. As Atwell (1988, p. 8) stated, "I propose that we acknowledge that many of the structures and values that we accept on our campuses are actually obstacles to the educational success of minorities." Atwell further points out that much of what is needed to provide a genuinely hospitable, conducive, and supportive environment for students of color is not provided for white students. Hence, it may be too much to ask [expect] institutions to provide these conditions for students of color.

In responding to the need for increasing retention and access of African-American students, one possibility that arises is national legislation and policy making. A stimulating debate directed by leaders in higher education as well as at the federal and state levels is needed. If diversity and pluralism must become one of the goals of higher education in an expanding global economy and labor market, then the need for change must be realized by our institutions of learning—both higher education and lower schooling.

Although we can legislate actions, we cannot legislate attitudes and commitments, and it is attitudes and commitments at institutions that need to change. Many institutions have created affirmative action and equal opportunity policies and practices for well over 20 years; what lacks, however, is the commitment to enforce these policies and practices. Increasing the number and participation of African-American and Latino students in higher education will not occur until serious commitments are made toward these goals by the leadership at institutions.

Basic public policy issues need to be addressed, and indeed some new policy making may be appropriate. For example, colleges and universities can begin by strengthening their linkages with elementary and secondary schools in inner-city areas, where the largest populations of students of color reside. Atwell (1988) notes that higher education institutions are obligated to work with these schools, not to rescue them or share great wisdom, but because their futures are inextricably tied to one another. Often when colleges and universities have exemplary programs to pilot, they invariably look to suburbs, where more resources and facilities are available for elementary and secondary schools. Colleges and universities must concentrate their collective institutional resources and efforts on inner-city areas and their residents. Such areas are where improvements could begin toward the preparation of students of color for college admission and retention.

Similarly, the gap between two-year community colleges and four-year institutions must be narrowed or eliminated for students of color. A number of critical points have been identified where significant attrition occurs in the educational process of African-American and Latino students (Astin, 1984; Christofell, 1986; Lang, 1988). One of these critical points is transfer from community college to completing the baccalaureate degree at four-year college. Community colleges are far exceeding four-year colleges in providing access and retention of students of color. Further, they continue to bear a disproportionate share of the burden of providing educational opportunities for these students. In brief, colleges and universities must assume more responsibility for developing bridges to attract and transfer students to their institutions from the community college system.

Student access and retention are educational processes; they are not merely programmatic functions. The success of these processes should not be measured by the number of African-American and Latino students being enrolled and graduated from colleges and universities. Rather, they should be measured by the structural and functional changes in the institution to accommodate the diversity of skills, cultural backgrounds, adeptness, and historical legacies that students of color bring with them. Moreover, they should further be measured by the articulation of the institution's commitment to access and success of its diverse student body.

Traditional strategies have failed to meet the needs of African-American and Latino students and infuse pluralism into higher education. Most African-American and Latino students are nontraditional students; therefore, it is unrealistic to use traditional strategies with these students. As a consequence, nontraditional strategies should be employed to respond to affirmative action regulations, educational finances, curricula and pedagogy organization, test and instruction, and expectations. Richardson (1989, p. 48) identified nontraditional strategies that can assist predominantly white colleges and universities in promoting access and retention of African-American and Latino students, namely:

Early intervention in public schools to strengthen preparation and improve students' educational planning.

Summer "bridge" programs to accustom minority students to college-level coursework and the campus atmosphere before they begin college.

Special orientation programs to help with choice of courses and registration.

Tailored financial-aid programs, including policies that recognize students who may not be able to contribute as much in summer earnings to their aid package if they participate in bridge programs.

Strong academic-assessment programs, coupled with courses designed to offset gaps in preparations.

Adequate tutoring services, learning laboratories, and organized "monitoring" programs.

Career guidance to translate nonspecific educational goals into programs of study where the coursework and desired outcomes are clearly linked.

Conclusion

When we assess the role that academic institutions have played in the struggle for equality for students of color, we realize that their role has not exemplified intellectual let alone moral leadership. They have not been role models for the rest of society. Rather, they have reproduced and sometimes legitimized the same prejudices and social injustices that have been prominent among the poor and unintellectual masses, despite their presumed wealth of information and knowledge production. This fact is quite apparent in the present handling of access and retention of African-American and Latino students in lower schooling in general and in higher education in particular.

Equal access and retention of students of color are serious problems with very serious consequences for the social, economic, and political stability of our nation. Can our institutions of higher learning foster the production of knowledge needed to solve these perplexing social, economic, and political problems? When we consider that as a nation our workforce is growing more ethnically and racially diverse, can we afford not to educate well all of our citizens? If access and retention are not guarantees for all citizens, we need to rethink our educational system's priorities.

References

Allen, W. R. (1986a). Blacks in Michigan higher education. In *The state of black Michigan: 1987,* J. T. Darden & C. Mitchner (Eds.), pp. 53–68. East Lansing: Urban Affairs Programs, Michigan State University.

Allen, W. R. (1986b). *Gender and campus race differences in black student academic performance, racial attitudes, and college satisfaction.* Atlanta: Southern Education Foundation.

Allen, W. R. (1992). The color of success: African-American college student outcomes at predominantly white and historically black public colleges and universities. *Harvard University Review* 62(1):26–44.

Astin. A. W. (1975). *Preventing students from dropping out.* San Francisco: Jossey-Bass.

Astin, A. W. (1982). *Minorities in higher education: Recent trends, current prospects and recommendations.* San Francisco: Jossey-Bass.

Astin, A. W. (1984). Minorities in higher education. In *Equality postponed: Continuing barriers to higher education in the 1990s,* Stephen H. Adolphus (Ed.), pp. 35–55. New York: College Entrance Examination Board.

Atwell, R. H. (1988). *Minority participation in higher education: We need a new momentum.* Washington, D.C.: American Council on Education.

Banks, J. A. (1977). *Multiethnic education: Practices and promises.* Bloomington, IN: Phi Delta Kappa.

Bayer, A. E. (1972). *The Black college freshmen: Characteristics and recent trends.* Washington, D.C.: American Council on Education Research Reports, No 3.

Blackwell, J. E. (1982). Demographics of desegregation. In *Race and equity in higher education,* Reginald Wilson (Ed.)., pp. 28–70. Washington, D.C.: American Council on Education.

Boyd, W. M. (1974). *Desegregating America's colleges: A nationwide survey of Black students, 1972–1973.* New York: Praeger.

Brown v. Board of Education of Topeka, 347 US 483 (1954).

Carnoy, M. (1994, Autumn). Why aren't more African Americans going to college? *Black Issues in Higher Education* 5:66–69.

Chang, M., Witt, D., Jones, J., & Hakuta, K. (2000). Compelling interests: Examining the racial dynamics in higher education. *Report of the American Educational Association Panel on Racial Dynamics in Colleges and Universities.* Palo Alto: Stanford University.

Christoffel, P. (1986, October). *Minority access and retention: A review. (Research and Development Update).* New York: College Entrance Examination Board.

Clewell, B. C. & Ficklsen, M. S. (1986). *Improving minority retention in higher education. A search for effective institutional practices.* Princeton, NJ: Educational Testing Service.

College Board (1999). *Reaching the top: A report of national task force on minority high achievement.* New York: College Entrance Examination Board.

Cuban L. (1990, January- February). Reforming again, again, and again. *Educational Researcher* 19(1):3–13.

Cuyjet, M. J. (1997). *Helping African American men succeed in college: New directions for student services.* San Francisco: Jossey-Bass.

Elam, J. C. (1988). *Black in higher education overcoming the odds: National association for equal opportunity in higher education.* New York: University Press of America.

Fleming, J. (1984). *Blacks in college.* San Francisco: Jossey-Bass.

Gaither, G. H. (1999). *Promising practices in recruitment, remediation, and retention. New directions for higher education.* San Francisco: Jossey-Bass.

Gordon, E. W. (1995, Summer). The promise of accountability and standards in the achievement of equal educational opportunity. *Teacher's College Record* 96(4):751–756.

Hebel, S. (2000, February 4). Clinton tax break proposal favors the middle class, college officials say, *Chronicle of Higher Education,* pp. A34-A35.

Lang, M. (1988). The Black student retention problem in higher education: Some introductory perspectives. In *Black student retention in higher education,* M. Lang & C.A. Ford (Eds.), pp. 3–12. Springfield, IL: Charles C. Thomas.

National Commission on Excellence in Education (1983). *A nation at risk: The imperative for educational reforms.* Washington, D.C.: U.S. Department of Education.

Nettles, M., Gosman, C., Thoeny, A., & Dandridge, B. (1985). *The causes and consequences of college students' attrition rates, progression rates and grade point averages.* Nashville, TN: Higher Education Commission.

Niba, J. N. & Norman, R. (1989). *Recruitment and retention of black students in higher education. National Association of Equal Opportunity in Education.* New York: University Press of America.

Obiakor, F. E. (1990, November). *Crisis in minority education.* Paper presented at the National Social Science Association (NSSA) Conference, Washington, D.C.

Obiakor, F. E. (1991, February). *Crisis in the education of minorities.* Paper presented at the Multicultural Fair, The University of Tennessee at Chattanooga, TN.

Obiakor, F. E. (1992, August). Multiculturalism in higher education: A myth or reality? *Resources in Education* 27(8):104.

Obiakor, F. E. (1993, April). *American 2000 reform program: Implications for African American at-risk students.* Paper presented at the 71st International Convention, San Antonio, TX.

Obiakor, F. E. & Barker, N.C. (1990, October). *Educating the black male: Renewed imperatives for black and white communities.* Paper presented at the 15th Annual National Conference of the Society of Educators and Scholars, Wichita, KS.

Obiakor, F. E. & Lassiter, R. F. (1988). After the scholarship: Retention and academic achievement of black students in white colleges. *Minority Voices* 11(1):22–23, 25.

Obiakor, F. E., Steinmiller, G. & Barker, N. C. (1993, March). *The politics of higher education: Perspectives for minorities in the 21st century.* Paper presented at the Annual Arkansas Association of Colleges for Teacher Education (AACTE) Spring Conference, Little Rock: AR.

Office of Education Research and Improvement, U.S. Department of Education (1999). *The Condition of Education.* Washington D.C.: GPO.

Orfield, G. & Paul, F. (1988, Fall-Winter). Declines in minority access: A tale of five cities. *Educational Record,* pp. 57–62.

Richardson, R. C. (1989, January). If minority students are to succeed in higher education, every rung of the ladder must be in place. *Chronicle of Higher Education* 35(18):A48.

Turner, W. H. & Rosen, N. L. (1979). *Traditionally black institutions: A profile and an institutional directory.* Washington, D.C.: National Center for Educational Statistics.

Underwood, C. (1998). *Task force on black eligibility: A review of the literature.* Berkeley: University of California at Berkeley.

Webster, D. W., Sedlacek, W. E., & Miyares, J., (1979). A comparison of problems perceived by minority and white university students. *Journal of College Student Personnel* 20(2):165–170.

4

ALTERNATIVES TO RACE-BASED ADMISSIONS IN HIGHER EDUCATION

EXAMINING X-PERCENT PLANS IN CALIFORNIA, TEXAS, AND FLORIDA

Eugene L. Anderson

President Johnson's rationale for affirmative action in his 1965 Howard University speech, let us recall, was that it was unfair to take someone who has long been "hobbled by chains" and put him at the starting line in a race and say "you are free to compete with all the others." And yet affirmative action in admission to elite colleges amounted to precisely that. It put ill-prepared African-American students at the starting line and told them that they were free to compete with students who entered with calculus, several Advanced Placement credits and combined College Board scores often above 1400 (Thernstrom & Thernstrom, 1997, p. 395).

Some of public perception about affirmative action in college admissions is shaped by opinions such as this quote from the Thernstroms. Opponents of affirmative action are active in the courts and state legislatures across America. These legal and political attacks on affirmative action in the college admissions process are changing how colleges and universities select students. The goal of creating a racially diverse campus in the 21st century is now threatened by these attacks on affirmative action. These attacks and the deafness of the federal courts to the concerns of African Americans force those committed to racial diversity and equity in higher education to reexamine the admissions policies at selective public colleges and universities. This chapter focuses on the X-percent plans three states recently adopted following the forced or voluntary end of affirmative action in those states. The chapter also addresses the controversy over merit and the use of standardized tests in the admissions process. Finally, the chapter discusses two alternatives to X-percent plans if affirmative action is banned across the United States.

For decades those in higher education took the SAT or ACT test score gap between black and white students as a sign of the inequity in the quality of education at the primary and secondary level (Hanford, 1991; Nettles, Perna, & Millett, 1998). For some, the belief was that the use of affirmative action in college admissions was necessary not only because of the historical discrimination of higher education institutions, but also because of the historical and present discrimination in the provision of adequate K-12 public education. Affirmative action was the only way that the test score gap would not be used to foster the continued disadvantage of blacks and other minorities. The attack on affirmative action turns this rationale upside down and demands the evaluation of admissions policies that rely heavily on a measurement tool that places African Americans at a disadvantage (Crouse & Trusheim, 1988; Nettles, Perna, & Millett, 1998).

Controversies over Standards and Merit

In fact, the dominance of standardized tests in selection is a relatively recent development. The civil rights revolution, and the introduction of affirmative action programs, occurred at the same time that society was formalizing a "meritocracy" based on education and standardized testing (Guinier & Sturm, 1996, p. 965).

Since the passage of the Civil Rights Act of 1964 there existed a conflict over the role of race in college admissions, based on Title VI and the Fourteenth Amendment of the Constitution, which guarantees equal protection under the law for all regardless of race or ethnicity. Because most selective colleges and universities rely on standardized test scores, admissions policies for these institutions use affirmative action to overcome the disparate impact of standardized tests on minority students. Because of this use of affirmative action to overcome the disparate impact of standardized tests, some believe that affirmative action admits less qualified blacks while turning away better qualified whites (D'Souza, 1995; Sowell, 1984; Thernstrom & Thernstrom, 1999).

Critics consider that affirmative action in college admissions is a racial preference that clearly violates the equal protection clause of the Fourteenth Amendment. Public colleges and universities were protected legally from this criticism because of the Supreme Court's ruling in *Regents of the University of California v. Bakke* (1978). The Supreme Court's ruling in this case established a complicated and conflicting precedent for future courts. The court upheld the ruling of the lower court that the special admissions program of the University of California at Davis (UC-Davis) Medical School was not permissible under the law. Four of the five justices, Stevens, Burger, Stewart, and Rehnquist, voting in the majority on this issue agreed that the admissions plan violated Title VI of the Civil Rights Act of 1964. The fifth justice, Powell, did not interpret Title VI to suggest color-blind policies. Based on his interpretation of Title VI, racial classifications that do not discriminate should be examined under the Equal Protection Clause of the Fifth Amendment. Based on the Equal Protection Clause, Powell found the UC-Davis medical school admission plan unconstitutional. The other four justices in the majority on this issue did not review the admissions plan on constitutional grounds because they believed it was not necessary since the plan violated Title VI. Justice Powell was the only justice to vote in the majority on both issues. On the second issue about the future use of race by UC-Davis Medical School, Justices Powell, Marshall, Brennan, White, and Blackmun, reversed the lower court ruling that the use of race was not permissible under any circumstances. All five justices, except Powell, believed that if the use of race in college admissions met an intermediate level of scrutiny it was permissible. Justice Powell in his opinion stated that set-asides and quotas were not constitutional, but the use of race along with other variables was allowable in order to achieve a diverse learning environment (Spann, 2000).

For some time Justice Powell's opinion stood as the legal protection of affirmative action in college admissions. In the 1990s this legal protection was weakened as the composition of some federal district courts became more conservative (Masters, 2000). In March of 1996, the Fifth Circuit Court of Appeals overturned the lower district court's ruling in *Hopwood v. Texas* (1996). The appeals court found that the University of Texas School of Law discriminated against whites by giving racial preference to certain minority groups. *Hopwood v. Texas* (1996) was a major victory for opponents of affirmative action and it encouraged lawsuits in other states because it revealed the vulnerability of affirmative action in college admissions in the courtrooms of conservative judges. In 1998 the First Circuit Court of Appeals upheld a lower court ruling that race cannot be used in determining admission to a selective admissions public high school in Boston, despite a legacy of segregation in the city's schools (Ferdinand, 1998).

In July of 2000 two separate rulings showed that the conservative nature of judicial rulings in school admissions cases is continuing. In Georgia, a U.S. District Court found the University of Georgia's admissions policy violates the Constitution because the use of race as a positive variable for select racial groups gives an unfair advantage to certain minorities (Rankin & McCarthy, 2000). In Florida, a judge upheld Governor Jeb Bush's plan to end affirmative action in higher education. The judge wrote that, "affirmative action is no longer needed to ensure equal access to higher education" (Selingo, 2000). In addition to Georgia, Boston, Florida, and Texas, affirmative action policies in school admissions are under attack in Maryland and Michigan. The remote fear of legal action caused several major universities such as the University of Virginia and the University of Massachusetts to significantly diminish the use of race in their admissions process (Bennefield, 1999).

One argument in support of affirmative action is that such a policy is necessary because standardized tests such as the SAT are racially and economically biased and place low-income students and certain minorities at a disadvantage. The white-black test score gap and rich-poor test score gap are extremely controversial topics that are heavily debated with little consensus among supporters and opponents of affirmative action. According to Jencks (1998) standardized tests have five types of biases: labeling bias, content bias, methodological bias, prediction bias, and selection bias. Environment is a major factor in aptitude, which means that such tests place students from environments different from the test designers at a disadvantage (Jencks, 1998).

Scholars and writers on both sides of the issue come back to the cultural bias issue while ignoring a more problematic issue, the continued misuse of standardized test scores in the admissions process. Because of the increasing burden of reviewing thousands of applicants many selective colleges and universities rely significantly on standardized test scores (Nettles, Perna, & Millet, 1998). Relying on test scores in the college admissions process is extremely problematic for several reasons. First, because standardized tests are statistical estimates of student ability, there is an error of measurement. According to George Hanford, President of the College Entrance Examination Board (College Board), "The SAT's error of measurement is such that two times out of three, the score a student gets on a particular form, or edition, of the test will be within about 30 points one way or the other of the true score. That phenomenon may seem to suggest that SAT scores aren't all that reliable, but that's pretty reliable—indeed very reliable—for a test" (Hanford, 1991, p. 33).

The second problem with relying significantly on the standardized tests is related to the issue of reliability or predictive validity. According to Hanford, despite the error of measurement the SAT is "pretty reliable." Opponents of affirmative action usually support the use of standardized tests in the admissions process based on the predictive validity of the tests. According to D'Souza (1995, p. 309):

> Yet the general conclusion of psychologists and psychometricians is that the SAT predicts college performance reasonably well. In technical terms, the predictive validity of the SAT is approximately 0.50. (A score of 1 would indicate a perfect correlation between SAT scores and college grades.) Taken in conjunction with high school grades, the SAT is an even better predictor of academic success at the university level (D'Souza, 1995, p. 309).

This statement by D'Souza is similar to statements in publications by the College Board (Bridgeman, McCamley-Jenkins, & Ervin, 2000). D'Souza does not properly explain what "0.50" means. By stating that "a score of 1 would indicate a perfect correlation between SAT scores and college grades," he suggests that a predictive validity of 0.50 means that half of the variation in students college grades are explained by their SAT.

However, what D'Souza suggests is not correct because 0.50 is the multiple correlation coefficient, mathematically referred to as r. The multiple correlation coefficient r does not explain the variance between the independent variable (SAT score) and the dependent variable (freshman college grades). In the beginning of any good statistics text, the author will warn against making the mistake that "r is irrelevant in the regression model. Therefore, interpreting r as indicating the linear relation between X and Y is inappropriate" (Pedhazur, 1997, p. 39). It is r^2 that gives the proportion of variance of the dependent variable explained by the independent variable. To find out what the variance explained is we must square 0.50 because 0.50 is r. When squared 0.50 is 0.25, which is the amount of variation in college grades (dependent variable) impacted by SAT score (independent variable). Simply stated, SAT scores only explain 25 percent of the variation in freshman grades.

Despite this low explanation of variance, selective colleges and universities keep a significant number of students of all races out because of a statistical estimate of how they will perform. This is extremely significant because the College Board and colleges and universities draw charts of predictability based on students' SAT scores and their freshman grade point average (GPA). Such a matrix is impressive, especially when tabulated using thousands of students' test scores and college grades. However, the matrix is only as good as the predictive validity of the data. Using such a matrix with a predictive validity as low as 0.25 to determine college admissions leaves many unanswered questions and makes many false assumptions. Although combining high school GPA with SAT scores improves the multiple correlation coefficient (r) to 0.61, the r^2 is still small, 0.37 (Bridgeman, McCamley-Jenkins, & Ervin, 2000).

The X-Percent Factor

Because of the increasingly conservative disposition of the federal courts, there is little prognosis of success for proponents of affirmative action (Spann, 1990). Selective public institutions must reevaluate their admissions policies if they are committed to racial diversity, because any alternative that addresses race directly will come under legal challenge. Following the end of affirmative action in California the African-American presence in the freshman cohort at the University of California at Berkeley (UC-Berkeley) decreased from about 8 percent [7.8%] in 1997 to less than 4 percent [3.8%] in 1999 (Cooper, 2000). Despite voting to end affirmative action in college admissions in 1995, the University of California Board of Regents maintain that they continue to be committed to campuses as diverse as the state (Karabel, 1998). One of the first efforts by the state to maintain diversity was to increase the quality of minority student preparation so that more students of color are able to gain admission to the flagship institutions in California. Because the focus of this chapter is the admissions policy, no discussion will be given to the topic of precollegiate and college preparatory programs.

California, Texas, and Florida are leading the nation in implementing what is referred to as X-percent or percentage plans. These plans guarantee a top percentage of graduating students from each high school in the state admission to a public college or university. These alternative admissions policies are seen as a way to maintain diversity after ending affirmative action. The logic of the X-percent plans is that because most high schools are racially segregated, guaranteeing admission to a certain percentage of students from every school will bring in students of color regardless of standardized test scores.

The California program is called the Eligibility in the Local Context program (ELC). This program guarantees the top 4 percent of graduating students in each high school admission to one of the eight University of California schools. The program includes both public and private high schools. In high schools with separate academic programs, ELC eligibility is determined for graduating students from each program. For example, in determining ELC eligibility for a high school with a magnet program, a top 4 percent is determined for both the general program and the magnet program. According to the ELC website:

The plan [ELC] was developed to recognize that student achievement is relative to the educational opportunities available at individual schools. . . . Students deemed eligible through ELC will be guaranteed a place at one of UC's eight undergraduate campuses, though not necessarily the campus of their choice. Students must complete remaining eligibility requirements prior to enrollment (http://www.ucop.edu/sas/elc/overview.html).

In the effort to maintain diverse campuses in the university system, the ELC program is an extremely poor effort. The program contains two major flaws that limit its ability to increase the percentage of African Americans on University of California campuses following the end of affirmative action in California. The two major problems with the ELC plan are the lack of student choice and the high eligibility threshold. Because students in the top 4 percent must meet individual university guidelines to gain admission, the program does little to maintain an ethnically diverse campus at the most prestigious schools in the University of California System (UC System). The eight University of California schools are not considered equal in resources and prestige. The lack of student choice in the ELC program is significant because despite the overall quality of the UC System, UC-Berkeley and the University of California at Los Angeles (UCLA) are nationally recognized as among the best universities in the country. According to *U.S. News and World Report* college rankings, both UC-Berkeley and UCLA are ranked in the top 25 of all National universities (http://www.usnews.com/usnews/edu/college/corank.htm). These institutions accept less than a third of all applicants. At the other end of the UC System are the University of California at Riverside (UC-Riverside) and the University of California at Santa Cruz (UC-Santa Cruz). Both of these institutions are ranked in the second tier and accept about 80 percent of applicants. The average combined SAT score for African-American students in California for 1999 was 864. The SAT score average for white and Asian students was 1,075 and 1,034. With an average SAT score of 864 many ELC-eligible African-American students will be forced into the less prestigious University of California schools. The ELC program will leave UC-Berkeley and UCLA significantly less racially diverse than before the end of affirmative action.

The second major flaw of the ELC program is that the 4 percent eligibility for the program is so small that it offers little change in the normal composition of admitted students. The top 4 percent are the best of the best. As a statement of quality most universities cite the percentage of their students who were in the top 10 percent in their high school class. Despite the variance in SAT averages for the eight University of California schools, at least 90 percent of the incoming freshmen at each school were in the top 10 percent of their graduating class. Automatically admitting the top 4 percent to one of these schools does little to change these numbers.

The ELC plan has one advantage. Without the ELC plan students at many schools located in low-income communities would fail to achieve a SAT score sufficient for admission to any of the University of California schools. Many high schools located in low-income urban communities are underfunded because of a low local tax base. The lack of financial resources and rapid increase in student enrollment in cities such as Los Angeles create overcrowded classrooms, where the task of teaching and learning is difficult (Booth, 2000). The conditions at many schools serving low-income students are so detrimental to the educational process that the American Civil Liberties Union filed a suit in May 2000, claiming that the state failed to provide a minimum quality of education to low-income students in urban schools (Sahagun & Helfand, 2000). The quality of education in these schools is exacerbated by the loss of experienced teachers and an inability to attract talented new teachers. A school can be so academically inadequate that top students fail to score above 900 on the SAT. The lowest average SAT scores in the UC System are 940-1,200 at UC-Riverside. Even ELC-eligible students in poor urban high schools who fail to obtain an average score on the SAT, will gain admission to one of the University of California campuses. The inclusion of all schools in the ELC plan addresses the issue of access for all students who reach the highest goals established by their high school.

Overall the ELC plan is a poor substitute for affirmative action in maintaining racial diversity throughout the University of California System. The plan does increase access to the UC System for African-Americans students from urban schools; however, many of these students will be relegated to the lowest tier of the UC System. Because the ELC plan fails to disperse African-American students throughout the UC System, the black student population at UC-Berkeley and UCLA will remain small. Although the ELC plan increases the access of low-income students to the UC System, the plan may fail to increase the percentage of blacks in the entire University of California System to the numbers prior to the end of affirmative action. The automatic admission of students from schools located in low-income minority communities might crowd out better prepared black students from academically challenging schools who fail to make the top 4 percent cut. The increase in access for low-income African-American students satisfies a policy aimed at increasing access along the economic spectrum. However, as long as the total number of African-American students admitted under the ELC plan is not equal to the number of blacks admitted under the previous affirmative action policy, the ELC plan will fail to maintain racial diversity.

An X-percent plan similar to the California program is being implemented in Florida. The Florida plan is called the Talented 20 program and is a part of Governor Jeb Bush's One Florida Plan. The One Florida Plan is aimed at addressing the state's history of legal discrimination in government contracting and college admissions. The Florida plan is similar to the California plan because students who are eligible do not gain admission to the school of their choice; that decision is based on institutional standards. The biggest difference between the Florida and California plans is the number of eligible students. Florida includes the top 20 percent from Florida public high schools, which is a significantly larger number than the top 4 percent in California. In a high school senior class of 300 students, the Florida plan increases the number of eligible students by 400 percent over the California ELC plan. According to the Florida Board of Regents:

> The Talented 20 Program would provide the future pathway for all Florida students, regardless of race, ethnicity, gender, economic circumstances, or zip code, to reach their highest educational aspirations (*Talented 20 report*, 2000, p. 2).

Just as in California, if students gaining admission to the State University System of Florida are sorted based on institutional standards, few African-American students will gain admission to one of the state's flagship institutions, the University of Florida or Florida State University. This lack of access to the most prestigious public universities in the state is more severe in Florida because unlike the University of California System, several of the public universities in Florida are near the bottom of national rankings. The University of South Florida and Florida International University rank in the 3rd tier of national universities. Florida Atlantic University and the University of Central Florida are ranked in the 4th tier of national universities. Also unlike California, the dispersion of Talented 20 students is impacted by two unique institutions.

Florida Agricultural and Mechanical University (Florida A&M) is one of the historically black colleges and universities (HBCUs). Florida A&M is rated as one of the top HBCUs in America and is highly respected for its engineering and business schools. As an institution committed to providing top quality educational opportunity to African-American students, Florida A&M combines both flexible admissions standards with the ability to attract top African-American students from across the country. The average SAT score in 1996 was 1,036, partly due to the school's ability to attract many National Achievement Scholars (African-American students with the highest SAT scores). In 1995,

Florida A&M enrolled more National Achievement Scholars than any other school in the country. While attracting the top African-American students from around the country, Florida A&M reserves almost a third of its freshman class for students who would not normally qualify for admission (Evelyn, 1998). The second unique institution in Florida is the newly established Florida Gulf Coast University. This institution opened its doors in the fall of 1997 to meet the growing educational and high-tech skilled-labor needs of Florida's growing Gulf Coast region. As with any new institution, Florida Gulf Coast University suffers from a lack of an alumni network, reputation, and prestige.

Currently, African-American students are 7 percent of the undergraduate enrollment at the University of Florida and 12 percent at Florida State University. This level of African-American enrollment was achieved with affirmative action as a part of the admissions process. Under the Talented 20 program, without the use of affirmative action, these percentages will probably decline. The average combined SAT for African-American students in Florida is 854, whereas the average score for whites is 1,041. The average SAT range at the University of Florida is 1,120-1,320. The average SAT range at Florida State University is 1,040-1,240 (http://www.usnews.com/usnews/edu/college/corank.htm). While the top 20 percent from predominantly black high schools all over the state will gain automatic admission to state institutions, few will be able to meet the admissions standards of the University of Florida or Florida State University. The African-American population at these two flagship institutions will also be affected by the fact that some black students able to gain admission to these schools will choose to go elsewhere because of their belief that they will be among a small minority. The presence of Florida A&M as another top-quality option will likely exacerbate this flight of top black students from the two flagship institutions.

Following the *Hopwood v. Texas* (1996) decision, which ended affirmative action in Texas, the state legislature passed an X-percent plan. According to the official state website for the Texas plan, "the legislation that created this admission policy was in response to the Hopwood v. Texas court decision. As a result of that decision, criteria on which university admissions decisions are made must be race-neutral" (Texas Higher Education Coordinating Board, 2000). The Top 10 Percent rule (Texas plan) was created by the Texas Higher Education Coordinating Board and adopted in October 1997. Under the Texas plan students in the top 10 percent of their graduating class at public and private high schools receive automatic admission to a public college or university in Texas. Eligible students in Texas can choose which public college or university they wish to attend.

The Texas plan is different from the Florida and California plans because eligible students in Texas have the power of choice. Student choice increases access for some students of color in Texas and maintains the level of racial diversity from the affirmative action years (U.S. Commission on Civil Rights, 2000). Although eligible students in Texas can select either of the flagship institutions, the University of Texas at Austin (UT-Austin) or Texas Agricultural and Mechanical University (Texas A&M), the impact of the Texas plan is small. The number of African-American students eligible under the Texas plan is not significant because the plan only includes the top 10 percent. Analysis of the projected public high school graduates for the 1995-1996 academic year shows that only 4 percent of African-American high school graduates were in the top 10 percent of their class (Holley & Spencer, 1999). Even if all of the 901 black students eligible under the Texas plan entered either UT-Austin or Texas A&M, the percentage of African-Americans students would not be significant. If half, 450, entered UT-Austin, based on the undergraduate enrollment figures for 1999, African-American students would make up only 6.4 percent of the university. This hypothetical 6.4 percent is twice the percentage enrolled during the first year under the Texas plan, 1998. However, it is not significant when one considers that 13.8 percent of the population in Texas was African American in 1995 (Institute, 1997).

The Texas plan still does not improve access for many of the state's most academically prepared African American students in predominantly white middle-class high schools. Black students in magnet programs or academically challenging and competitive public and private schools who are not in the top 10 percent are forced to go through a race-neutral admissions process. Proof that this is occurring can be found in the declining acceptance rate for African-American students after implementation of the Texas plan. Following the end of affirmative action and the implementation of the Texas plan the acceptance rate for black students at UT-Austin decreased from 57 percent in 1996 to 46 percent in 1999 (U.S. Commission of Civil Rights, 2000).

All three percentage plans must be examined in comparison to the policy they replaced—affirmative action. While all three plans open access to higher education to the most economically distressed communities, they fail to meet the goals of racial and ethnic diversity at every institution in the three state university systems. The plan in California limits choice and includes an extremely small percentage of graduating students. The plan in Florida includes a significant number of students but fails to give them the ability to select where they enroll. The plan in Texas gives students choice but only includes a small percentage of students. Another major problem with all three programs is that each state program, as a legal substitute for affirmative action, is based on the continued residential and educational segregation of each state.

A Class-based Alternative

Another alternative commonly mentioned in the debate over racial diversity in higher education is class-based affirmative action. Supporters of this policy do not believe that all college admissions decisions should be based on academic variables such as grades and standardized test scores. Class-based affirmative action suggests that, after centuries of racial oppression, America's problems of unequal opportunity and disadvantage are largely economic problems. Support for this alternative is partly based on the belief that race-based affirmative action places the burden on lower-income whites or Asians who are not responsible for past discrimination. Examples of the unjust burden placed on Asians and whites are described by opponents of race-based affirmative action. According to D'Souza (1991, p. 24):

> When high school senior Yat-pang Au received his rejection letter from the University of California at Berkeley in 1987, he was incredulous. . . . Yat-pang's credentials were not in question. He graduated first in his class at San Jose's Gunderson High School with a straight A average; his SAT scores were 1,340 . . . he ran a Junior Achievement company; won varsity letters in cross country and track; was elected to the student council and school Supreme Court.

One fundamental flaw of class-based affirmative action is that it makes the assumption that only blacks living in poverty suffer from a lack of equal opportunity. Class-based affirmative action assumes that the children of professional middle- and upper-income African Americans are above the legacy of racism and oppression in America. Another major flaw with class-based affirmative action is that it ignores the value of racial and ethnic diversity. Opponents of race-based affirmative action argue that affirmative action's goal of a diverse campus assumes that black people all think one way and that way is different from the way whites or Asians think. According to one critic of race-based affirmative action, "skin color does not equal ideas, and ethnicity does not equal experiences. . . . Moreover, since the invention of the printing press, it has not been necessary to meet people in order to learn their perspectives" (Clegg, 2000, p. B8). Clegg's argument is a ridiculous simplification of culture, which is an extremely complex issue.

Admittedly there is a construct called black culture, just as there is a European culture, Latino culture, and Asian culture. These cultures are not mutually exclusive and they certainly are within themselves vibrant and constantly changing. For example, within black culture there are variations based on regions of the United States. There also exist recent immigrant cultures within black culture such as West Indian culture and African culture. Clegg is correct that skin color does not always equal ideas. Within any ethnic group, there exist people who ascribe to the culture of another ethnic group or a combination of cultures based on a multiethnic heritage. This is all rather complicated and is better understood through experiences, which is one of the goals of race-based affirmative action. Affirmative action does not assume that all blacks are alike. Opponents of race-based affirmative action created a myth of diversity, which is expressed in the quote from Clegg. The reality of diversity is that only through a racially diverse learning environment will students learn just what opponents of affirmative action say, which is that not all black students think and act alike.

If implemented, class-based affirmative action will lead to lower representation of African-American students at selective institutions (Bowen & Bok, 1998; Kane, 1998). In support of class-based affirmative action Kahlenberg (1996) argues that colleges can maintain the same level of racial diversity as race-based affirmative action if the policy is properly structured. According to Kahlenberg (1996, p. 166):

> Assume, for example, that a university now informally sets aside ten seats for blacks in a class of one hundred. Under a new class-based affirmative action program, assume the university sets a goal of forty seats for students who come from the bottom 50 percent economically. Even if 75 percent of the class preference seats go to nonblacks, there is no net loss of black seats. The absolute number of African Americans is still ten.

Mathematically Kahlenberg's example is correct. However, his solution is extremely implausible. Kahlenberg assumes that an institution would be willing or able to afford the financial cost of enrolling 40 students of every 100 from the bottom 50 percent economically. Besides the high cost of enrolling 40 percent of students from the lower half of the economic scale, a college would lose some students able to pay a much larger share of their expenses. For wealthy institutions such as Harvard University, Kahlenberg's plan is plausible, but for the majority of other institutions, especially public institutions, the plan is nearly impossible considering the decrease in funding from state legislatures (Kane, 1999).

A Bold Alternative

In the debate over the use of the SAT in the college admissions process some simply accept the SAT as the best option available. According to Kahlenberg (1996, p. 157):

> Of course, standardized tests do not come close to measuring everything that is important—creativity, character, leadership. And they certainly do not predict who will be a good lawyer, doctor, or businessperson. But until someone devises such tests, we are stuck with muddling along and doing the best we can with what we have.

Are the current admissions policies in many selective colleges and universities the best option available? All the alternatives to affirmative action discussed earlier still maintain the heavy reliance on standardized tests in the admissions process. Perhaps a new, slightly different race-neutral admissions policy that does not utilize standardized tests is the key to maintaining diversity and providing equal opportunity following the repeal of affirmative action in some states. Selective admissions colleges have long gone beyond focusing only on a student's high school performance. In the 1800s individual colleges, primarily in the Northeast, administered their own admissions tests to ensure that entering students knew the body of information that the college faculty felt necessary in order to advance to postsecondary work (Fine, 1946; Fuess, 1950). The change to standardized tests was the result of a movement in college admissions that focused on comprehensive examinations "by which they meant examinations not based mainly on the memorization or mastery of assigned subject matter, but rather designed to test a candidate's ability to reason independently and to compare and correlate the material of a broad field of study" (Fuess, 1950, p. 79).

In a country where there is not enough room at selective institutions for everyone desiring admissions, the use of standardized tests seem not only appropriate, but necessary. However, the issues of race, class, equity, and justice significantly alter the context of college admissions in America. In seeking to select better students, the SAT complicates efforts for equity and diversity. The only solution then is for selective colleges and universities to eliminate the use of standardized test scores in the selection process. According to one study by the College Board, "indeed, high school average grades are usually a better predictor than the test scores" (Schrader, 1971, p. 120).

The concern with focusing too much on high school grades is that school curricula and grading standards are not consistent across a state let alone the nation. One way of addressing this problem is to build closer ties between higher education and primary and secondary education. Giving public colleges and universities a role in developing K-12 curricula helps to reduce the discrepancy in content and standards throughout a state. Despite the belief that high school courses and grading standards are not consistent across the country, the variance in freshman (college) GPA explained by high school GPA is slightly higher than the variance in freshman (college) GPA explained by the SAT—0.29 compared to 0.27 (Bridgeman, McCamley-Jenkins, & Ervin, 2000). An r^2 of 0.29 is still small; however, it is better than using the SAT alone. Using both high school GPA and SAT scores together does have a significantly higher r^2, 0.37. However, the issues of cultural bias and other nonacademic factors that affect SAT scores are too significant to outweigh the minor advantage of using both SAT and high school GPA in the college selection process. At least a high school GPA is based on a student's ability to do a certain level of work consistently for three to four years. A high school GPA based on weighted courses rewards students for rigorous course selection and makes the road to college clear. Classes at some high schools are significantly less rigorous than at other schools; however, state and local governments are working to change this. Focusing on high school grades is similar to the logic behind the X-percent plans in California, Florida, and Texas, "there is general American acceptance of the notion that hardworking students should not be deprived of an equal chance at the best public higher education opportunity because their schools did not offer them a chance to take certain courses" (U.S. Commission on Civil Rights, 2000).

Conclusion

The conservative climate in the United States has caused a loss of progress in the quest for diversity and equality in higher education. The attack on affirmative action has given rise to alternative admissions policies in public higher education. Already these alternative admissions plans are failing to halt the decline in minority enrollments at selective institutions. Alternative admissions policies aimed at diversity will continue to be analyzed and scrutinized as more information is available. The state of race-based admissions is due to the unsettled issue of race in America. There are no easy answers because the issue of race in America is complicated and as old as the nation.

References

Bennefield, R. M. (1999, October 14). Running for cover: Fear and paranoia surrounding affirmative action lawsuits unjustified, experts say. *Black Issues in Higher Education* October 14:22–24.

Booth, W. (2000, April 18). A problem crowds in on L.A. schools. *The Washington Post*, p. A03.

Bowen, W. G., & Bok, D. (1998). *The shape of the river: Long-term consequences of considering race in college and university admissions.* Princeton: Princeton University Press.

Bridgeman, B., McCamley-Jenkins, L., & Ervin, N. (2000). *Predictions of freshman grade-point average from the revised and recentered SAT I: Reasoning test* (2000–1). New York: The College Entrance Examination Board.

Clegg, R. (2000, July 14). Why I'm sick of the praise for diversity on campuses. *Chronicle of Higher Education*, p. B8.

Cooper, K. J. (2000, April 2). Colleges testing new diversity initiatives. *Washington Post*, p. A04.

Crouse, J., & Trusheim, D. (1988). *The case against the SAT.* Chicago: University of Chicago.

D'Souza, D. (1991). *Illiberal education: The politics of race and sex on campus.* New York: The Free Press.

D'Souza, D. (1995). *The end of racism: Principles for a multiracial society.* New York: Free Press.

Evelyn, J. (1998, January 8). Ten stories that made a difference in 1997. *Black Issues in Higher Education* 14:14–17.

Ferdinand, P. (1998, November 20). Race-based school policy struck down. *Washington Post*, p. A04.

Fine, B. (1946). *Admission to American colleges.* New York: Harper & Brothers.

Florida Board of Regents (2000) Talented 20 report. [World Wide Web]. Florida Board of Regents. Available: http://www.borfl.org/borpubs/equity_education/equity_in_education.asp [2000, August 14].

Fuess, C. M. (1950). *The College Board: Its first fifty years.* New York: Columbia University Press.

Guinier, L., & Sturm, S. (1996). The future of affirmative action: Reclaiming the innovative ideal. *California Law Review* 84(953):953–1036.

Hanford, G. H. (1991). *Life with the SAT: Assessing our young people and our times.* New York: The College Entrance Examination Board.

Holley, D., & Spencer, D. (1999). The Texas ten percent plan. *Harvard Civil Rights-Civil Liberties Law Review* 34(245):245–278.

Hopwood v. Texas, 78 F3d 932 (1996).

Institute, F. D. P. R. (1997). *The African American Education Data Book*, Vol. I: Higher and Adult Education. Fairfax, VA: The College Fund/UNCF.

Jencks, C. (1998). Racial bias in testing. In *The black-white test score gap*, C. Jencks & M. Phillips (Eds.), pp. 55–85. Washington, D.C.: Brookings Institution.

Kahlenberg, R. D. (1996). *The remedy: Class, race, and affirmative action.* New York: Basic Books.

Kane, T. J. (1998). Misconceptions in the debate over affirmative action in college admissions. In *Chilling admissions: The affirmative action crisis and the search for alternatives*, G. Orfield & E. Miller (Eds.), pp. 17–31. Cambridge, MA: Harvard Education Publishing Group.

Kane, T. J. (1999). *The price of admission: Rethinking how Americans pay for college.* Washington, D.C.: Brookings Institution.

Karabel, J. (1998). No alternative: The effects of color-blind admissions in California. In *Chilling admissions: The affirmative action crisis and the search for alternatives*, G. Orfield & E. Miller (Eds.), pp. 33–50. Cambridge, MA: Harvard Education Publishing Group.

Masters, B. A. (2000, July 5). 4th circuit judges steering to the right. *The Washington Post*, p. B01.

Nettles, M. T., Perna, L. W., & Millett, C. M. (1998). Race and testing in college admissions. In *Chilling admissions: The affirmative action crisis and the search for alternatives*, G. Orfield & E. Miller (Eds.), pp. 97–110. Cambridge, MA: Harvard Education Publishing Group.

Pedhazur, E. J. (1997). *Multiple regression in behavioral research: Explanation and prediction*, 3rd ed.. Orlando, FL: Harcourt Brace & Company.

Rankin, B., & McCarthy, R. (2000, July 26). Admission policy at UGA faces more suits. *Atlanta Journal & Constitution*, p. 1C.

Regents of the University of California v. Bakke, 98 Sup. Ct. 2733 (1978).

Sahagun, L., & Helfand, D. (2000, May 18). ACLU sues state over conditions in poor schools. *Los Angeles Times*, p. 1.

Schrader, W. B. (1971). The predictive validity of college board admissions tests. In *The College Board admissions testing program: A technical report on research and development activities relating to the Scholastic Aptitude Test and Achievement Tests*, W. H. Angoff (Ed.), pp. 117–145). New York: College Entrance Examination Board.

Selingo, J. (2000, July 21). Judge clears Florida plan on affirmative action. *Chronicle of Higher Education*, p. A24.

Sowell, T. (1984). *Civil rights: Rhetoric or reality?* New York: William Morrow.

Spann, G. A. (1990). Pure politics. *88 Michigan Law Review*, 1971–2033.

Spann, G. A. (2000). *The law of affirmative action: Twenty-five years of Supreme Court decisions on race and remedies.* New York: New York University.

Texas Higher Education Coordinating Board (2000). *Top 10 percent eligible for automatic college admission.* [World Wide Web]. Texas Higher Education Coordinating Board. Available: http://www.thecb.state.tx.us/divisions/grpi/topten.htm [2000, August 13].

Thernstrom, S., & Thernstrom, A. (1997). *America in Black and White: One nation, indivisible.* New York: Simon & Schuster.

Thernstrom, S., & Thernstrom, A. (1999, February). Racial preferences: What we now know. *Commentary* 107:44.

U.S. Commission on Civil Rights (2000). *Toward an understanding of percentage plans in higher education: Are they effective substitutes for affirmative action.* [World Wide Web].U.S. Commission on Civil Rights. Available: www.usccr.gov/percent/stmnt.htm [2000, August 13].

5

DEVELOPING ACADEMIC WARRIORS

THINGS THAT PARENTS, ADMINISTRATORS, AND FACULTY SHOULD KNOW

James L. Moore III

Without regard to race or gender, many of the factors that contribute to academic success of African-American students are often identified for all college students at predominately white institutions (PWIs). What distinguish African-American students from their Caucasian counterparts are the added burdens of racism, discrimination, and negative stereotypes. These oppressive forces constantly convey messages of intellectual incompetence, which at times have debilitating effects on the academic identity and achievement of African-American students. More often than not, success in college has less to do with aptitude in cognitive measures (e.g., high school grade point averages [GPAs], standardized achievement tests [SATs], and class rank) than noncognitive measures such as self-efficacy, motivation, commitment, and persistence. The author of this chapter postulates that academic success for African-American students is determined in large measure on how they respond to racism when it occurs, adjust to the academic and social environment, and navigate through the culture of their PWI. Nevertheless, it is essential that they devote the necessary time, effort, and energy to their academic studies. This level of commitment is not limited to one particular strategy; in fact, it may manifest in one or a combination of the following strategies: (1) getting extra help from professors, tutors, and peers; (2) spending more time reading and going over homework assignments; (3) studying with class-mates (both African American and Caucasian); and/or (4) utilizing other resources around campus designed to increase academic performance. This chapter focuses on African-American students who have the academic back-ground and ability to be successful in PWIs but who are not always reaching their potential academically. First, the author presents a historical overview of African-American students on PWIs. Second, he identifies the hidden obstacles to academic success. Third, the author highlights factors that commonly hin-der academic persistence and achievement of African-American students. Fourth, the author provides a short overview of motivation and persistence of African-American students. Fifth, recommendations are provided to assist par-ents, administrators, and faculty in helping transform African-American stu-dents into "academic warriors." The recommendations are designed to em-power African-American students to take responsibility for their own academic performance.

Historical Overview of African-American Students at PWIs

Since the 1960s, the enrollment patterns of African-American students have dra-matically shifted from historical black institutions (HBIs) to PWIs (Harvey & Williams 1993; Tidwell & Berry, 1993; Townsend, 1994). Many scholars (Allen, 1992; Tidwell & Berry, 1993) attribute the change of demographics to *Brown vs. Board of Education of Topeka*. This monumental case significantly changed the landscape of higher education by declaring that "separate but equal" was unconstitutional. It mandated that all public educational institutions abolish their segregation policies (Scott, 1995). As a result, PWIs began developing recruiting initiatives, educational opportunities, and partnerships with African-American institutions to attract talented African-American students to their respective universities (Davis, 1998; Tidwell & Berry, 1993; Townsend, 1994). Many of these efforts were successful in attracting African-American students to PWIs; however, a disproportionate number of students had difficulty adjusting and persisting through the curriculum (Fleming, 1984; Fordham & Ogbu, 1986; Weber, 1992). Much of the difficulty was directly or indirectly related to African-American students' negative interpersonal experiences at PWIs.

Just as in the 1960s, adjustment tribulations are still common among African-American college students who attend PWIs (Tinto, 1993). Some of the challenges are generalizable to all college students, and others are specific to African-American students (Allen, 1992). African-American students often feel isolated and alienated at PWIs (Delphin & Rollock, 1995; Schwitzer et al., 1999; Sedlacek, 1987). Research results suggest that a significant portion of the African-American students who attend PWIs leave by their sophomore year in college (Jackson, 1992). Nettles (1987) attributes the poor retention to PWIs not adequately meeting the needs and expectations of African-American students. Nettles further explains that the needs of African Americans are quite different from their Caucasian counterparts. Therefore, one could make the case that PWIs need to create retention initiatives that are applicable to African-American culture.

When comparing African-American students who attend HBIs with those who attend PWIs, Davis (1994) found that the students who attended HBIs had higher GPAs than those who attended PWIs. One possible explanation for these findings is that HBI students receive more contact from professors and are encouraged more than their peers who attend PWIs (Cokley, 1999; Fleming, 1984; Weber, 1992). Gloria et al.(1999) found, in their study, that social support, university comfort, and positive self-beliefs were highly associated with the persistence of African-American students at PWIs. Although the three variables predicted persistence, social support and university comfort were the strongest predictors. These findings substantiate past research conducted on African-American college students (Fleming, 1984, 1990; Scott, 1995).

In a qualitative study, Schwitzer and his colleagues (1999) found that African-American students felt less supported and nurtured in their respective PWIs than in their communities and high schools. The authors also found that these students were less likely to approach their instructors for help unless the instructor was of the same gender, race, and/or both. Students' reservations were directly related to their fears of being perceived as needing help because of their race. Such reluctance is common among African-American students at PWIs. Howard and Hammond (1985, p. 18) suggest that this behavior is "rooted in the fears and self-doubt engendered by a major legacy of American racism: the strong negative stereotypes about black intellectual capabilities."

The Masked Obstacles of Academic Achievement

College life on the margins is an unpleasant reality for African-American students at PWIs. Many Caucasian professors and students harbor negative stereotypes about African-American students' academic ability and potential. These stereotypes manifest in professors paying less attention to African-American students and/or ignoring them altogether (Moore, 2000; Simms, Knight, & Dawes, 1993; Trujillo, 1986). Caucasian students' negative perceptions are also indicated by their behaviors. It is not uncommon for them to express reluctance in working on projects and studying with African-Americans (Moore, 2000). Unfortunately, many African-American students, regardless of the PWI they attend, are confronted with these unpleasant realities. They are constantly faced with the task of "beating the odds" and transcending assaults on their humanity and academic ability (Moore, 2000). These insidious attacks are both blatant and subtle; nevertheless, the effects are often detrimental to their academic motivation and educational outcomes (Ford, 1996).

Howard and Hammond (1985) posit that "black inferiority" is communicated in different venues of society. Furthermore, the two authors suggest that the stigma of inferiority follows African-American students everywhere they go, especially in specific academic arenas (e.g., engineering, mathematics, and science). The effects often negatively inhibit their confidence and motivation. As a result, many of these students adopt unsuccessful practices that cause them to make unwise academic decisions and sometimes fail academically (Hrabowski & Maton, 1995; Moore, 2000). Results of several studies (Moore, 2000; Scott, 1995) suggest that those who fail feel like they are letting their families and race down. These are common feelings expressed by ethnic minorities who embrace a collectivistic worldview and ideology of life. Therefore, failure is not without sociological, psychological, and emotional repercussions.

Howard and Hammond (1995) assert that everyone encounters failure, but unexpected failure affects students differently from expected failure. For example, a student who is confident in his or her ability but happens to fail at a task is likely to attribute his or her failure to not working hard enough. On the contrary, a student who is expecting to fail is likely to attribute his or her failure to lack of ability and is likely to hesitate approaching the task again. It is clear that expectancy and cognition play a tremendous role on educational outcomes, especially for African-American students. In more detail, Howard and Hammond (1985, p. 20) lament:

> The negative expectancy first tends to generate failure through its impact on behavior, and then induces the individual to blame the failure on lack of ability, rather than the actual attribution in turn becomes the basis for a new negative expectancy. By this process the individual, in effect, internalizes the low estimation originally held by others. This internalized negative expectancy powerfully affects future competitive behavior and future results.

Steele (1997), a renowned social psychologist at Stanford University, refers to this notion of behavior as the "stereotype threat." He first coined the term to explain the structural barriers and achievement gaps of capable African-American students. He suggests that African Americans' academic achievement has less to do with their academic ability than with the threat of negative stereotypes about their capacity to achieve. The premise of Steele's theory begins with the assumption that negative societal perceptions about African Americans can negatively impact the intellectual and identity development of individual group members. The stereotype threat occurs most often when one is pursuing a career or education that is not perceived as the norm of reference. "This predicament threatens one with being negatively stereotyped, with being judged or treated stereotypically, or with the prospect of conforming to the stereotype" (Steele, 1997, p. 14). More importantly, it intensifies the fears and uncertainties of the person being negatively stereotyped (Howard & Hammond, 1985).

Motivation and Persistence

Research results (Bowser & Perkins, 1991; Moore, 2000; Scott, 1995) indicate that motivation and persistence have a profound influence on academic performance. "Certain variables consistently associated with persistence are included in an integrationist theory of persistence" (Donovan, 1984, p. 244). The variables are typically associated with learning environments, academic problems, relationships with instructors, and interactions with other students (Wilson-Sadberry, Winfield, & Royster, 1991). Sedlacek (1983) identifies eight noncognitive variables that are exceptional in predicting academic success of African-American college students. These variables are: (1) a positive self-concept; (2) understanding and dealing with racism; (3) a realistic self-appraisal; (4) the preference of long-range goals to immediate needs; (5) the availability of a strong support person; (6) successful leadership experiences; (7) demonstrated community service; and (8) nontraditional knowledge.

According to Simms, Knight, & Dawes (1993, p. 259), "these variables are offered as potential areas for faculty members to consider when working with minority students as ways to promote success and increase retention in post-secondary institutions." Scott (1995) found in her study that motivation and effort were key factors in the academic performance of African-American students. In addition, she discovered that good study habits combined with clear goals positively contributed to the academic success of African-American students. When making between-group comparisons (e.g., below 2.0 GPA group, 2.0–3.0 GPA group, and 3.0 GPA and above group), Scott (1995) discovered that each sample group recognized the importance of these factors, but approached them differently. For example, Scott (1995, p. 98) states:

> The successful students [3.0 and above] talked about investing extra study time, using campus resources, studying with peers, and talking to professors. The satisfactory students [2.0–3.0] also engaged in similar activities but not to the extent as the successful group. The less successful students [2.0 or less] admitted that academics were not a priority and that they had not spent adequate time on their studies.

Tinto (1975) hypothesizes, using Durkheim's (1951) theory of suicide, that academics and social life influence the educational outcomes of college students. He further articulates that lack of integration in the two variables can or will lead to low persistence. In other words, an individual's degree of integration into the academic and social environment determines in large measure whether or not the individual is going persist through college (Wambach, 1993). For example, Tinto (1975, pp. 91–92) states:

> When one views the college as a social system with its own value and social structures, one can treat dropout from that social system in a manner analogous to that of suicide in the wider society . . . social conditions affecting dropout from the social system of the college would resemble those resulting in suicide in the wider society; namely insufficient interactions with others in the college and insufficient congruency with the prevailing value patterns of the college collectivity . . . lack of integration into the social system of the college will lead to low commitment to that social system and will increase the probability that individuals will decide to leave college and pursue alternative activities.

Parental and Familial Support

Transitioning to college is a stressful period for many students (Lafreniere, Ledgerwood, & Docherty, 1997). Whether it is meeting new friends, finding classes, or being away from family for the first time, both African-American and Caucasian college students need support. More often than not, support comes from parents and other family members. These individuals often are called on to provide encouragement, guidance, and reassurance about college and the student's potential. Regardless of the reason, results of several studies suggest that parents positively influence academic achievement (Hrabowski, Maton, & Greif, 1998; Moore, 2000; Scott, 1995; Taylor, Hinton, & Wilson,

1995). Strong parental support manifests into greater levels of confidence, effi-cacy, and motivation in the student. For example, Smith and Hausfaus (1998) discovered that minority students did better in math and science when their parents were involved and supportive of their education.

Hrabowski and Maton (1995) found similar results, when comparing three different cohorts in the Meyerhoff Scholars Program[1] (N = 69) with compara-ble historical cohorts. The two authors discovered that the Meyerhoff Scholars had significantly higher overall GPAs (3.5 versus a 2.8). They also found that the scholars even outperformed prior cohorts in specific science and math courses (means of 3.4 and 2.4, respectively). Many of the components of the program (e.g., recruitment, bridge program, scholarship support, faculty involvement, etc.) were mentioned, but family involvement was identified as the most important ingredient for its success. For example, parents were kept informed of their child's academic progress. In addition, they were regularly invited to participate in university activities and special events (Hrabowski & Maton, 1995). Another study on the Meyerhoff Program (Hrabowski, Maton, & Greif, 1998), involving the scholars (N = 60) and their parents, identified the parental factors that most impacted the success of the scholars. In the quali-tative study, the following factors were identified "(1) the importance of read-ing, beginning with parents (especially mothers) who read to their sons at a young age, (2) the parents' view that education is both necessary and valuable, (3) active encouragement on the part of parents toward academic success, (4) close interaction between the parents and their son's teachers, (5) strong parental interest in homework, and (6) considerable verbal praise" (Hrabowski, Maton, & Greif, 1998, p. 194). The authors also found that both the students and their parents were virtually on the same page about critical parenting com-ponents such as love, encouragement, discipline, and reassurance. These differ-ent modes of support were all considered necessary for success.

According to many researchers (Baker, McNeil, & Siryk, 1985; Baker & Siryk, 1984), adjusting to college can be categorized into four factors: "(1) *aca-demic adjustment* to college-level educational requirements; (2) *institutional adjustment* or commitment to college pursuits, academic goals, and eventual career direction; (3) *personal-emotional adjustments* or the need to independ-ently manage one's own emotional and physical well-being; and (4) *social adjustment* to roommate, peer, faculty, and other interpersonal relationships" (Schwitzer et al., 1999, p. 189). Interestingly, all of the different adjustments

---

1. The program is a million-dollar retention initiative at the University of Maryland Baltimore County designed to increase the number of African-American males in scientific disciplines (e.g., mathematics, engineering, and sciences).

play a tremendous role in causing students to question their academic ability, lose their motivation, and/or fail out of college. Hrabowski and Maton (1995) found that parents and other family members were instrumental in helping African-American students adjust to PWIs. They helped foster enthusiasm and increase efforts of students.

A growing body of research indicates that parental and familial support has advantageous effects on students' academic performance (Hrabowski, 1991; Hrabowski & Maton, 1995; Sanders, 1998; Scott, 1995; Taylor, Hinton, & Wilson, 1995) and career development (Blustein et al., 1991; Fisher & Griggs, 1995; Fisher & Padmawidjaja, 1999; Young & Friesen, 1992). Therefore, African-American students who have strong parental and familial support are more likely to be successful in PWIs. Hrabowski (1991) discovered, in his research with the Meyerhoff Scholars Program, that parents were an important resource in making the program successful. Many of the parents were actively involved with the program and the university. As a result, the Meyerhoff Family Association was founded.

Recommendations for Parents

African-American students often lack role models and mentors at PWIs (Sedlacek, 1998). The faculty and administrators are perceived as unapproachable and unfriendly. Many African-American students have to rely on their parents, friends, or other family members for guidance and encouragement. Unfortunately, advice from parents who are not college educated or college informed, such as some college-educated parents, can sometimes be detrimental. Such advice may lead to making unwise academic decisions. However, there is a role for parents who have limited or abundant educational experiences. These parents' role may vary from providing social, financial, spiritual, or moral support. Many research studies support the fact that all three forms of support are needed in helping African-American students persist through PWIs (Moore, 2000; Scott, 1995: Hrabowski, Maton, & Greif, 1998). Regardless of the kinds of support given, it is clear that parental guidance plays a tremendous role in the academic success of African-American students. Drawing on Moore's (2000) research, African-American parents should consider the following points when supporting and helping their child persist through college:

- Every attempt should be made to make sure that their child has appropriate resources, supplies, and support to excel educationally.

- Parents should use facilitative strategies when encouraging their child. Such strategies are good in affirming the child's sense of confidence and conveying the message that success is achievable, even in dire circumstances.

- Parents should set high expectations for their child academically and for life in general. In other words, parents should model the behaviors that they desire from their child.

- From an early age, parents should help their child develop a positive racial identity. Such an identity helps African-American students transcend negative perceptions and stereotypes.

- Since parental support is important in the persistence of African-American students, parents should provide a lot of guidance and encouragement. Such encouragement can occur by sending a nice letter, email, and/or making a telephone call to their child.

- Every attempt should be made to be actively involved in the child's college experience. In other words, parents should attempt to attend special events on campus (e.g., Parents Weekend) to keep abreast of the university's climate, policies, and important dates.

- Every attempt should be made to connect with different resources on campus. By doing this, parents can help university faculty and administrators identify potential problems as they relate to their child.

Recommendations for Administrators and Faculty

To improve the retention and graduation rates of African-American students, it is imperative that administrators and faculty not only learn what factors affect persistence, but the initiatives that are most appropriate for helping them succeed at PWIs. An overview of the literature indicates that most programs and retention initiatives focus on African-American students rather than the racism harbored on PWI campuses. The following recommendations are made to administrators and faculty in improving the persistence of African-American students. Many of the recommendations focus primarily on the administrators and faculty.

- Every attempt should be made to include parents and other significant family members in retention and academic efforts, especially since parents play a tremendous role in the persistence of

African-American students at PWIs. This can be achieved by sending personal invitations to parents when special events are taking place on campus.

- Faculty members and advisors should closely monitor the academic progress of African-American students, so they can avoid making unwise academic decisions. Keeping good academic records and having a sound data base system to alert them when students are not on track can easily achieve this.

- Efforts should be made to connect African-American students with faculty and administrators, so they will have access to a wider network of relationships. Having special social events that allow students to meet different faculty in their departments and around campus can easily accomplish this task.

- Collaborative relationships should be made between African-American alumni and the students. Such interactions could help the students in developing contacts for future employment.

- Efforts should be made to enhance faculty and advisors' understanding of challenges that African-American students experience at PWIs. This could easily be achieved through seminars and workshops.

- Faculty should be given names of the offices around the campus that specialize in working with African-American students. These offices can serve as a resource for the faculty.

Summary

The nature of PWIs is inherently difficult for most students, regardless of race and/or gender, but it is clear that African-American students have many obstacles stacked against them that go beyond academics. Many of these obstacles are directly or indirectly related to stereotypes and negative perceptions perpetuated by the dominant culture. These stigmas often inhibit or cause African-American students to doubt their academic ability. In effect, it takes resourcefulness as well as a resilient personality to transcend these hurdles.

What is obvious about African-American students is that they are black. To fully understand their psychosocial and academic needs, it is important that parents, administrators, and faculty understand how blackness intertwines with American culture in America, how they are interpreted by society, and internalized by African-American students (Moore, 2000). Generally speaking, when people are born, "they are socialized by members of their community to fit into the social order" (Vontress, 1992, p. 459). This notion of conceptualization suggests that the development of African Americans is socially constructed. Vontress (1992, p. 459) states:

> Socialization is holistic. At birth, it is primarily physical. Parents and others who attend children feed, change, bathe, and burp them. Gradually, attendants introduce social controls. They spank, scold, and instruct newcomers in the ways of the group. By responding to the special qualities of children, adults help them to develop an understanding of their individual uniqueness. Consequently children come to perceive their emotional, intellectual, psychological, and social dispositions. From contact with authority figures, they also acquire an intangible self that allows them to transcend the immediate environment and to connect spiritually with departed ancestors, powerful deities, and other inexplicable forces in their lives.

Vontress's quote suggests that authority figures such as the family and community are instrumental in showing a child the way of the group and world. For African Americans, this process of socialization is not only critical for succeeding in PWIs but society in general. In other words, during early childhood, African Americans need to be taught how to be resourceful in increasing their life opportunities (White & Cones, 1999). Through my work as an educator and researcher, I am convinced that "academic warriors" are not born but developed through strong rearing practices and careful planning. However, I do believe faculty and administrators can do a better job facilitating and enhancing the persistence and growth of African-American students.

References

Allen, W. (1992). The color of success: African-American college student outcomes at predominately white and historically black public colleges and universities. *Harvard Educational Review* 62(1):26–44.

Baker, R., McNeil, O., & Siryk, B. (1985). Expectations and reality in freshman adjustment to college. *Journal of Counseling Psychology* 32:94–103.

Baker, R., & Siryk, B. (1984). Measuring adjustment to college. *Journal of Counseling Psychology* 62(1):179–189.

Blustein, D. L., Walbridge, M. M., Friedlander, M. L., & Palladino, D. E. (1991). Contributions of psychological separation and parental attachment to the career process. *Journal of Counseling Psychology* 38(1):39–50.

Bowser, B., & Perkins, H. (1991). Success against the odds: Young black men tell what it takes. In *Black male adolescents: Parenting and education in community context,* B. P. Bowser (Ed.), pp. 183–200. Lanham, MD: University Press of America.

Brown v. Board of Education of Topeka, 347 US 483 (1954).

Cokley, K. (1999). Reconceptualizing the impact of college racial composition on African American students' racial identity. *Journal of College Student Development* 40(3):235–245.

Davis, J. E. (1994). College in black and white: Campus environment and academic achievement of African American males. *Journal of Negro Education* 63(4):620–633.

Davis, J. E. (1998). Campus climate, gender, and achievement of African American college students. *African American Research Perspectives* 4(1):40–46.

Delphin, M. E., & Rollock, D. (1995). University alienation and African American ethnic identity as predictors of attitudes toward, knowledge about, and likely use of psychological services. *Journal of College Student Development* 36(4):337–346.

Donovan, R. (1984). Path analysis of a theoretical model of persistence in higher education among low-income black youth. *Research in Higher Education* 21(3):243–259.

Durkheim, E. (1951). *Suicide.* Glencoe, IL: Free Press.

Fisher, T. A., & Griggs, M. B. (1995). Factors that influence the career development of African-American and Latino youth. *Journal of Vocational Education Research* 20(2):47–66.

Fisher, T. A., & Padmawidjaja, I. (1999). Parental influence on career development perceived by African American and Mexican American college students. *Journal of Multicultural Counseling and Development* 27(3):136–152.

Fleming, J. (1984). *Blacks in college: A comparative study of students' success in black and white institutions.* San Francisco: Jossey-Bass.

Ford, D. Y. (1996). *Reversing underachievement among gifted black students: Promising practices and programs.* New York: Teachers College Press.

Fordham, S., & Ogbu, J. (1986). Black students' school success: Coping with "burden of acting" white. *The Urban Review* 18:176–206.

Gloria, A. M., Kurpius, S. E., Hamilton, K. D., & Wilson, M. S. (1999). African American students' persistence at a predominately white university: Influences of social support, university comfort, and self-beliefs. *Journal of College Student Development* 40(3):257–268.

Harvey, W. B., & Williams, L. E. (1993). Historically black colleges: Models for increasing minority representation. In *Racial and ethnic diversity in higher education,* C. S. Viernes-Turner, M. Garcia, A. Nora, & L. I. Rendon (Eds.), pp. 233–240. Needham Heights, MA: Simon & Schuster.

Howard, J., & Hammond, R. (1985). Rumors of inferiority. *The New Republic* 193(11):17–21.

Hrabowski, F. A. (1991). Helping gifted black males succeed in science. *Journal of Health Care for the Poor and Underserved* 2(1):197–201.

Hrabowski, F. A., & Maton, K. I. (1995). Enhancing the success of African-American students in the sciences: Freshman year outcomes. *School Science and Mathematics* 95(1):19–27.

Hrabowski, F. A., Maton, K. I., & Greif, G. L. (1998). *Beating the odds: Raising academically successful African American males.* New York: Oxford University Press.

Jackson, G. A. (1992). Why they continue to fail, black students in white colleges—The dark side of higher education: A review of the literature. *Journal of the National Council of Educational Opportunity Associations* 7(1):14–19.

Lafreniere, K. D., Ledgerwood, D. M., & Docherty, A. L. (1997). Influences of leaving home, perceived family support, and gender on the transition to university. *Guidance and Counseling* 12:14–18.

Moore, J. L. (2000). The persistence of African-American males in the college of engineering at Virginia Tech. Ph.D. diss., Virginia Polytechnic Institute and State University.

Nettles, M. T. (1987). Black and white college student performance in majority white and majority black academic settings. In *Title IV regulation of higher education: Problem and progress,* J. Williams (Ed.), pp. 49–63. New York: Teachers College Press.

Sanders, M. G. (1998). The effects of school, family, and community support on the academic achievement of African American adolescents. *Urban Education* 33(3):385–409.

Schwitzer, A. M., Griffin, O. T., Ancis, J. R., & Thomas, C. R. (1999). Social adjustment experiences of African-American college students. *Journal of Counseling & Development* 77:189–197.

Scott, D. W. (1995). *Conditions related to the academic performance of African American students at Virginia Polytechnic Institute and State University.* Ph.D. diss., Virginia Polytechnic Institute and State University.

Sedlacek, W. E. (1983). Teaching minority students. In *New directions for teaching and learning, 16,* J. H. Cones III, J. F. Noonan, & D. Janha (Eds.), pp. 39–50. San Francisco: Jossey-Bass.

Sedlacek, W. E. (1987). Black students on white campuses years of research. Special issues: Blacks in U.S. in higher education. *Journal of College Student Personnel* 28(6):484–494.

Sedlacek, W. E. (1998). Admissions in higher education: Measuring cognitive and noncognitive variables. In *Minorities in Higher Education 1997–98,* D. J. Wilds, & R. Wilson (Eds.), pp. 47–68). Washington, D.C.: American Council on Education.

Simms, K. B., Knight, D. M., & Dawes, K. I. (1993). Institutional factors that influence the academic success of African-American men. *Journal of Men's Studies* 1(3):253–266.

Smith, F. M., & Hausfaus, C. O. (1998). Relationship of family support and ethnic minority students' achievement in science and mathematics. *Science Education* 82:111–125.

Steele, C. M. (1997). A threat in the air: How stereotypes shape intellectual identity and performance. *American Psychologists* 52(6):613–629.

Taylor, L. C., Hinton, I. D., & Wilson, M. N. (1995). Parental influences on academic performance in African-American students. *Journal of Child and Family Studies* 4(3):293–302.

Tidwell, R., & Berry, G. L. (1993). Higher education and the African-American experience: Historical perceptions and the challenge for change. *College Student Journal* 27(4):465–471.

Tinto, V. (1975). Dropout from higher education: A theoretical synthesis of recent research. *Review of Educational Research* 45:89–125.

Tinto, V. (1993). *Leaving college: Rethinking the causes and cures of student attrition.* Chicago: University of Chicago Press.

Townsend, L. (1994). How universities successfully retain and graduate black students. *Journal of Blacks in Higher Education* 4:85–89.

Trujillo, C. M. (1986). A comparative examination of classroom interactions between professors and minority and non-minority students. *American Educational Research Journal* 23(4):629–642.

Vontress, C. E. (1992). The breakdown of authority: Implications for counseling young African American males. In *Counseling American minorities: A cross-cultural perspective,* D. R. Atkinson (Ed.), pp. 457–473. Dubuque, IA: W. C. Brown & Benchmark.

Wambach, C. A. (1993). Motivational themes and academic success of at-risk freshmen. *Journal of Developmental Education* 16(3):8–10, 12, 37.

Weber, J. (1992). Creating the environment for minority student success: An interview with Jacqueline Fleming. *Journal of Developmental Education* 16(2):20–22, 24.

White, J. L., & Cones, J. H. (1999). *Black man emerging: Facing the past and seizing a future in America.* New York: W. H. Freeman.

Wilson-Sadberry, K. R., Winfield, L. F., & Royster, D. A. (1991). Resilience and persistence of African-American males in postsecondary enrollment. *Education & Urban Society* 24(1):87–102.

Young, R. A., & Friesen, J. D. (1992). The intentions of parents in influencing the career development of their children. *Career Development Quarterly* 40:198–207.

PART TWO

RETAINING AFRICAN-AMERICAN ADMINISTRATORS

6

A NEW TEST FOR DIVERSITY

RETAINING AFRICAN-AMERICAN ADMINISTRATORS AT PREDOMINANTLY WHITE INSTITUTIONS

Jerlando F. L. Jackson

Racial equity is still a major hurdle facing higher education institutions in the United States. Despite three decades of efforts on the part of the nation's postsecondary institutions, African Americans still face special problems navigating their careers in academe (Jackson, 2000; Turner & Meyers, 2000). Race is a salient concern as it pertains to higher education institutions' abilities to thrive in the new millennium. African-American faculty and administrators are not only underrepresented in academic institutions, but their retention also poses a problem (Menges & Exum, 1983; Silver, Dennis, & Spikes, 1989). Of these two aforementioned groups, the one that receives the least amount of attention as it relates to retention is administrators. Oliver and Davis (1994, p. 61) observed that "the retention of African-American administrators in PWIs [Predominantly White Institutions] is short-lived owing to the personal harassment and indignity people of color experience in the discharge of normal duties." The purpose of this chapter is to explore the concept of retention as it relates to African-American administrators at PWIs. This is achieved by analyzing three construct areas: (1) college and university administration and African Americans; (2) retention in higher education; and (3) the findings of a study detailing practical steps for retaining African-American administrators at PWIs.

College and University Administration and African Americans

What Is College and University Administration?

The administration and governance of higher education institutions are broken down into three specialty areas: academic affairs, student affairs, and administrative affairs (Sagaria, 1988). Academic affairs include positions such as president, academic deans, and vice president or provost of research. Student affairs include positions such as vice president for student affairs, dean of students, and director of financial aid. Administrative affairs encompass positions such as vice president for finance, director of alumni affairs, and the director of computer services (Moore & Sagaria, 1982). In the context of this chapter the word administrator is a person in a managerial or policy-making capacity that may have a line or staff function. A line function is part of the institution's hierarchy and someone to whom others report. This person also reports to a supervisor. Staff functions fall outside of the institution's hierarchy with no one reporting to this person. Quite often the person with the title "assistant to" is in the role of a staff person.

African-American Administrators at PWIs in the Literature

The presence or lack of African Americans in the administration of a college or university provides a sense of whether an African-American student will or will not feel welcomed at the institution. In reviewing the literature on African-American administrators at PWIs, one quickly realizes very little exists. The presence of a measurable number of African Americans in college and university administration is a recent phenomenon (Wilson, 1989). African Americans, as did other people of color, often came into higher education institutions as directors of TRIO programs (i.e., Ronald E. McNair and Talent Search), affirmative action officers, director of minority student affairs, and so forth. These positions fall in the realm of student affairs that do not carry the same status as department chairs and deans, which are considered academic affairs. Thus, such positions are not seen as the mainstream of administration (academic affairs), and rarely do persons in these positions get considered for top-level positions such as president or provost. Academic affairs is considered mainstream because its members define criteria for the university curriculum, students' admissions requirements, and faculty qualifications. In spite of the talents of many people in these positions, their creations from outside the institutions and their peripheral structure in the university make not only their continuance vulnerable, but they have been valued less by "mainstream" academic administrators.

The lack of diversity in the administration of colleges and universities is a mirror image of society. Reginald Wilson (1989, p. 85) made this profound statement:

> It is ironic that the two institutions most identified with preserving the nation's ethical mores and democratic philosophical values—the church and the university—are the two institutions most resistant to diversity and democracy in their practices and in their leadership.

Crawford (1983) and Moore (1982, 1983) reported that more African-American males held administrative positions than did African-American females. As a result, the majority of the literature examines African-American women administrators, in an attempt to help increase the numbers and decrease the negative experiences for this population. African-American women administrators face dual burdens of sexism and racism (Singh, Robinson, & Williams-Green, 1995; Williams, 1989; Wilson, 1989). Mentoring was a consistent method suggested in the literature as an important means of increasing both the number of African Americans in general serving as administrators in higher education and the percentage of those who reach senior level positions (Johnson, 1998; Judson, 1999).

Powell (1992) provides a description of a detailed model of how one state system of higher education attempted to increase the presence of African Americans within administrative positions. He suggests that three practices have been historically used to prepare administrators: formal study, in-service programs, and informal study (Booth, 1987). Formal study includes graduate programs intended to award a degree in administration (i.e., education, higher education, business, and public administration). In-service programs for preparing administrators include seminars, conferences, workshops, and so forth. Informal study includes independent study methods whereby the incumbent performs extended research to obtain the necessary skills. Bridges (1996) examined the personal background and perceptions of African-American administrators. He recommends that for African Americans who aspire to positions in administration the following personal characteristics, career decisions, and activities are important: educational preparation; communicating in writing and speaking, setting goals, and developing and strengthening self-confidence; and being involved in a mentoring relationship is imperative.

Retention

The discussion of retention in higher education has become increasingly more important, particularly as it pertains to African Americans at PWIs (Cabrera et al., 1999; Turner & Meyers, 2000). The next section outlines the retention literature on African Americans in higher education, discusses barriers to retention, presents a framework for job satisfaction, and conceptually constructs a definition for retention as it relates to administrators.

Retention Literature

The largest portion of the retention literature is dedicated to students (Allen, Epps, & Haniff, 1991; Holmes et al., 2000; Loo & Rolison, 1986; Nettles, 1990; Pascarella & Terenzini, 1991). Even with this large body of literature, PWIs continue to have problems with integrating students of color; even more germane to this discussion is the integration of African-American students into the ethos of the academy. In order for colleges and universities to carry out their "promissory note" to benefit society and to be true to their mission statements, they must provide a "good faith" effort to equally prepare all citizens of the United States.

One strand of the retention literature focuses on the "involvement of the student" to assist with retention (Kuh et al., 1991; Pascarella & Terenzini, 1991; Tinto, 1993). Astin's theory of student involvement (1984, 1996) began the discussion around the proposition that if students invest their time and energy in the learning process and are involved in the social and academic life of the university, they would more likely remain and complete their degrees. Closely aligned to this thought is Turner's (1994) observation that academic success for African-American students is tied to their comfort level with the institution.

The second strand of the retention literature places attention on the validation process of students. Rendon (1994) introduced the notion of validation as a means to help retain students of color. The model presents two categories of validation: out-of-class and in-class agents. These two agents are used to validate the students' worth and place in the institution. Holmes et al., (2000) present a model conceptualized specifically for African-American students at PWIs. The model is based on the premise that the success of African-American students at PWIs is a function of both in and out of class experiences, which begins at the point of first contact. The guiding principle of this model is the student's validation with the institution. The model places more emphasis on the institution's influence over the student's pre-enrollment characteristics. Holmes et. al. (2000) posit that what happens to students after they enter college has a greater impact on retention than other factors.

A third area in the retention literature is the integration of the student into the university. Tinto's (1993) theory is based on the notion that the student's interaction with the educational environment directly affects how and whether the integration is paramount to the student's persistence. Tinto suggests that the individual's departure results from interactions between the student and the educational environment over time. Integration is a key element in providing an inclusive and welcoming environment of African Americans at PWIs. Further, Holmes et. al. (2000, p. 43) state:

> The problem has intensified to the point that if immediate action is not taken to increase the number of African American students receiving college degrees, especially at the Ph.D. level, the higher education community as well as the nation at large will suffer.

This statement provides a logical transition for exploring retention factors of African-American faculty.

Why faculty of color stay in academe was addressed in the text of *Faculty of Color in Academe: Bittersweet Success* (Turner & Meyers, 2000). They found that despite subtle discrimination, faculty of color have the same reasons as their white counterparts for staying in academe. The most commonly articulated reasons were love of teaching, supportive administrative leadership, sense of accomplishment, importance of mentors, collegiality, commitment to community, and relating to other faculty of color. Furthermore, the book suggested that the strategies for faculty of color having successful academic careers were networking, workshops, creating social ethnic groups, mentoring—pairing with senior faculty, and better support for research and publications, which is very similar to the findings of the Jackson and Rosas (1998) study that specifically examined successful scholars of color.

Just as a number of students and faculty of color have been attracted to PWIs, so have administrators of color (Davis, 1994). Unfortunately, administrators of color along with the other two aforementioned groups, leave these institutions prematurely. Davis (1994) informs us that these talented groups become disenchanted with PWIs, and move to historically black colleges and universities (HBCUs), or leave academe altogether. There are a number of indicators that colleges and universities focus on to assess the level of institutional commitment to diversity (e.g., number of students of color enrolled); however, Davis (1994, p. 3) directs our attention to another area of consideration:

> The litmus test for institutional commitment to diversity is the number of senior-level administrators of color remaining at the institution with a tenure of four or more years. Certainly, five years or more reflect an excellent benchmark for institutional commitment to diversity.

It is believed that administrators of color can warm the "chilly" campus climates for students of color at PWIs. If colleges and universities intend to hire and retain administrators of color, an institutional commitment to cultural diversity must be present. Institutions should not just be satisfied with their increase of "cultural capital" by making the hire; the true test for the institution is its commitment for retention.

Barriers to Retention

Barr (1990) identified barriers to the recruitment and retention of competent and qualified administrators. Although the original list was developed specifically for student affairs administrators, it has applicability to academic and administrative affairs as well. The barriers are lack of professional identity, lack of a career path, working conditions, compensation, competition from outside the academy, and competition from within the academy.

A lack of professional identity exists because of the uncertainty with the requisite skills, knowledge, and competencies needed for college and university administration. College and university administration lacks a clear rank and promotion system for position advancement. A limited number of administrative positions exist at one institution; therefore, advancement often requires the individual to move to another institution. Working conditions for administrators are of concern because typically administrators work at an unrelenting and fragmented pace. In addition, there is a high expectation for performance, which requires administrators to be available when needed, which extends the work week beyond 40 hours.

Compensation becomes a problem when administrators work long hours and weeks without additional compensation. When comparing the number of hours per week against the dollar amount earned, administrators tend to be on the bottom of the pay scale. Competition from outside the academy exists because there are higher compensation packages and a more predictable career path in the marketplace. Furthermore, competition from within the academy exists because jobs with similar titles and duties may pay more; therefore, individuals will move about internally as well.

Job Satisfaction

Although older research, Herzberg and his associates have delineated useful findings on employee satisfaction that is relevant today. Workers' attitudes toward their jobs provide insight into the factors that lead to job satisfaction (Herzberg, Mausner, & Snydermen, 1964). As a result of the research on workers' attitudes and motivation launched by Herzberg and his associates, the Motivation-hygiene theory was developed (Herzberg et al., 1974). Simply put, the Motivation-hygiene theory classifies all human needs into two sets: pain avoidance and growth. A distinction is made between the types of incentives that will satisfy these two sets of needs. Within the context of the workforce, the only incentives that satisfy the pain-avoidance needs are environmental or external to the job (i.e., working conditions and security), which are called hygiene factors. The factors are termed as such because they are maintenance factors and are primarily preventative. The incentives that satisfy the growth needs are internal to the job (i.e., achievement and responsibility), which are called motivator factors. Herzberg, Mausner, and Syndermen (1964) recognized that an affective difference exists qualitatively in the satisfaction of the growth and pain-avoidance needs.

Fourteen factors were identified from the respondents in reference to sources of good or bad feelings about their jobs. The factors are (not listed in any rank order): recognition, achievement, possibility of growth, advancement, salary, interpersonal relations, supervision-technical, responsibility, company policy and administration, working conditions, work itself, factors in personal life, status, and job security. Recognition is a special notice or attention because of the job. Achievement is any form of success, accomplishment, or attainment on the job. The possibility of growth included the likelihood of advancement upward within the organization or onward to another organization. The advancement factor differs only with the actual change in status or position.

The salary factor involved increases in wage or salary. The interpersonal relation factor dealt with the interactions with other people (i.e., supervisor, subordinate, and peers). The supervision-technical factors referred to the supervisor's willingness or unwillingness to delegate or teach responsibilities to the person of question. Responsibility is the person's satisfaction with being given responsibility for his or her own work and the work of others. The company policy and administration factor included the characteristics of the company's overall policy and administration.

The working conditions referred to the physical conditions of work, the amount of work, and the facilities available for working. The work itself factor was the actual doing of the job. Factors in personal life were aspects of the job that affected the personal life. Status was a factor when "status" was attributed to the job. Job security included such considerations as tenure and company stability or instability. The five factors (satisfiers) that were found to be associated with job satisfaction were: achievement, recognition, work itself, responsibility, advancement, and salary. Subsequently, it is expected the major contributors (dissatisfiers) to job satisfaction are the remaining ten factors (see Table 6.1).

Herzberg (1979) proposed four approaches to job enrichment. First, the orthodox job enrichment, which is the traditional hierarchy approach with the managers planning the work and motivating the people to work. In the first enrichment approach the attempt is to give the worker longitudinal grasp of work. Second is the sociotechnical systems approach. This approach uses semiautonomy and work rotation within a job, to provide a variety of tasks

Table 6.1 Percentage of Each Factor Identified as Source of Good or Bad Feelings About Job (N = 228)

Factor	Total*
1. Achievement	41
2. Recognition	33
3. Work itself	26
4. Responsibility	23
5. Advancement	20
6. Salary	15
7. Possibility of growth	6
8. Interpersonal relations—subordinate	6
9. Status	4
10. Interpersonal relations—supervisor	4
11. Interpersonal relations—peers	3
12. Supervisor-technical	3
13. Company policy and administration	3
14. Working conditions	1
15. Personal life	1
16. Job security	1

Source: Adapted from F. Herzberg, B. Mausner, & B. B. Synderman (1964). *The motivation to work,* 2nd ed. New York: John Wiley & Sons.
*The percentages total more than 100 because more than one factor can appear in any single sequence of events.

and gives individuals a larger picture of the whole concept. The third is participative management. The primary need for personal involvement can be satisfied through worker participation and will provide the commitment necessary to motivate workers. The last approach is industrial democracy. This approach promotes the philosophy of democracy, and the main objective is to foster presentation and involvement in all the decision-making organizations to provide ownership.

Situating Administrators in the Retention Discourse

What does it mean to retain administrators? The two other populations (faculty and students) covered in this book have clear definitions of retention. The retention of African-American students is to successfully matriculate toward the completion of the degree program (i.e., undergraduate, graduate, and professional school). As for faculty, retention can be divided into two phases. The first phase requires the faculty member to secure tenure within seven years at the institution. Phase two is to ultimately maintain the faculty at the institution with continued movement up the professoriate ascension, which include full professor, distinguished professor, university professor, and so forth. For these two groups retention is an obvious product (degree or tenure). Therefore, what is the product for administrators?

A definition for the retention of administrators is not available in the literature. The definition could be conceptualized in a myriad of ways. For example, one may suggest that to retain administrators is to keep them at the same institution their whole careers. Another may argue that retention would consist of the administrator staying at the institution until given a promotion at another institution. However, for the purposes of this chapter retention will be conceptualized around the length of tenure in the position. Therefore, the length of tenure of an African-American administrator is compared against his or her white counterparts. As stated earlier, Davis (1994) communicates that African-American administrators meeting the five-year milestone are a clear indication of the institution's commitment to administrative diversity. Additionally, Moore (1983) found in her extensive study of higher education administrators in general that five years was a breaking point. Fifty-three percent of the administrators in her study held their current position for five years or less. This provides support for concentrating on the length of tenure in the position for African-American administrators at PWIs.

It must be noted that administrators do leave institutions for reasons that are beyond the control of the college or university. The connection of the administrator's length of employment with the institution's commitment to diversity is solely based on the barriers of retention that can be addressed by the institution. Therefore, the product for the retention of administrators is equity. The goal is to equally maintain administrators at PWIs in the position in comparison with their white counterparts.

Study
Method

The study was designed to determine practical steps that would enable PWIs to retain African-American administrators. The method section includes a description of the participants, data collection, and data analysis.

Participants   A panel of experts was established based on professional success and experience in college and university administration. Participants for the study were recommended on the basis of their professional roles and/or recognition by their peers and their familiarity with college and university administration. Fifteen administrators were invited to participate on the panel of experts, 10 administrators actually participated in the study. Demographic data on the participants show that six (60%) were male and four (40%) were female. The employment distribution was as follows: five worked in academic affairs (50%), four worked in student affairs (40%), and one worked in administrative affairs (10%).

Data Collection   A modified, two-round Delphi technique was used as a method to collect data for this study (Delberq, Van de Ven, & Gustafson, 1975). This process is essentially a series of questionnaires, with subsequent questionnaires based on responses to preceding questionnaires. The intent of the modified, two-round Delphi technique process was to develop practical steps that PWIs could use to retain African-American administrators. The first round consisted of the development of the first list of practical steps. The first questionnaire in the Delphi technique allowed participants to write responses to a broad question.

The second round consisted of the integration of recommended steps into one comprehensive list and the redistribution of that list to the panel of experts. This round of the process primarily served as a clarification step to check the accuracy of ideas presented from the panel. Participants were asked to comment on the usefulness of the list and to provide further information that may have been needed to improve the list. The questionnaires were administered via electronic mail.

Data Analysis   The analysis of data collected in this study passed through three interrelated stages: (1) data reduction, (2) data display, and (3) conclusion and implications (Keeves, 1988, p. 518). Data reduction was managed through the identification of emergent themes from the participants' recorded responses. The displayed data consisted of the practical steps supplied by the participants. The conclusion and implications are materialized through the development of the final comprehensive list of practical steps and the discussion of them.

Results: Practical Steps for the Retention of African-American Administrators at PWIs

Commit to the Principles of Diversity and Affirmative Action

Colleges and universities can include a diversity educational component to all institutional training programs for their personnel. This sends a message that the institution truly wishes its members to be understanding of differences and appreciative of those differences. More specifically, it shows that the institution values the African-American perspective. As a result of this commitment, the institution should reach out to the African-American local community in fostering fairness and diversity. This commitment should be institutionalized into the culture prior to implementing the subsequent steps.

Use Recruitment as a Retention Strategy

Retention of African-American administrators begins with an institution's recruitment and hiring practices. A university that has well thought out and printed practices for recruiting and hiring staff of color sends a positive, welcoming, and supportive message to incoming and current staff. Recruitment for administrators can be viewed through two lenses: (1) the "grow your own" strategy; developing leadership opportunities for entry and midlevel African Americans; and (2) external recruitment; seeking candidates from outside the institution for administrative positions. Institutions must go a step beyond just having these policies in place; they must move toward reaching and maintaining goals and objectives for their desired diversity mix. Examples of positive recruiting and hiring practices include: (1) Senior university administrators sending out recruitment letters encouraging colleagues at other institutions to submit qualified candidates of color; (2) ensuring that search committee members are trained, educated, and knowledgeable of the university's desired diversity goals and EEO/AA policies; (3) reopening the search and aggressively attempting to diversify the pool if necessary to meet goals; and (4) describing the institution's work environment challenges and rewards (particularly as they pertain to diversity issues).

Provide Equity in Wages and Salaries

Colleges and universities should provide competitive wages and salaries; such compensation shows a commitment to the person in the position. Salary issues should be evaluated as they relate to recruiting and retaining African-American administrators. Often administrators can be lured away by other institutions willing to offer more benefits. Wages and salaries have to be sufficient and equitable. Timely, equitable, and sufficient increases are important to all personnel.

Provide an Orientation Program

This orientation process could simply include two components: community and campus orientation. Community orientation would consist of community leadership informing the new administrator about the present network systems (i.e., churches, social groups, etc.). Campus orientation would be a reception to introduce the administrator to the students, faculty, and staff of the college or university. The orientation phase could possibly provide a transition to the mentoring phase of retention. The formal or informal process of pairing the mentor/mentee dyad can begin at this point.

Develop a Mentoring Program for Junior and Senior Management

Provide mentoring opportunities with dedicated university officials who will take the time to nurture African-American administrators. This experience will provide knowledge of the political environment that is very important in terms of acclimating to the campus and its culture. Just the simplest things such as unspoken dress codes (i.e., long sleeve white shirts worn consistently) should be identified if they are an important fiber of the campus culture.

Foster Open Lines of Communication Between the Administration Hierarchy and Staff

Professionals value feedback and input about their work. However, the feedback and input must be constructive and encouraging in nature and should come from upper-level administration. None of the feedback should be done in a patronizing manner. Sincere support and feedback of the administrator's performance are most valuable in fostering a feeling of belonging and of being a valued member of the team. This enables administrators to feel supported when they have to make a difficult decision. For example, many institutions can be schizophrenic when it comes to their mission statements. Generally, there are two variations of the mission statement: philosophical and operational. These variations for the most part are in conflict with one another, particularly when an African-American administrator is learning to negotiate the environment.

Empower the Administrator to Perform His or Her Job

Utilizing a team concept of management will allow for greater inclusion in decision making and policy formulation. Ultimately, the administrator must be given the power to make changes when necessary when it comes to the over-all direction of his or her operating unit and the institution as a whole. Micro-management is a frustrating situation for any administrator. The empower-ment of administrators will establish a nurturing campus ecology among all constituencies.

Promote the Pursuit of Professional Advancement and Development (i.e., Learning and Research)

Colleges and universities should support and endorse the professional aspira-tions of African-American administrators. Encouraging career development and advancement such as participating in professional organizations is very important. This is especially true if there is a desire to maintain affiliations with multicultural subgroups within these organizations, which can assist in maintaining cultural roots if that is an important factor to self-identification. Furthermore, colleges and universities should reward administrators' efforts with promotions and new and expanding responsibilities. Institutions should endorse the American Council on Education (ACE) Fellowship program in assisting administrators who aspire to campus presidencies and other senior positions. In addition, institutions should develop their own internship pro-gram for career enhancement for African-American administrators.

Conclusion and Implications

When colleges and universities are implementing the above steps or similar ones, they must bear in mind that diversity exists within the African-Ameri-can community as well. Differences exist among African Americans as to political affiliation (democratic, republican, and independent), geographic (rural, urban, and suburban), social preferences, and so forth. The match between these background characteristics and an institutional environment are as important as they are for students and faculty entering these environments. Following are several implications for the practical steps.

First, PWIs should provide the opportunity for African Americans to personally and/or professionally define "quality of life." Sometimes it is assumed that African-American administrators need larger salaries, or need to be at large or prestigious universities, or in close proximity to urban centers. Allowing administrators the opportunity to define their own quality of life gives them the opportunity to share what they value and how their values relate to the institution. Also, by knowing what administrators value, the institution may better serve their interests by directing meaningful assignments to them. Lastly, PWIs can appropriately reward the administrators for their work because they understand what is important to the administrator.

Second, PWIs should recognize that for the most part, African Americans work in a dichotomous world: one African American and the other majority white. The vast majority of PWIs still maintain vestiges of the old systems that were designed primarily for white men. There is a different "face" that many African Americans have learned to wear in these "old system" environments in order to successfully negotiate them. Although many African Americans have learned to negotiate these types of environments, there can still at times be feelings of alienation. By raising their awareness to the presence of these environments, PWIs can greatly enhance the experience of African Americans at their institutions.

Third, PWIs should be careful not to "ghettoize" African-American administrators. Many times institutions call on them to provide expert opinion on or intervene in issues that involve some aspect of race and ethnicity. These issues may not be within their normal scope of responsibilities; therefore, these issues can become burdensome. On the other end of the spectrum, caution should be exercised not to "set anyone up for failure" by delegating assignments to and/or placing African Americans in positions for which they do not have the appropriate aspiration, skills, ability, or potential. These conscious or unconscious "setups" can be professionally and personally demoralizing.

In conclusion, three constructs were used to situate or introduce African-American administrators in the retention discourse. Construct one provided an explanation of college and university administration, which painted the background on which the chapter is based. Secondly, it provided an overview of the literature on African-American administrators at PWIs. Construct two outlined various methods of retention presented in the literature germane to students, faculty, and administrators. Next, this construct introduced barriers of retention, followed by a discussion of job satisfaction anchored in the industrial psychology literature. Lastly, this construct presented a definition for retention as it pertains to African-American administrators. Construct three delineated practical steps that would enable PWIs to retain African-American administrators. It should be noted here that there is a consistent theme in the findings provided in constructs two and three, which is an indicator that sound retention strategies are transferable to different settings and populations.

PWIs are urged, as the title implies, to view diversity through a broader lens. The number of people from diverse populations infused in the power and decision-making structure is a good indicator of an institution's commitment to diversity. Clearly, it is important to focus on the number of students and faculty remaining at institutions of higher education. However, it is those elevated to the levels of leadership that the institution is truly saying it supports. It is quite possible that this diverse presence in the administration of the college or university could strengthen the representation of the other two populations (i.e., faculty and students). In the final analysis, the question is: Will your institution pass the test?

References

Allen, W., Epps, E., & Haniff, N., Eds. (1991). *College in black and white: African American students in predominantly white and historically black public universities.* Albany, NY: SUNY Press.

Astin, A. W. (1984). Student involvement: A developmental theory for higher education. *Journal of College Student Personnel* 25:297–308.

Astin, A. W. (1996). Involvement in learning revisited: Lessons we have learned. *Journal of College Student Development* 37:123–134.

Barr, M. J. (1990). Growing staff diversity and changing career paths. In *New futures for student affairs: Building a vision for professional leadership and practice,* M. J. Barr, M. C. Upcraft & Associates, pp. 160–177. San Francisco: Jossey-Bass.

Booth, L. R. (1987). *The university system of Georgia's administrative development program: A means to increase the pool of black administrators.* Ph.D. diss. University of Georgia.

Bridges, C. R. (1996). The characteristics of career achievement perceived by African American college administrators. *Journal of Black Studies* 26:746–767.

Cabrera, A. F., Nora, A., Terenzini, P. T., Pascarella, E., & Hagedorn, L. S. (1999). Campus racial climate and adjustment of students to college. *Journal of College Student Development* 35:98–102.

Crawford, A. (1983). *Skills perceived to lead to success in higher education administration.* (ERIC Document Reproduction Service No. ED 232 519.)

Davis, J. D., Ed. (1994). *Coloring the halls of ivy: Leadership & diversity in the academy.* Bolton, MA: Anker Publishing Company.

Delberq, A. L., Van de Ven, A. H., & Gustafson, D. H. (1975). *Group techniques for program planning.* Glenview, IL: Scott Foresmen.

Herzberg, F. (1979). New perspectives in the will to work. *Personnel Administrator* 24:72–76.

Herzberg, F., Mathapo, J., Wiener, Y., & Wiesen, L. E. (1974). Motivation-hygiene correlates of mental health: An examination of motivation and inversion in a clinical population. *Journal of Consulting and Clinical Psychology* 42:411–419.

Herzberg, F., Mausner, B., & Snydermen, B. B. (1964). *The motivation to work,* 2nd ed. New York: John Wiley & Sons.

Holmes, S. L., Ebbers, L. H., Robinson, D. C., & Mugenda, A. G. (2000). Validating African American students at predominantly white institutions. *Journal of College Student Retention: Research, Theory, & Practice* 2:41–58.

Jackson, J. F. L. (2000). Administrators of color at predominantly white institutions. In *Brothers of the academy: Up and coming African Americans earning our way in higher education,* L. Jones (Ed.), pp. 42–52. Sterling, VA: Stylus Publishing.

Jackson, J. F. L., & Rosas, M. (1999). Scholars of color: Are universities derailing their scholarship. Minneapolis, MN: *Keeping Our Faculties Conference Proceedings,* pp. 86–107.

Johnson, G. G. (1998). African American women administrators as mentors: Significance and strategies. *Initiatives* 56:49–56.

Judson, H. (1999). A meaningful contribution. In *Grass roots and glass ceilings: African American administrators in predominantly white colleges and universities,* W. B. Harvey (Ed.), pp. 83–112. Albany, NY: SUNY Press.

Keeves, J. P., Ed. (1988). *Educational research methodology and measurement: An international handbook.* Elmsford, NY: Pergamon Press.

Kuh, G. D., Schuh, J. H., Whitt, E. J., & Associates. (1991). *Involving colleges: Successful approaches to fostering student learning and development outside the classroom.* San Francisco: Jossey-Bass.

Loo, C., & Rolison, G. (1986). Alienation of ethnic minority students at a predominantly white university. *Journal of Higher Education* 57:58–77.

Menges, R. J., & Exum, W. H. (1983). Barriers to the progress of women and minority faculty. *Journal of Higher Education* 54:123–144.

Moore, K. D. (1982). The role of mentors in developing leaders for academe. *Educational Record* 63:23–28.

Moore, K. D. (1983). The top line: A report on presidents', provosts', and deans' careers. In *Leaders in transition: A national study of higher education administration.* University Park, PA: Center for the Study of Higher Education. (ERIC Document Reproduction Service No. ED 346 082.)

Moore, K. D., & Sagaria, M. A. D. (1982). Differential job change and stability among academic administrators. *Journal of Higher Education* 53:501–513.

Nettles, M. T. (1990). Success in doctoral programs: Experiences of minority and white students. *American Journal of Education* 98:495–522.

Oliver, B., & Davis, J. D. (1994). Things they don't teach you about being a dean. In *Coloring the halls of ivy: Leadership & diversity in the academy,* J. D. Davis (Ed.), pp. 59–70. Bolton, MA: Anker Publishing Company.

Pascarella, E. T., & Terenzini, P. T. (1991). *How college affects students.* San Francisco: Jossey-Bass.

Powell, J. V. (1992). Increasing equity in administrative leadership: A regents model. *Equity and Excellence* 25:67–76.

Rendon, L. I. (1994). Validating culturally diverse students: Toward a new model of learning and student development. *Innovative Higher Education* 19:33–51.

Sagaria, M. A. D. (1988). Administrative mobility and gender: Patterns and prices in higher education. *Journal of Higher Education* 59:306–326.

Silver, J., Dennis, R., & Spikes, C. (1989). *Employment sequences of Blacks teaching in predominantly white institutions.* Atlanta, GA: Southern Education Foundation.

Singh, K., Robinson, A., & Williams-Green, J. (1995). Differences in perceptions of African American women and men faculty and administrators. *Journal of Negro Education* 64:401–408.

Tinto, V. (1993). *Leaving college: Rethinking the causes and cures of student attrition,* 2nd ed.. Chicago: University of Chicago Press.

Turner, C. S. V. (1994). Guest in someone else's house: Students of color. *Review of Higher Education* 17:355–370.

Turner, C. S. V., & Myers, S. L. (2000). *Faculty of color in academe: Bittersweet success.* Needham Heights, MA: Allyn & Bacon.

Williams, A. (1989). Research on black women college administrators: Descriptive and interview data. *Sex Roles: A Journal of Research* 21:99–112.

Wilson, R. (1989). Women of color in academic administration: Trends, progress, and barriers. *Sex Roles: A Journal of Research* 21:85–97.

7

STRATEGIES FOR OVERCOMING THE BARRIERS OF BEING AN AFRICAN-AMERICAN ADMINISTRATOR ON A PREDOMINANTLY WHITE UNIVERSITY CAMPUS

Raphael M. Guillory

The changing face of the United States will reflect a very different image in the years to come. The United States is becoming a multicultural society in which the descendants of European immigrants will no longer determine the dominant culture. Our American tapestry will be characterized not only by the Anglo-based cultures of the past, but also by those of its ethnic minorities (Kellett, 1994). Demographers predict that people of color—African Americans, Asian Americans, Hispanic Americans, and Native Americans—will become the majority population in many states early in the millennium. In the late 1990s, immigration from various areas worldwide has altered the U.S. racial and ethnic portrait (Firebaugh et al., 2000). With this change has come a greater demand for fair representation and more opportunities in education. Answering the call to meet the needs of our growing diverse population are institutions of higher education, but they have met with mixed results. For example, from 1985 to 1995, the minority full-time faculty in higher education increased 47.7 percent, compared with a 9.9 percent increase for white (non-Hispanic) faculty. Minorities made up 12.9 percent of all full-time faculty in higher education in 1995 (Wilds & Wilson, 1998). From 1985 to 1995, undergraduate enrollment of African Americans, Hispanic Americans, Asian Americans, and Native Americans increased 2.7 percent to an all-time high of 3.6 million students (Wilds & Wilson, 1998). However, despite these encouraging statistics, one area in higher education where minorities still lag behind is at the administrative level. This lag is especially the case on predominantly white university campuses where administrators of color account for only 2.5 percent of all administrators at predominantly white colleges and universities (Konrad & Pfeffer, 1991).

Institutions of higher education have a civic responsibility to meet the needs of our growing ethnically diverse U.S. population. Representation in the administrative ranks commensurate with the community served is not only a civic but a moral responsibility. Although there have been notable attempts to ameliorate the status of minority administrators, the current anti-affirmative action wave that is sweeping throughout mainstream colleges and universities, leaves many people of color wondering whether there is still a true commitment to the advancement of minorities in higher education, not only at the faculty and student levels but also where the power truly exists—at the administrative levels. In response to the need to advance more people of color, in particular African Americans, who are the focus of this chapter, to administrative positions at predominantly white colleges and universities, this chapter addresses the overall status of minorities in management positions nationwide; the effects of most common barriers to advancement for African-American administrators at mainstream colleges and universities; and strategies to strengthen and encourage young African-American administrators to surmount the institutional and organizational barriers that pervade predominantly white colleges and universities.

Career Progress

African Americans, in particular, constitute about 12 percent of the American population, or one in eight (Carr-Ruffino, 1996). The U.S. Department of Labor predicted that African Americans would be about 22 percent of the new workforce in the 1990s. From 1978 to 1990 there was a 52 percent increase in the number of African Americans who occupied positions as managers, professionals, and government officials. The greatest progress has been in government jobs. In 1980, two-thirds of African Americans holding jobs as managers and professionals were working for the federal government (Carr-Ruffino, 1996).

In 1986, Korn/Ferry found that of 1,362 senior executives only 29 percent were women and 13 percent were people of color, a total of 3 percent at a time when women and people of color made up 51.4 percent of the workforce. According to one survey reported by Braham, in 1979, blacks occupied 0.2 percent of the senior executive positions and that figure had increased to only 0.3 percent by 1985. Another survey reported by Braham (1987) actually showed a decrease in blacks at senior management levels during the same period: from 0.4 percent to 0.2 percent. In addition, blacks have lost momentum in management overall. Blacks made up only 4.9 percent of the management ranks in 1987 compared with 4 percent in 1980.

These statistics indicate that moving into the senior administrative ranks is still a problem for some traditionally underrepresented groups. For African Americans, moving beyond middle management is an even greater problem for most nontraditional managers who confront the "glass ceiling." Although the U.S. government reports that 30 percent of corporate middle management is made up of women, blacks, and Hispanics, these groups make up less than 1 percent of chief executives and those who report directly to them (Wren, 1995).

Barriers to Career Advancement

African-American administrators experience a myriad of barriers and organizational pitfalls that their white counterparts are not subjected to. Institutional racism, cultural insensitivity, and marginalization are just few of the manifold encumbrances that define the experience of an African-American administrator at predominantly white colleges and universities. Although the types of barriers are much less egregious and overt today than a few decades ago, they are no less damaging to the dreams and aspirations of many African-American administrators striving to create their own professional niche.

There are several reasons why African Americans have been unable to ascend the organizational hierarchy in higher education. Since the literature on barriers to advancement for African-American administrators at mainstream colleges and universities is limited, I discuss barriers to advancement for African Americans from a generic organizational perspective.

A commonly held barrier is *prejudice* which refers to attitudinal bias and means to prejudge something or someone on basis of some characteristics. Another barrier is *discrimination,* which refers to behavioral bias toward a person based on the person's group identity (Cox, 1993). Together, the effects of prejudice and discrimination can form a formidable barrier to occupational advancement for African-American administrators.

In a study conducted on executives in corporations, the majority of executives apparently believe that prejudice and discrimination do influence career outcomes in organizations. For example, in-depth interviews with 50 middle and senior managers in a division of a Fortune 500 firm revealed that 80 percent believed that experiences at work were influenced by group identities such as racioethnicity and gender (Cox, 1993).

The effects of prejudice and discrimination are also apparent in other areas of organizational life. For instance, their effects can be seen in interpersonal trust, which is an important ingredient for effective human relations and performance in organizations. The historical relations between whites and blacks have created a trust barrier to successful interaction and communications. Another area that prejudice and discrimination affect is processing feedback. According to Cox (1993, pp. 82-83), "When a person believes that feedback received is a mixture of prejudice and realistic performance evaluation, it becomes difficult to determine what areas need to be changed." The effects of prejudice and discrimination are also evident in employee motivation. Cox (1993, pp. 82-83) claims, "Individuals may not believe that performance ratings will adequately reflect effect and therefore motivation may suffer. Even if the evaluation performance is not influenced by group identities, motivation will still be hampered if employees believe that outcomes are not strictly performance-based but somewhat dependent on group identity prejudice."

Another commonly held barrier to career outcomes is institutional bias. Institutional bias refers to preference patterns that are inherent in how we manage organizations that often inadvertently creates barriers to full participation by organization members from cultural backgrounds that differ from traditional majority groups (Cox, 1993). Examples of institutional bias are *individualistic reward systems,* which are the antithesis of the collectivist or communal culture that is often synonymous with African-American culture. Another form of institutional bias is the "similar-to-me" phenomenon, which suggests selection decisions are heavily influenced by the extent to which the decision makers view the job candidate as being like himself or herself (Cox, 1993). Another form of institutional bias occurs in the form of informal networks. Because of the importance of informal contacts, recommendations, and referrals as a source of information for occupational advancement, individuals such as women, nonwhite men, persons with disabilities, and others who are not majority group members will struggle to participate in informal communications and social networks, thus helping their careers.

Describing sundry barriers that continue to hinder the ability of talented African Americans to climb the organizational hierarchy can go on and on.

Other barriers such as stereotyping, racial discrimination, and glass ceiling effects on occupational mobility are themes that resonate in the literature. The point is that African-American administrators continue to struggle to create their own professional niche while simultaneously paving the way for future generations of worthy African Americans to occupy positions of political power and influence at mainstream colleges and universities. However my focus is not on the barriers that many African-American administrators continue to face, but on strategies to overcome these barriers. The strategies presented in this chapter are practical and helpful to the advancement of not only young African-Americans administrators, although they are the focus of this chapter, but also members of underrepresented groups in higher education. The strategies will provide tactics to help maneuver through the organizational maze and transcend institutional bureaucracy.

The Strategies

Before I delve into the strategies, I would like to preface by suggesting that it is extremely difficult, if not impossible, to advance your career without community support. Developing a community of black faculty, administrators, and students is critical to successful acclimation within a predominantly white university environment. The community provides the social support to discuss work-related or diversity issues, creates a milieu that fosters open and honest communication, and cultivates working and collaborative relationships. However, the key to successful community building is consistent participation among group members. This can be accomplished by appointing a committee responsible for maintaining open communication of meeting times and agenda items. A certain rate of attrition can be expected due to loss of interest, job responsibilities, or other commitments. But this should not discourage or deter the core members of the group from providing an enclave in which the black community can take refuge.

Strategy 1 Enhance Your Expertise: Going Beyond the Scope of Your Responsibility

Mastering your job duties and responsibilities, obviously, is mandatory in order to keep your job. As a supplement, a good habit to develop is to enhance your expertise by going beyond the scope of your responsibility through familiarizing yourself with departmental policies, regulations, and guidelines and understanding how each individual in your department fulfills his or her role.

In addition, identifying the latest research in your area through literature reviews of academic books, journal articles, or periodicals will also enhance your expertise. The purpose is to prepare as though you will become the senior administrator of your department. By doing this you can stand out at meetings, using your expertise as a vehicle to your advancement. Develop a reputation of being the one who has all the answers. Keeping yourself abreast of the latest issues, policies, and research can enhance your credibility and help you become marked for advancement.

Strategy 2 Align Yourself with Successful Mentorship

An effective way to overcome institutional barriers is to seek successful African-American mentorship. Aligning yourself with successful African-American mentorship is crucial in becoming successful at a predominantly white university campus. Despite the abysmal statistics mentioned earlier, there are pioneers within mainstream higher education who can serve as a guide through the institutional maze that has discouraged great potential in many young African-American administrators. Whether one goes through the administrative or academic route, there are those African Americans who have been successful in overcoming the barriers that pervade predominantly white colleges and universities. The key is to develop and cultivate a relationship by seeking advice and knowledge from such individuals. These individuals can become a resource who can help you break through institutional barriers by providing contacts to other job opportunities, letters of reference, and so on. However, it is important to choose your mentor carefully. Veteran African-American administrators can become bitter and cynical from years of prejudice and discrimination. My intention is not to belittle their struggles, but to make young African-American administrators aware that seeking mentorship from such individuals can distort your perception of positive progress. If not chosen carefully, your mentors can inoculate you with a negative attitude that can hinder your career at mainstream institutions of higher education.

Strategy 3 Enhance Your Credibility: Earn Advanced Degrees

It is difficult to discuss this issue without sounding condescending or patronizing. My purpose is not to belittle or explain the obvious, but rather to encourage those who are on the fence or debating as to whether they should pursue an advanced degree such as Master's degree, Ed.D., or Ph.D., or some other terminal degree. There are numerous factors that contribute to the lack of advanced degrees among African-American administrators, most of which are financial and occupationally based. Some may feel that pursuing an advanced degree while working for the institution is too difficult. Factors such as the time needed to complete class assignments, hours during the day or night to take classes, or the money to finance their education all need to be taken into account when making this decision. Fortunately, many mainstream colleges and universities in the country allow their employees to take classes while working for the institution, on the condition that they will be able to maintain their job duties and responsibilities.

This section is of primary importance for young administrators starting out in higher education. As an administrator, credibility is the only real currency of value in higher education. Obtaining the appropriate credentials in higher education is critical to earning the respect necessary to be effective in the administrative arena. Whether we like to admit it or not, colleges and universities, like organizations around the world, are classist institutions, meaning that unless one is a part of a certain class or group, it is easy to become ostracized or marginalized. In higher education, having a Ph.D., Ed.D., Master's degree, or some other terminal degree, increases your credibility and helps you ascend up the professional hierarchy. This may be an obvious assertion; however, many African-American professionals who have a Bachelor's degree and are trying to advance their careers in higher education will find many obstacles hindering their progress without an advanced or terminal degree. This is not to suggest that those who do not have advanced degrees are any less capable of doing an effective job. Unfortunately, university administrators at predominantly white institutions do not take young African-American administrators seriously enough as credible professionals if they do not hold advanced degrees. I have seen many young, talented African-American professionals unable to gain the respect and administrative advancement they deserved solely on the basis of their lack of advanced degree status. The best these individuals could do is make lateral occupational moves to other institutions, only to find themselves facing the same occupational roadblocks they faced at their previous institution. The purpose behind this message is to encourage African Americans to pursue advanced degrees while working for a college or university.

Strategy 4 Create Coalitions with Key Political Figures in the Organization

One area that needs to be addressed is the political aspect of organizational life within higher education. Politics is often seen as a pejorative term. Politics occurs in the form of "wheeling and dealing" where people from divergent views attempt to advance their specific interests (Morgan, 1997). It is a permanent fixture of organizational life. As an African-American administrator, politics can be a useful means of ascertaining one's career goals, through the art of consultation and negotiation.

An effective way of accomplishing this task is to build coalitions with key political figures within higher education. According to Morgan (1997, p. 160):

> Organizations are coalitions and coalition building is an essential dimension of almost all organization life. Coalitions arise when groups of individuals get together to cooperate in relation to specific issues, events, or decisions or to advance specific values and ideologies. Coalition development offers a strategy for advancing one's interests in an organization, and organization members often give considerable attention to increasing their power and influence through this means. Sometimes, coalitions are initiated by less powerful actors who seek the support of others. At other times, they may be developed by the powerful to consolidate their power; for example, an executive may promote people to key positions where they can serve as loyal lieutenants.

By investigating the background and research interests of senior-level administrators such as the president, provost, vice provost, dean, or department chairs and building coalitions, you can position yourself for advancement in the event that your services will be called on for a particular program or project. Senior administrators will not consider you if they do not know who you are. Set up meetings with senior administrators to introduce yourself and discuss career goals. The goal is to keep yourself at the forefront of their minds. It is within these coalitions that young African-American administrators can politically maneuver up the institutional hierarchy and place themselves in positions of political power and influence.

Strategy 5 Avoid Being Marginalized: Work from a Broad-Base Position

Working from a broad base refers to working from a position within a mainstream college or university that has broader, culturally neutral focus where the duties and responsibilities are not tailored exclusively to people of color. I want to preface my argument by first stating that minorities working in positions in higher education that cater toward serving solely multicultural populations is not necessarily a bad career move. Departments such as the division of minority affairs, or office of multicultural relations should be occupied by people of color. Such positions in higher education are a quantum leap from what was being offered to people of color as recently as 30 to 40 years ago when certain mainstream colleges and universities were still struggling with integration. Multicultural-focused divisions have their place within the higher education milieu because: (1) their presence on a mainstream campus reminds the rest of the university that minority people do exist; (2) they provide a place where students can connect with other minority students; and (3) they provide an opportunity for people of color to get their foot in the door of a mainstream institution. However, working from a broad-base position allows African-American administrators to create a nexus with the powerful figures that a narrow-focused position may not offer. This is not to say that developing a relationship with powerful figures is impossible from a narrow-focused position. It is just more advantageous to build relationships from broader positions, where not every issue deals with race, although this is an important issue. You do not want senior administrators to think that diversity issues are the *only* issues you are capable of handling. Demonstrate that you can work on a broader range of issues such as academics, politics, research interests, university advancement, and so on.

Some researchers actually believe that such narrowly tailored positions are efforts to disenfranchise minorities. For example, Wilson (1980) argues that white men seek to exclude black men and women as competitors for prestigious jobs, as suggested by the social closure argument. One way to minimize encroachment into privileged positions is to channel black men and women into "racialized" or marginalized jobs (Muame, 1999). This form of racial segregation in higher education keeps African Americans essentially marginalized, having little to no power within the mainstream university system. By keeping African Americans channeled into these racialized jobs, African Americans are unable to make progress up the occupational ladder. The problem with these assignments was summarized by Jones (1986, p. 89):

> Too often Black managers are channeled into The Relations as I call them—the community relations, the public relations, the personnel relations. These may be important functions, but they are not gut functions that make the business grow or bring in revenues. And they are not the jobs that prepare an executive to be a CEO. If this experience is typical, the channeling of Black workers into racialized jobs reserves the more visible and policy-oriented jobs are reserved for Whites. Moreover, the impact of segregation will be magnified if there is evidence that the university neglects or devalues jobs that are increasingly associated with minorities. The effect suggests that African Americans are hired into and then allowed to languish in racialized jobs.

Holding in such racialized jobs in higher education for long periods of time can actually cause you to be pigeonholed occupationally. This can limit your ability to find work outside such fields. The purpose behind this discussion is to encourage young African-American administrators to seek positions where they can influence and affect change within the university while at the same time move up the occupational ladder.

Strategy 6 *Cultivating Leadership Potential*
The idea of cultivating leadership potential as a strategy for overcoming the barriers of being an African-American administrator on a predominantly white campus does not seem to make sense at face value. Cultivating leadership potential in African Americans can actually work to benefit both those who have the vision to cultivate leadership among the African-American citizenry and the citizenry itself. To better explicate my rationale for using leadership as a means to overcome institutional barriers, I first describe different types of leadership.

In many contemporary organizations, the most appropriate leader is one who can lead others who can lead themselves (Manz & Sims, 1991). This perspective suggests a new measure of a leader's strength–one's ability to maximize the contributions of others through recognition of their right to guide their destiny, rather than the leader's ability to bend the will of others to his or her own (Manz & Sims, 19951). Through mentoring, encouraging, and cultivating leadership among young African-American faculty, students, and staff, African-American administrators are creating a culture of leadership that stresses community, consensual validation, and positive reinforcement. This is a selfless form of leadership that gives African-American administrators opportunities to enhance the potential of up-and-coming leaders, but also gives them the chance to reveal their ability to not only mobilize their community but to demonstrate effective leadership. This is critically important because of the limited opportunities given to African-American administrators to demonstrate their skill to be productive.

According to Kotter (1990, p. 9), "Leaders almost always have had the opportunities during their twenties and thirties to actually try to lead, to take a risk, and to learn from both triumphs and failures. Such learning seems essential in developing a wide range of leadership skills and perspectives." As the maxim goes, "perception is reality." Predominantly white colleges and universities are extremely image conscious and if the university is perceived as an institution that promotes and advances people of color to senior administrative positions, that is an advantage for the university economically since there is potential for attracting more diverse faculty, staff, and students.

Strategy 7 Learn to Develop Fund-raising Skills

Another method of overcoming institutional barriers is to develop the ability to raise money through fund raising or grant writing. These extremely valuable skills are a top priority for mainstream colleges and universities. Nothing speaks more loud and clear to mainstream institutions than money. It may seem like a shallow and superficial way to gain the type of respect needed for advancement up the institutional ladder, but fund raising forces university brass to see any administrator, regardless of race or ethnicity, as a valuable contributor to university advancement. Money is a universal language that does not discriminate and turns outsiders into real players in the administration game. Grant writing or fund raising can increase the potential for advancement for African-American administrators exponentially.

One effective way to develop fund-raising skills is to identify departments on campus such as a foundation office that is responsible for soliciting gifts from potential donors. Develop a relationship with a program officer in the department who would be willing to help you understand the dynamics of fund raising, such as engaging potential donors, identifying potential candidates, and so on. If your schedule permits, offer to work on projects that will enhance your fund-raising skills. Anything that will help you to understand the nuances of fund-raising will increase your marketability.

Another way to learn how to raise money is through grant writing. Most mainstream colleges and universities have a grant or research development office that specializes in negotiating contracts with funding agencies from federal, state, foundation, and corporate sources. They also provide instruction on how to write grants successfully. Billions of dollars in awards can be earned from funding each year. These offices can provide instructional videos and other materials that teach the basics of grant writing as well as provide strategies to gain a competitive edge. Grant and research development offices can also identify potential funding sources or agencies that would be interested in funding your project. In addition, you can also take classes in grant writing at your college or university as well as attend grant-writing workshops.

Concluding Remarks

The point to all this is to make senior administrators at predominantly white university campuses see you as a potential asset to the university, which means developing those skills that are deemed valuable or marketable such as the skills previously mentioned. Some of the work may be extremely boring and tedious but its rewards are invaluable to young African-American administrators who seek to acquire these skills.

As African-American administrators, developing valuable skills is more important than ever with the recent resurgence of antidiversity campaigns on mainstream college and university campuses across the country, which take the form of "merit-based" or "reverse discrimination." For example, the passage of Proposition 209 in the state of California and Initiative-200 in the state of Washington, both laws that ban affirmative action programs at state-funded institutions sends a clear message that the pendulum is swinging in the direction against minority advancement. In another recent case, a Florida judge ruled to uphold the governor's controversial plan to end affirmative action in university admission. This is a precursor to a growing trend at mainstream colleges and universities that will be a disadvantage for minority people in higher education. In the face of these challenges, W. E. B. DuBois' "The Talented Tenth" best summarizes our commitment to the advancement of people of color:

> Can such culture training of group leaders be neglected? Can we afford to ignore it? Do you think that if the leaders of thought among Negroes are not trained and educated thinkers, that they will have no leaders? On the contrary a hundred half-trained demagogues will still hold the places they so largely occupy now, and hundreds of vociferous busybodies will multiply. *You have no choice;* either you must help furnish this race from within its own ranks with thoughtful men of trained leadership, or you must suffer the evil consequences of a headless misguided rabble. . . .

As African Americans, we have no choice but to take up the mantle of leadership and continue to press forward. This is a call to all African-American administrators to rise up, develop creative strategies to overcome institutional barriers, and acquire the necessary skills that mainstream institutions deem valuable so that when we are in senior administrative positions, we can determine the direction of our divisions and influence university policy on issues that are pertinent to the advancement of underrepresented groups. Mainstream colleges and universities are beginning to turn a deaf ear to the cries of minorities in general. We must continue to be creative in the fight against the detrimental effects of institutional barriers that cripple our career outcomes.

References

Braham, J., (1987). Is the door really open? *Industry Week* (November 16): 64–70.

Carr-Ruffino, N. (1996). *Managing diversity: People skills for a multicultural workplace*. USA: Thomas Executive Press.

Cox, Jr., T. (1993). *Cultural diversity in organizations: Theory, research, & practice*. San Francisco: Berrett-Koehler Publishers.

DuBois, W.E.B. (1903). *The talented tenth. The Negro problem*. New York: James Pott & Company.

Firebaugh et.al., (2000). Diversity and globalization: Challenges, opportunities, and promise. *Journal of Family and Consumer Sciences* 92(1):27–36.

Jones, E. W., Jr. (1986). Black managers: The dream deferred. *Harvard Business Review* 64:84–93.

Kellett, C., (1994). Family diversity and difference: A challenge for change. *Journal of Home Economics* 86(3):3–11.

Konrad, A. M., & Pfeffer, J. (1991). Understanding the hiring of women and minorities in educational institutions. *Sociology of Education*, 64(3):141–157.

Korn/Ferry International (1986). *Korn/Ferry's international executive profile. A survey of corporate leaders in the 80s*. New York: Korn/Ferry International.

Kotter, J. P. (1990, May–June). What leaders really do. *Harvard Business Review*.

Manz, C., & Sims, Jr., H. P. (1991) *Organizational Dynamics*. New York: American Management Association.

Morgan, G., (1997). *Images of organization*. Thousand Oaks, CA: Sage Publications.

Muame, D. J. (1999). Occupational segregation and the career mobility of white men and women. *Social Forces* 77:1433–1449.

U.S. Department of Labor. (1987, May). *Work force 2000*. Washington, D.C.: Employment and Training Administration, U.S. Department of Labor.

Wren, J. T., (Ed.). (1995). *The leader's companion: Insights on leadership through the ages*. New York: The Free Press.

Wilds, D. J. & Wilson, R. (1998). *Minorities in higher education, 1997–98*. Sixteenth annual status report. Washington, D.C.: American Council on Education.

Wilson, W. J. (1980). *The declining significance of race: Blacks and changing American institutions*, 2nd ed. Chicago: University of Chicago Press.

8

RETAINING AFRICAN-AMERICAN ADMINISTRATORS

A Subconscious Deluge of Neglect or a Conscious Subterfuge to Reject?

J. W. Wiley

Introduction

> In spite of the meager rewards, however, the idea of leadership looms high in the Negro mind. It always develops thus among oppressed people. The oppressor must have some dealing with the despised group, and rather than have contact with individuals he approaches the masses through his own spokesman (Woodson, 1993, p. 115).

Yes, this is an intriguing quote to have chosen for a conversation on the retention of African-American administrators. When Carter G. Woodson expressed this sentiment in 1933 in his book *The Mis-Education of the Negro* he would not have realized that his words would still ring true 70 years later. The idea of leadership still looms large in the minds of African Americans. We are arguably still oppressed, albeit more mentally than physically, unless economic oppression is physical. But what warranted this quote and ignited this dialogue was the manipulation that the oppressor had over the spokesman. This often is the plight of African-American administrators when it comes to certain types of programs they manage, direct, or administrate. They are selected by their management, usually white management, for their skills in communicating to certain constituencies. Often the significant "skill" they possess is the color of their skin.

As Woodson implied, African-American administrators usually are leaders within their communities because it is a priority to them. They are leaders because they endeavor to be leaders. They are leaders because the positions they find themselves in usually necessitate a responsibility for them to be leaders. As a matter of fact, if they did not exhibit a certain degree of leadership ability, they probably would never ascend to the position of administrator at a major college or university. However, leaders sometimes lead in their respective environments but then become followers outside of those communities. Regrettably, for a multitude of reasons, leadership is sometimes co-opted. Consequently, what appears to be leadership by an administrator is often nothing more than a member of the team implementing the team plan. Even worse, sometimes it is a figurehead carrying out the plans of the administration while attempting to convey an aura of authenticity amidst an ambiance of despair.

Why is the possibility of manipulation by management of an African-American administrator in academia a concern? Within this context the import is significant because it can be seen as a detrimental factor against successful retention practices. The lack of autonomy that results from an inability to obtain your management's support can ultimately prove stifling when you want to implement programs that you believe in or that would directly benefit your constituency. The frustrations your management must have with an apparent lack of confidence in your abilities can be psychologically and emotionally debilitating. Faced with this harsh reality, there is a concern that the sometimes coveted role of administrator, which ideally equates to leader, is nothing but a duplicitous term that really means pawn, or even worse, servant. What other term should be used to define the administrator who is hired to function as the mindless operator of a preset agenda? And yes, servant does add an additional element of anxiety to the analysis when the administrator is of color. In institutions that have abysmal representation of underrepresented administrators, manipulation of the few who are there does not enhance the possibilities of retaining them.

In his book *Reflecting Black,* Dyson (1994, p. 151) suggests that a certain amount of subterfuge occurs around "those subjects."

> On elite college campuses the implications of difference, diversity, and pluralism are heatedly debated, but their hard lessons are mostly avoided or dissolved in the discourse of merit, objectivity, or standards.

Dyson's reference to an avoidance of the topics of difference, diversity, and pluralism on college campuses underlines the reasons that many black administrators are designated to head these initiatives or engage their respective constituencies. Conversations on these subjects are seldom welcomed in the workplace. Academic institutions are comfortable appropriating diversity as a marketing tool and a weighted expression of the institution's sensitivity and sophistication. However, when the rubber hits the road the institutions are disconnected from the operations that perpetuate the success and failure of the so-called welcome participants. Then it is left to the black administrators to represent the administration such that the often disenfranchised "diversity people" will be happy enough to represent the university. Welcome to the game called representation!

Considerations such as these are often the determinants to the success or failure of retaining African-American administrators. The pressure involved in appeasing management that may or may not care about the humanity of the project is juxtaposed against members of the served group accosting the integrity of the administrator. Let there be no mistake: the "Uncle Tom" jacket is an extremely difficult article of clothing not to be fitted for. Anthropologist Marc Cohen, author of *Culture of Intolerance,* endorses the notion that someone who appears to have achieved success is "likely to be accused of brown-nosing or trying to make everyone else look bad" (Cohen, 1998, p. 88). He insists that this is the price society levels on those who are successful or even "overtly generous."

Many of these factors can be mitigated completely if an institution is aware of its contribution to such awkward and unfortunate scenarios. The reality of an African-American administrator as the sole or one of a few administrators of color at a university is harrowing enough given the academic institution and its surrounding environment. But denial or refusal to discuss issues that are critical concerns in larger society can sometimes be the deciding factor as to whether the administrator leaves or stays. Often that departure is not the result of a better opportunity seeking out the administrator, but more so of him or her looking for a better opportunity.

Mitigation of retention failures can also occur if, in the initial conversations (perhaps the first interview), the administrative candidate explicitly states what his or her goals and objectives actually are. His or her goals then can be contrasted with the necessarily articulated goals and objectives of the institution or department. This will then generate enough of a response or reaction from the interviewer that potential disconnects might reveal themselves earlier rather than later.

There are other factors that can contribute to the failure of retention efforts beyond the manipulation of an administrator, communication disconnections, singular status within an organization, portrayal as a figurehead, and so forth. An additional aspect to consider will be what I call the 53rd card in the American deck: the race card! Since there are only supposed to be 52 cards, it is an indication that something is amiss and will be revealed systematically throughout this conversation. However, when the basic thesis of this paper is revealed, in its various forms, you will have the major reason for the failure of retention of African-American administrators.

According to W. E. B. DuBois:

> Is it going to be possible in the future for races to remain segregated or to escape contact or domination simply by retiring to themselves? Certainly it is not. Race segregation in the future is going to be impossible primarily because these races are needed more and more in the world economy (Fonrer, 1991, p. 184).

The Bilinguality of Black Folk

Two assessments of African-American administrators that actually are the point of departure for my analysis were the chapters written by Larry L. Rowley and Jerlando F. L. Jackson for the Lee Jones project titled, *Brothers of the Academy*. In his book, Jones canvassed up-and-coming black male academics for their insights and perspectives on many facets of the academy. Why Jones did this appears to be prima facie:

> The purpose of *Brothers of the Academy* is to highlight and showcase African American Brothers who have achieved in their chosen careers despite the odds. This book will not only profile twenty-six African American Brothers of the academy, it will also provide the readers with tangible examples of how these Brothers have progressed in their chosen careers (Jones, 2000, p. xxi).

Jones also provided evidence for two very different communities that, through the voices of the participants in his project, show that communication within the black community is very laden with theory and that black folk are bilingual. That the theory is the lived experience of a legacy of slavery resonates in everything that African Americans do and say within the confines of a racist state. The bilingual reality is evidenced in how viscerally black folk "feel" one another when sharing their experiences of infiltrating economic, social, and political spaces that they helped to create but often have little access to. Omi and Winant (1994) endorse this sentiment in their discussions on racial formation. They concur that in America there exists at least two languages, one that reflects the trauma of the black, or "other," experiences in America, and another that reflects the white inability to relate to the scars of enslavement and its aftermath. According to Omi and Winant (1994, p. 71):

> The absence of a clear source "common sense" understanding of what racism means has become a significant obstacle to efforts aimed at challenging it. Bob Blauner has noted that in classroom discussions of racism, white and non-white students tend to talk past one another. Whites tend to locate racism in color consciousness and find its absence colorblindness. In so doing, they see the affirmations of difference and racial identity among racially defined minority students as racist. Non-white students, by contrast, see racism as a system of power, and correspondingly argue that blacks, for example, cannot be racist because they lack power. Blauner concludes that there are two "languages" of race, one in which members of racial minorities, especially blacks, see the centrality of race in history and everyday experience, and another in which whites see race as "a peripheral, nonessential reality."

Omi and Winant's point addresses student perspectives, but those perspectives cannot be far removed from the perspectives of administrators. A close friend who happens to be an esteemed anthropologist admitted that he believed he had colorblindness with respect to race. Within minutes we were immersed in dialectic that found me positing the existence of his admittedly naive position against my assertion that if he could see disability, sexual orientation, and class distinction, then race should be ascertainable to him as well. I then cautioned him that whether race is a factor in the way an organization treats its administrators or not, because of America's history regarding race, regrettably it becomes an issue in the mind of most African-American administrators.

In their reformulation of racism, Omi and Winant define racist projects as such only if they "create or reproduce structures of dominance based on essentialist categories." It is in the acceptance of their physical capabilities of seeing racism only as colorblindness that whites open themselves up to accusations of essentialism. Not being limited, necessarily, to processing racial skin the way most of us have causes irreconcilable differences between all who do see color and are colorblind regarding race.

So, what does it mean to be bilingual in America and yet not have your language recognized as such? It means that you can edit a book the way Jones did,

have black folk read it and understand the context, the pretext, and the subtext, and know they would be able to relate to it fully because it is an experience that they have lived. On the contrary, it is also recognizing that most non-
blacks do not speak this language and therefore may understand 80 percent of
the context, 70 percent of the pretext, and only 20 percent of the subtext.

It should not be surprising that white folk are bilingual also. They speak
from a position of privilege from which the most privileged of black folk will
never speak. Even those whites who are disadvantaged can still communicate
that privilege, though they may not access it for whatever reasons. It is amaz-
ing that in articulating a reality of language within this paper you may have
experienced a dialectical moment that permeated itself with an original thesis
of black bilinguality, an antithesis of white bilinguality, and a synthesis that
perhaps black folk are trilingual.

Recognizing a Mob When You See One

Jackson (2000) and Rowley (2000) highlighted similar realities while detailing very different realities of the academy and its ability to retain African-
American administrators. Rowley, in his article titled "African American Men
in Higher Education" looks at both faculty and administrative retention,
though his focus is more on faculty of color than on administrators of color.
His data reflects the poor graduation statistics of baccalaureate degrees, and
the abysmal attainment of graduate degrees by African-American men. They
also reflect exactly where black faculty are employed and how disproportionately their representation is at premier institutions. The data are significant because many of the black administrators that institutions endeavor to
retain are also faculty. Many of the administrators desire to become faculty
one day. Many of the administrators were once faculty and the institution
could not retain them in that capacity or the administrators decided to
enhance their experiences and join the ranks of the faculty. The fact that
Rowley's data do not offer administrative statistics does highlight the fact
that administrative retention is the first cousin to faculty and student retention. Therefore, analysis on this subject is normally folded in under the
purview of an exhaustive attempt at retention.

Rowley anoints the challenges that confront the retention process as
"dialectical in nature," with a healthy respect for contradictory propositions
on the subject that may challenge original theses and allow for potential synthesis of the varying ideals. In this spirit, his position is assailed with the hope
that our different perspectives can be synthesized.

Rowley's declaration of the significance that an appreciation of history can have as an influence on the endeavors of an aspiring administrator is directly on target and much more significant than one might gather on a first reading. As an aspiring black philosopher, my recognition of DuBois' journey toward his graduate degrees at that time in American history made my journey a bit less treacherous. However, my journey and that of Rowley's were journeys to becoming scholars, not administrators. Administrative retention must be moved out of the back seat of automobiles driven by faculty [retention] and student retention. To ensure that a benefit will be obtained from historical exploration for black administrators there needs to be systematic processes that provide opportunities for administrators to connect with one another the way faculty and students do.

Jackson (2000), in his article "Administrators of Color at Predominantly White Institutions," provides systematic organizational alternatives for retention, but they are more constructed to support faculty. The Minority Faculty Recruitment Incentive Program (MFRIP), New Faculty Mentoring Program (NFMP), and the Target of Opportunity Program (TOP) are all proffered as worthy of consideration as resources to assist in the recruitment and retention of black academic professionals (Jackson, 2000, p. 46). This is definitely neither a disparagement of the organizations nor of my colleague's efforts, but MFRIP and NFMP specifically decry themselves as academic entities in their titles. An administrator seeking refuge or solace in an organization may never venture there, unless he or she had faculty aspirations and was so distraught with the situation that he or she would seek nurturing wherever it is available. An institution, especially one seeking support for its black administrators, may choose not to seek support from these organizations either. Why is this? Because consistent with statistics, these senior administrators would be non-black (white). In recognition of the fact that there is nothing to gain by being coy regarding retention, we should not be coy in stating some obvious facts about retention. It is a rarity when nonblack folk (in this case, white) are comfortable enough with themselves to clearly state that they do not know something, or more importantly, that black folk know more. When this does occur, you have found a nonblack person whom you need to befriend because you are more apt to see a pink elephant in tights than to run across many more individuals such as this in your lifetime. Seriously, black intellectuals do not acknowledge their ignorance of matters that often either, so when race or culture is a factor in determining knowledge and everyone endeavors to be a genius, on some level we are talking human nature. But white folk would most likely be unfamiliar with these organizations.

Jackson's article also highlights the criticality of consistently maintaining affirmative action policies throughout the duration of African-American administrators' appointments. In addition, Jackson asserts the importance of demonstrative support from the university president, including acknowledgment of the administrators' contributions to the university. He also recommends public presidential recognition of black administrators and their efforts to succeed. This type of appreciation is definitely a strategy for enhancing retention of African-American administrators. However, I caution you not to believe the hype too quickly. The sayings "don't let the smooth taste fool you" and "beware t ie handshake that hides a snake" are still good advice. Words do not mean a thing if actions are not backing them up. Putting it differently and with a not so subtle acknowledgment to a colleague, "the bottom line is results; anything else is rhetoric."

Still, the problems that exist for administrators of color are often unique to them and need to be treated as such. The days of monolithic solutions to problems for black folk ended around the same time blacks realized that braids, dreads, the Afro, the Fade, bald heads, and perms were all appropriate if they were what blacks chose to wear, and inappropriate for those who did not desire that look. Translated, organizations that are designed to address the troubles of black folk in a certain line of work will not necessarily cure what ails black folk in other professions simply because the common denominator is that they are all black.

The Right Questions Will Not Get You Lynched

In any negotiations for a position it is important for the prospective administrator to *know how many staff,* if any, will report to him or her and in what capacity they will be available, as well as whether or not they will report directly. Also, it is important that employees who are not direct reports are aware that they could be identified as resources. While this may appear inconsequential (and to some degree it is), the ramifications of a new administrator having to introduce indirect underlings to their soft line assignments is an unnecessary headache and one that often arises due to insufficient communication by management.

Awareness of *budget realities* is critical. Knowing what the operating budget is for the organization or projects that you will direct or manage should be ascertained prior to the acceptance of any opportunity. Knowing if the university is going to provide you with a credit card or telephone card for the expenses you incur on behalf of the university is important to know.

Answers to these questions can make a significant difference to the sanity of a relatively inexperienced administrator who might be financially strapped trying to absorb some of the financial burdens of his or her organization on his or her personal credit card. Also, knowing what the future budget plans of the organization are can be significant in terms of both short- and long-term planning. The mere fact that the administrator is asking questions regarding the strategic planning of the operation is a statement about the administrative maturity of the individual. Failure to initiate and accomplish these suggestions contributes to a potentially distasteful situation, potentially fraught with distrust, monetary inadequacies, and unnecessary concerns that should have been alleviated up front. Both the hiring management and the prospective administrator have a responsibility to ensure that these conversations occur. Not only are these processes important in alleviating unnecessary stress. They enhance the potential of retaining the administrator.

Office location might appear to be one of the most insignificant considerations when assessing retention, but it very well might be one of the most important aspects of a new job to consider. Often you can determine quite a bit about the value of an operation or the importance of the position by where it is placed or situated in an institution. That fact, combined with the fact that your office is the first impression you make on clients and colleagues and is the space where you have been designated to live for many hours a week, makes this an aspect that should not be taken lightly. In addition, many operations allow newly hired administrators to purchase new furniture when their positions are new to the organization or when the budget allows for it. Conversely, old furniture can project an image of disinterest in the administrator and how he or she is perceived. Finally, new furniture and a prime office location can often be a very strategic "feel good" move by an organization; it makes a statement that, in actuality, is not necessarily strong or significant, but nevertheless appears to exemplify that fact that the recipient feels good.

Equipment in the age of technology is just as critical to the success of an operation as furniture. Antiquated office equipment is a telltale sign that the company you are considering probably is not performing well. Your articulation of your need for office equipment that you think is necessary for you or your staff to perform well on the job needs to be communicated. A high-tech fax machine, a flat-screen computer, a Palm Pilot, and a cellular phone all have their respective merits. The response from the prospective management team to your assessment of technical needs that they deem luxuries but you deem essential might be an indication of the level of sophistication or immaturity in the respective perspectives. Both parties should listen carefully to the positions that are articulated in these conversations to assist in the determination of whether the equipment should be purchased. Just because it might appear to be a toy to someone who is technologically impaired should not devalue the equipment if a strong case is presented regarding need for the purchase. Conversely, there might be very rational reasons for less or different equipment and new administrators should be mindful enough to recognize that their management should have a handle on these issues. Essentially, communication should assist in clearing up this snafu.

A *personal development line* within the budget is essential to the long-term success and sanity of an administrator. This request is one that many administrators are hesitant to ask for because of the perception of it as a perk. However, an organization that cannot accommodate it and does not provide solid rationale behind its inability to accommodate the request is not an organization that believes in investing in its personnel. Besides, a personal development line should enable an administrator to attend a conference or workshop that will enrich his or her professional perspective. The personal development opportunity is beyond the traditional business trip and the opportunity to enrich yourself and your organization or institution should not be lost.

Regarding *relocation packages:* Just as people encourage young couples to attempt to have all of their financial matters resolved before entering into marriage, a professional relationship can be viewed as a marriage of sorts. In this vein, it would be advantageous for the newly hired administrator and the prospective employer to be inquisitive and forthcoming, respectively, about the details of the hiring package. Relocation packages can be negotiated. Sometimes a financial ceiling may be mandated that cannot be surpassed, but that does not mean it cannot be circumvented. Creative conversation with your new employer might allow for certain expenses to be folded in outside of the relocation package. For example, an airplane flight, hotel accommodations, and meals for both the administrator and spouse might be allowable outside of the relocation package while the administrator is in the process of looking for living quarters. This option is not always offered by new employers but still might be available if requested.

The key to all of these preemployment conversations is the ability to preface and caveat. If you adhere to the theory that you can say anything you want to anyone if you only find the right way to say it, then conversations such as the ones described above should be no problem. This method, though, sometimes takes more time than most of us are willing to commit. However, the benefits that may result from this level of communication may have positive implications on the applicant's perspective toward himself or herself and his or her job, including the financial rewards obtained from simply asking for what he or she wants. The employer subsequently reaps the rewards of a satisfied new employee.

The timing for these negotiations varies. The safest time to have these conversations is after an offer has been made, and then they should be broached diplomatically. All of these topics lend themselves to the improvement of the professional environment of the administrator, starting with the first day of employment, which can itself easily be used as a preface to the conversation.

Administrators who do not negotiate for the above necessities immediately diminish their ability to perform by putting themselves at a disadvantage, especially in comparison with other administrators who are technologically equipped and capitalizing on opportunities at career development. Contentment at having the job without the requisite trappings will only last until after cashing those first few checks, and then watching with chagrin as your colleagues communicate and perform with the latest technology. Conversely, institutions should recognize that the little things are extremely significant in the grand scheme of things, and losing valued administrators over the failure to have them equipped and prepared is worse than not acquiring them in the hiring process. After all, you cannot lose what you never had, right?

Administrators interviewing their prospective employers about their respective management styles is very important and, even more so, strategic. It lets them know how comfortable you are with yourself. It makes a statement about how analytical you are and how much thought you have given to the possibility of joining their staff. It also can make them think about their management style, something they may never have considered. In articulating what their styles are they may discover them right then. It might inspire them to live up to the style they claim to exhibit, since they should be sophisticated enough to anticipate that if you were bold enough to ask them this question, you are probably bold enough at least to attempt to hold them to that style. At the very least it is one of those questions that often make managers who micromanage as uneasy as the interviewee is answering the ones he or she must address. If nothing else occurs, the micromanager, the invisible manager, and the manager who manages by committee will all provide the prospective administrator with prototypes of the type of manager he or she does not want to be.

Travel opportunities that are available to an administrator can vary. There are opportunities to travel that come down from the administrator's management and opportunities that arise from the nature of a project, job, or special assignment. African-American administrators often are in a different space with this reality because of the necessity to network with other administrators of color in order to attract diverse students, if that is an element of their function.

Retaining administrators is one concern. Strategies to retain administrators of color or, more specifically African-American administrators, is another. Many of the strategies mentioned previously apply. Some that have been mentioned would lose their potency at a historically black college or university (HBCU). However, the following strategies definitely apply more to administrators of color at predominantly white academic institutions because they begin to address some of those other issues that are significant factors in successful retention strategies.

Are You Planning on Claiming the Bounty on My Head?

Mixed messages from management to administrator can drive wedges between the administrator and the institution that employs him or her. Special situations such as those involving administrators who have not completed their Ph.D.s must be articulated explicitly. Major new assignments or frequent impromptu travel assignments from deans who claim to be supportive of administrators' educational endeavors are a significant indicator that the dean's interest in the administrators' success does not appear to be as great as it was when they were hired. With teamwork an essential element to the success of any organization, there are times when the Ab.D. or Ph.D. candidate must place his or her education on the back burner for the good of the university that employs him or her or for the good of the project that is critical. However, the signs that indicate the administrator's education will be much more on the back burner than the front are not difficult to detect. When they become that visible, then the issue truly is academic. At that point, efforts to retain the administrator are simply lip service.

This is a reality that becomes more significant for underrepresented administrators. Regardless of what is on their plates professionally, they will also have to make room for certain responsibilities that their white counterparts will often not face. A black administrator often must mentor students as if he is part of the faculty, if he is one of only a few black professionals on the campus. White administrators are never approached on the basis of being the only game in town unless they are employed at HBCUs, are self-identified gays or lesbians, or are visibly disabled. A black administrator must be available to black faculty for strategizing about their very existence in academia, especially when they are among the most disparate numbers in terms of race, ethnicity, and often even research interests. A black administrator will be asked to participate in searches, on committees, task forces, cabinets, and in various meetings, and he or she will be expected to participate. If he or she declines he or she runs the risk of not being a team player, having an attitude, or perpetuating the stereotype of black hostility.

Performance evaluations are often not given to administrators, especially those of color, because of the type of projects they manage. The manager of an administrator of color who is administrating federally funded programs is likely not to govern that administrator as closely, perhaps subconsciously justifying his or her hands-off approach with the knowledge that it is noninstitutional funding (soft money) anyway. However, regular evaluations should be given. How else will an administrator receive so-called career mentoring? How else will an administrator develop necessary skills for receiving professional criticism from an employer and the confidence and skills necessary to discuss that criticism, challenge it when appropriate, and plan for areas of improvement by means of appropriate training? A lack of performance evaluations from an employer can be directly related to a retention factor. Although it can suggest that the administrator is excelling in his or her responsibilities and does not require an evaluation, it can also suggest to the administrator that there is no true interest in his or her development. This becomes especially poignant for administrators of color who (often) have assignments on the margin of the institution's strategic plans; that is when all the pertinent behavior of upper management seems to endorse the marginalization.

Changes in assignments and promises that are not kept often come with the territory. Administrators and administrators of color need to understand that flexibility on their part is necessary and critical to any assignment. However, employers need to recognize that the nature of the beast is supply and demand. Those administrators of color on their staff, which usually number two or less, do not have to stay long in an environment where they are slaving for subsistence in obscurity, with an emphasis on the slaving.

Simply Passing Through the Big House

How realistic is it to actually hold a position that claims that failures of retention of African-American administrators cannot be distanced from a history of slavery? Times have not changed as much as we would like to think they have. More to the point, on some level, the scars of slavery are why we cannot distance ourselves from issues of race. If on no other level than the subconscious, black folk revisit aspects of this daily, as do white folk. When a woman has been molested is it hard to imagine that she does not mentally revisit it daily and to varying extents. When a child suffers abuse throughout his or her childhood, is it not difficult to imagine subconscious recurrence of these travesties. For black people, a history of actual societal, political, and psychological molestation and abuse has occurred and to varying extents is still occurring. The impact of the legacy of slavery and the role the ancestral slave owners played during that tumultuous period resonates with whites as well. When crime is perpetrated on anyone by a black person, because race is so problematic in this country, concerns arise regarding how much more difficult this will make life for many other American blacks who may suffer some form of backlash specifically tied to that transgression. So, many of today's whites may emotionally recoil at thoughts of deeds done by people who were not anything like them in ideology or identity, but now due to the concept of race are in the same historical category. In America, it is race that made the Italian, the Irishman, the Greek, and the Swede into brothers, not humanity. Hence, the legacy of slavery continues long after an emancipation proclamation and is manifested in a concept called race.

> The major institutions and social relationships of U.S. society—law, political organizations, economic relationships, religion, cultural life, residential patterns, etc.—have been structured from the beginning by the racial order (Omi and Winant, 1991, p. 79).

Race in America transcends the issues of class that predominate most other societies around the world. What started off as a social construction predicated on economics has become the one ailment America cannot seem to distance itself from. Without question, the issue of race is seen by many as a significant contributor to academic institution's failure to retain its administrators of color and its black administrators specifically.

> The tentative acceptance the Negro intellectual finds in the predominantly white intellectual world allows him the illusion that integration is real—a functional reality for himself, and a possibility for all Negroes. Even if a Negro intellectual doesn't wholly believe this, he must give lip service to the aims of racial integration, if only to rationalize his own status in society (Cruse, 1967, p. 453).

While Cruse's (1967) assessment of the situation for so-called Negroes is arguably somewhat dated, it does give an indication of how far we have failed to progress in our relationships with white folk. Cruse's statement from his book, *The Crisis of the Negro Intellectual,* that acceptance of the so-called Negro is an "illusion" is not misguided. Perhaps in the midst of the nihilism that surrounds and envelops the contemporary plight of the African-American administrator, he or she is left with no recourse but to rationalize his or her status in society. Dyson (1994, p. 150) tends to agree with Cruse's intimation that acceptance of race is subtle, if not illusory.

> The seventies and eighties witnessed the expression of racial hostility in subtle ways, indicating that racial transformation was not as substantial as many had formerly believed. In short, the character of American race relations permits the appearance of a level of success that can be easily exaggerated and exploited.
>
> Contemporary race relations are mired in the bog of a torturous irony: the passion and vision of liberals—whose intent it was to vanquish the obvious and vile manifestations of racial animosity—have now been co-opted by conservative intellectuals who conceal the abated but still malicious expressions of racism.

These illusions and subtleties manifest themselves in many different ways: Job titles that imply much more significance in worth to the institution than is actually found in the job responsibilities; representation at events that have no other purpose than to demonstrate the so-called "commitment to diversity" that every American academic institution has, but only a small percentage actually implement. The concealment of racism by the conservative intellectuals that Dyson (1994) speaks of poses an ugly question. Was the racism of the past that was much more blatant and overt easier for America to deal with because at least you could look it in the eyes? Conversely, the "abated expressions" extend a level of comfort that disarms and harms under the pretense of charm.

Jackson (2000, p. 50) is somewhat conservative, if not lenient, in his pronouncement of what precisely was the cause of the concealment he discovered.

> Many institutions are not facing the facts when it comes to administrative diversity. Some institutions will not open their eyes to the harsh reality. . . . Numerous deans and departmental chairs have verbalized that race and gender problems do not come into play in their academic units. This shows the denial expressed by many administrators. . . . Many administrators denoted that they did not know what they could do, if anything, to enhance the experiences of people of color.

Throughout his entire article Jackson is cautious, and almost hesitant to play the race card. Sometimes a spade needs to be called a spade. After all, black people were called spades often enough without the speaker's tongue in cheek.

Cohen (1998, p. 60) asserts that racial differences do not exist, opting to address issues of variation as cultural differences. However, for the purposes of my assessment regarding the difficulties of retaining black administrators, Cohen's (1998, p. 74) assessment of culture and the inherent difficulties that pertain to it are still germane to my argument.

> Being raised in middle-class American culture (or any other culture) makes it hard to comprehend other people's thinking and behavior. Worse, socialization can make us blind to the very existence of alternatives, reducing our tolerance of other cultures and our ability to think critically about our own assumptions. We assume that people who don't speak or behave as we do are ignorant or stupid. We assume that they are trying to be just like us but are failing in the attempt.

In essence, the assumptions people make are sometimes influenced by the fact that they place themselves in their own center with an expectation that everyone else will want, or should want, to emulate them. This notion is sometimes referred to as "the American way." West (1993a, 1993b) endorses the notion of going beyond traditional centers in his two-volume effort, *Beyond Eurocentrism and Multiculturalism.* In his essay "Decentering Europe," West (1993b, p. 137) agrees that many black scholars ride the tide of "decolonizing sensibilities that utilize, through organization, mobilization, and politicization of the populace under the leadership of people like Dr. King, power and pressure to influence institutions." West (1993b, p. 137) further asserts that this yields "intensive intellectual polemics and inescapable polarization. These polemics and polarization focus principally on the silences and the blindnesses and the exclusions of the male WASP cultural homogeneity and its concomitant notions of the canon." The way West's assessment translates into reality for both the institutions that employ black administrators and the administrators themselves is most interesting. The educational process that most African Americans have received over the past 30 years has contributed to a centering of blackness and a decentering of whiteness. This shift in the center contributes quite a bit of confidence to the way black people see and project themselves. It reveals itself in their attitudes and interactions with others, which is not problematic when the dealings are black on black. However, when black people operate from assumptions of blackness at the center and their dealings are with whites who have benefited from an existence in society that still has *them* centered as well, the "polemics," which West (1993b) talks about, occur over a fight for the center. Of course, the polemics often are an undercurrent, an unseen tension, in the halls of academia because intellect and sophistication mandate a certain level of behavior. And much of this tension is subconscious, shading the way we see one another, filtering in and out anxieties and aspersions that are never truly in front of us.

Cohen (1998, p. 106) asserts that cultural actions often have hidden purposes.

> Culturally defined actions have an official title and purpose but also lots of "riders" tacked on, often hidden and having a different purpose. It is sometimes hard to separate the primary intention from the riders. And the riders may be the reason the bill is passed or defeated, or why the cultural behavior continues or is abandoned. This is one reason why it is difficult to change (or even fully understand) any culture, including our own. You have to change all the "cultural riders" as well as the avowed purpose of any behavior. . . . Those who would change cultural rules have to make sure that they are picking up on the hidden as well as the expressed reasons for doing things a certain way. But that may be difficult precisely because people don't want to express the other motives or aren't even consciously aware of the hidden reasons that are the real basis for a decision. . . . Public dialogue in the United States is complicated by the fact that every group has purposes it will not express and even some that it cannot consciously perceive or articulate.

The "cultural riders" Cohen (1998) refers to are obviously complex in that they often are not discernible, and even when they are discernible, they still carry with them ambiguity. This ambiguity adversely contributes to additional levels of polemics and polarization. Polarization can occur both physically and mentally. The physical polarization manifests itself in the marginalization that is sometimes visible and sometimes only reveals itself to the well-trained, albeit paranoid, eye, which lends additional credence to the adage "just because you are paranoid doesn't mean you aren't being chased." An example of this can often be seen in efforts by institutions to diversify their curriculum or student body. If elements of diversity are inclusion and pluralism, then why do diversity initiatives often reach out only to underrepresented students or students of color? Diversity cannot truly function in a manner that benefits all unless a wide range of people are included in the conversation. Yet a marginalization occurs around diversity initiatives because many whites believe they do not necessarily need the exposure to diverse individuals, training, and curriculum, so they let the nonwhites engage in those issues. But it becomes a stilted engagement for those individuals who are interested in diversity because an important perspective is missing—the white perspective.

An intriguing irony about race is how subtly it affects people's perception of themselves and others, the nuances attached to it, and how harshly the reality of racism manifests itself. According to West (1993a, p. 206):

> Never forget that when Italians and Irish and Lithuanians arrived in America, they didn't know they were white. The Italians thought they were Italians. They learned they were white by looking at us which meant that's, in part, how they became Americans, because there is no discourse of whiteness and blackness in the southern part of Italy. They were on the way to becoming Americans. This is how we have shaped the national identity of the country and usually articulated in a conservative way.

So, in essence, West (1993a) is asserting that the mere existence of a black presence in America contributed to the defining of a nationality for white Americans at the expense of blacks being [further] ostracized. This "color definition" manifests itself in terms of retention as well. White administrators are not white until they are forced to deal with the realities of a colorless office or an office that now has acquired a tint of color. The increase in commitments to diversity that propagated within the academy over the last decade of the 20th century suddenly made the administrative wings of academic institutions feel that if the sun were to unceasingly shine in its hallways everyone would have to take cover. Everyone, that is, but those with enough melanin to withstand its rays, which still meant that everyone would have to take cover.

There is a detachment that accompanies not being included in lunches, not being invited to small dinner parties, having conversations diminish when you enter a room. None of these factors may be racially motivated in the least, but because of the fact that racism is so woven into the fabric of American society, it is painfully difficult to arrest paranoia in terms of racial happenstance. Were my grades as a graduate student influenced because of my different research topics that white faculty could not relate to or did not want to relate to? Has the size of my merit increases diminished somehow because of an overriding perception by my bosses that I make enough money already? And even then, is that predicated on an assumption about how much worth I have as a black person or how much wealth I should have? Will my promotions end at a certain level in an organization because it would never provide me access to the top position anyway? Overcompensation also occurs sometimes, and the sincere efforts to include sometimes appear to be bouts of tokenism instead of attempts to connect as humans.

The bottom line, though, is this: Retention is two-sided in intent. At least in the beginning, most administrators want to be retained and most employers have the intention of retaining their employees; otherwise what was the point of the hire? So with these thoughts in front of them, why do these parties get all bogged down in these "other issues"?

Rowley (2000) makes an excellent point in his assertion that the culture of intellectual life necessitates a "shared understanding among its members" for any possibility of success. Rowley (2000, p. 89) takes it further when he claims that "one must be properly socialized" in graduate school. Although there is merit in Rowley's point, black administrators should experience the socialization prior to their actual appointments; graduate school is not where this socialization process should begin. The networking that is necessary to make potential employers comfortable with the candidate is extremely important. After all, you are black and very different from the familiar. You closely resemble the face of crime in America, the troubled athlete, the black proletariat, the angry black student from high school or college. You are the sibling, parent, uncle, or aunt of a teen who listens to gangsta rap, and therefore you must have picked up violent tendencies from somewhere, right? While I am taking this to an extreme, do not delude yourself into believing that this type of thought does not occur. However, more profound socialization occurs before graduate school that conditions individuals to prepare for the trials, tribulations, and travails that await them or, sadly, that prepare them to introduce to others these tribulations.

Differences Between Uptown and Downtown Addresses

The *other issue* that permeates academic institutions to the detriment of African-American administrators is not race, nor is it culture. The issue is difference, as remarked by Omi and Winant (1994, p. 84):

> In racial terms, these relationships are structured by "difference" in certain ways: for example, minority officials may establish caucuses or maintain informal networks with which to combat the isolation frequently encountered in bureaucratic settings.

Outlaw (1988, p. 317) further comments on difference:

> What comes out of such a review is the recognition that though race is continually with us as an organizing, explanatory concept, what the term refers to—that is, the supposed origin and basis of racial differences—has not remained constant. The use of race "has virtually always been in service to political agendas, beyond more

'disinterested' efforts simply to understand" the basis of perceptually obvious (and otherwise not obvious, but real nonetheless) differences among human groups.

What people are truly afraid of is difference. They do not want to grow from it or get to know it. They only want to see either themselves, or themselves in other people, and if they cannot do that, then they would rather see nothing. They are human, not black or white. We all can relate to strength in numbers and wanting to feel comfortable with people who look like us.

Isolation is a factor for many black administrators. Many institutions recognize this isolation and attempt to implement programs that can make a positive difference in the lives of these administrators. Resentment can arise as a result of what may appear to be preferential treatment due to race. Management personnel sometimes try to level out imbalances in support systems that are afforded white administrators but not available to nonwhite administrators. When they do they run the risk of invoking resentment toward those nonwhite administrators. Resentful white administrators often simply are not sophisticated enough to notice and understand the privilege and advantage they have from being in an office environment where everyone has a paint job similar to their own. With academic institutions often employing black administrators for a multitude of reasons, none less than their perspectives, they often discover that perspectives reveal more than the institution bargained for. Conversely, black administrators enter into organizations wanting to fit in and then often discover that fitting in may require leaving because they realize that fitting in often necessitates a loss of identity. But identity does not have to be lost. We need only to subtract the adjective from all of the following phrases: racial differences and cultural differences, gender differences and sexual-orientation differences, religious differences, ideological differences, financial differences, and physical differences. What we are left with are differences. The most significant factor in the failure of retention is the differences that humans cannot reconcile. Once we make allowances for the fact that differences are additions and not subtractions, we will add quite a bit to this world.

Summary

The retention of African-American students on both the undergraduate and graduate level is a serious issue because they are our future leaders, parents, faculty, and administrators. The retention of African-American faculty is a serious issue because of the training and support they provide all students, their ongoing dialectic with knowledge, and the ability they have to relate to and engage black students. The retention of African-American administrators is a serious issue because they establish a discourse behind the scenes that permeates an institution in ways that often go unseen, unheralded, and sometimes, perhaps, unwanted. They often are the only mentors that black students have, and the only colleagues black faculty have whom they feel they can trust. And often they are the true lone wolves in the forest. The *other issues* that faculty can broach in their scholarship, at conferences, or in workshops are often not open for discussion for administrators, who then have little recourse but internalization. The *other issues* that students protest through campus newspapers, civil disobedience, and political maneuvers administrators attempt to change through policy, procedure, and positioning. Often administrators originate from the ranks of students and faculty, but once you become an administrator, on some level, it is like you have lost your student or faculty I.D.

I hope this chapter can assist in developing an appreciation for the often maligned and unsung heroes of retention considerations. My wish is that this chapter, or others like it, could become part of orientation packages distributed to underrepresented administrators at conferences and workshops throughout the country. I also believe that the benefits that could be garnered by academic institutions that honestly engaged themselves, their new employees, and their seasoned employees with this type of literature might be found to be immeasurable. In these times of technological advancements and cutting-edge theories, why are we bold and daring in so many diverse areas of our lives except when it comes to communication across diverse lines? Spike Lee had Larry Fishbourne exclaim loudly in the last scene of School Daze, "Wake up." Isn't it time we did?

References

Cohen, M. N. (1998). *Culture of intolerance*. New Haven, CT: Yale University Press.

Cruse, H. (1967). *The crisis of the Negro intellectual*. New York: Quill Publishing.

Dyson, M. E. (1994). *Reflecting black*. Minneapolis, MN: University of Minnesota Press.

Fonrer P. S., Ed. (1991). W. E. B. DuBois speaks. In *W. E. B. DuBois, Is race separation practicable?*, pp. 179–186. New York: Pathfinder.

Jackson, J. (2000). Administrators of color at predominantly white institutions. In *Brothers of the academy*, L. Jones (Ed.), pp. 42–51. Sterling, VA: Stylus.

Jones, L. (2000). Introduction. In *Brothers of the academy*, L. Jones (Ed.), pp. xv–xxvi. Sterling, VA, Stylus.

Omi, M., & Winant, H. (1994). *Racial formation in the United States.* New York: Routledge.

Outlaw, L. (1988). Philosophy, ethnicity, and race. In *I am because we are,* F. L. Hord & J. S. Lee (Eds.), pp. 304–326. Amherst, MA: University of Massachusetts Press.

Rowley, L. L. (2000). African American men in higher education. In *Brothers of the academy,* Lee Jones (Ed.), pp. 82–99. Sterling, VA: Stylus.

West, C. (1993a). Prophetic reflections: Notes on race and power in America. Monroe, ME: Common Courage Press.

West, C. (1993b). *Prophetic thought in postmodern times.* Monroe, ME: Common Courage Press.

Woodson, C. G. (1993). *The mis-education of the Negro* (6th ed.). Trenton, NJ: Africa World Press.

REFLECTIONS

DEVELOPING AN AFRICAN CENTER IN THE ACADEMY

Kipchoge N. Kirkland

Introduction

This reflective essay explores a few themes that discuss the development of an African center within academe from my perspective as an African-American education doctoral student. This reflective essay is created with several aspects in mind. I include a poetic reflection that discusses my thoughts and experiences while developing as an African-American scholar in predominantly European-American institutions. I then describe three conceptual perspectives, (1) recognition,(2) affirmation, and (3) action, that I have crafted for the purposes of critically understanding the development of a self-affirming, family-supporting, culture-uplifting worldview about people of African descent and others. Each of these three areas includes introductory thought-provoking statements shared by African Americans who I believe have developed powerful models to follow with regard to maintaining an African center within Eurocentric environments. These elders include Maria Stewart, W. E. B. DuBois, and Toni Morrison; their words have assisted me in writing this piece. This essay is my reflection of academic research, philosophical perspectives, and a cultural critique of the academy. I am grateful for this opportunity to share it with you all.

Reflection

DUEL Consciousness . . . A Brother's Response to the Academy

Kipchoge Kirkland, 2000

Boy! here they come with their PhDs and EdDs
talkin' that academic-ease askin' me
can I support my "hypothetical ethnography . . . either qualitatively or
quantitatively?"
knowin' full well that they want me to say something like
"Well statistically speaking there is still some data that I am seeking
to engage in an intellectual discourse that shows no remorse
for *my* people's cultural force"
while they are steadily tryin' to make me feel less than
and shifting to get me out of hand
prodding me into a mental matrix
where I won't be able to understand their subliminal context,
their critical text, and meta-analysis—shocking me into a mental paralysis.
In this place my mind, body, and soul get locked up with multiple flows
of Eurocentric inflections with little African cultural directions
and many times I have had to call on spiritual connections from the
Ancestors for answers!
For example, here's a sample,
Take those sisters and brothers who came first,
blazing trails and paths with their intellectual bursts,
passing through these academic halls with "Uplift the race!" on the
    mind . . .
Yeah, these cats were right on time!
They were "Keepin' it real!"
You see on campus, they knew how to deal
and at home it was their knowledge that they would spill
into the next generation giving them a feel
of what we might expect
from a higher education that could help us put our oppressors in check.
Yes Lawd! these cats

knew where the knowledge was at . . .
dueling on campus like mental Zulus
fighting for equal places where someday people like me and you
could engage in critical contemplation
which would lead us into thoughtful conversation
with the hope of a cultural transformation!
Yes, they would challenge the views about the world news
that centered on sisters and brothers of darker hues who were paying dues
from the deep imperial and colonial world powers . . .
And now, in this generation's finest hour . . .
You see young Black cats runnin' from the fight . . . takin' flight into
    places of residence trying to
leave no evidence,
so their neighbors won't know about the "new Black folks in town . . ."
Leaving many of their ways of getting down to the sounds
of Blues, Gospel, Black Speech, Black Teach,
and Creative Cultural Music in hopes to lose it
and gain some ill-informed fame
from attending prestigious institutions of cultural disillusions. . .
Distanced from the past, left with a thousand questions to ask
once caught in the center of a critical multicultural class!
Oh, the right of the fight has disheartened many . . .
but, for me there is an energy!
an overabundant supply which I can't deny
because within my people does this African center lie!
It glows and grows like a raging Sun . . .
and because I am in process, the "Struggle" is never done.
I have had to call on Elders, Family, Friends, Students
and African Poetry to hold me . . . more specifically, in terms of my
    identity,
I have had to engage in critical history
and the teachings of culturally relevant pedagogy to set my soul free . . .
Mentors have taught me the powerful reality
of developing a cultural duality
and have guided my way.

So in my response to the academy, here's what I'd like to say . . .
To all my colleagues, friends, and "homies"
take a few moments to reflect and connect with me about the academy.
It is a place of great potential while equally weighted with adversity
but, because of our cultural diversity we can impact it both
individually and collectively.
Beware of the cultural insensitivity of the dueling propensity
that seeks to render our folks unequal
and so . . . you must study long and hard for the freedom of our People!

Recognition

When I cast my eyes on the long list of illustrious names that are
enrolled on the bright annals of fame among whites, I turn my eyes
within, and ask my thoughts, "Where are the names of our illustrious
ones?"

—Maria Stewart (1833)

In my response to the academy I thought about Maria Stewart's words
"Where are the names of our illustrious ones?" Her words spoken a century
and half ago still ring true today for many of us who attend institutions that
are predominantly European American. In places such as these it is a difficult journey toward developing an African center because the environment is
not culturally constructed to foster such growth. Many of us are left asking
the questions "where are our people at and what can we do to change the
way it is?"

Although the relatively recent gains from the civil rights movement in the
sixties and seventies have provided people of color more opportunities to participate in the greater American community, we still have long way to go. On
predominantly European-American campuses across the United States it is a
difficult task to see conspicuous edifices that honor the contributions of people of color. Seldom do we find images and buildings dedicated to scholars of
African descent or any other alumni of color who have passed through the
halls of the academy. Seldom are we invited to hear about the contributions of
scholars or advocates of color that have contributed to development of some
philosophical practice that adds to the social fabric of the local, regional, or
national thought.

I am reminded of Randall Robinson's candid reflection about the nation's
capitol that has often omitted and made insignificant the existence and con-

tributions that African descendants have made toward the development of the United States. His words are powerful as he shares his thoughts from his book entitled *The Debt: What America Owes to Blacks*. Robinson specifically makes significant points with regard to slavery and the nation's capitol's response as he writes (2000, p. 6):

> This was the house of Liberty, and it had been built by slaves. Their backs had ached under its massive stones. Their lungs had clogged with its mortar dust. Their bodies wilted under its heavy load-bearing timbers. They had been paid only in the coin of pain. Slavery lay across American history like a monstrous cleaving sword, but the Capitol of the United States steadfastly refused to divulge its complicity, or even slavery's very occurrence.

Robinson's insightful words are a powerful reminder that we must continue to question and uncover American public institutions that downplay the presence of African descendants within their community. His words also challenge me to consider the history and experiences of African Americans who have attended predominantly European-American universities and colleges as the "first" during the 1800s, 1900s, and of course now. I wonder to what extent these African-American trailblazers have been considered as valued members of the academic community and whether they receive their support from their alma maters when they seek to develop the communities from which they come?

Many of the historical policies and practices such as the 1954 case *Brown v. the Board of Education of Topeka,* which sought to ensure African Americans equal access to a quality education, have recently begun to set a precedence in the United States. This country's commitment to educational equity and freedom for all people has been a gradual process. This process has contributed to the slow recognition and collaboration with the African American scholarly presence in Eurocentric academic institutions. This reality serves as an important context for African Americans moving toward developing an African center.

Another recognizable reality for African Americans participating in Eurocentric environments is illustrated in the presence of relationships students form with faculty of color on these campuses. For many students of color it is difficult to find mentors, professors, and elders who can provide substantive sustenance for one's intellectual *and* cultural survival. Due to the limited number of faculty of color in university departments, many students of color form relationships with faculty who are often outside of one's major department, or at other campuses entirely, and more likely than not with elders from within the extended and local community who have very little affiliation with the university or college. I might add that the relationships formed within the local community can become extremely difficult when attending institutions that are also located in predominantly European-American communities that have small populations of people of color and African Americans. It is equally important to note that those faculty that become supportive of your development are probably supporting several other "hungry" students who are in search of their cultural and intellectual exploration. Those of us who begin to recognize this reality also realize the impact on each of us, students and faculty, that we find to be equally troubling.

Students who recognize these difficult dynamics learn to become resourceful and respectful of time with faculty mentors. Those of us who are seeking culturally relevant scholarly support make extra efforts to spend quality time with these elders before class, following class, during scheduled appointments, and if possible away from campus to speak candidly and openly about our joys and frustrations of our journeys through the academy. When we do encounter scholars and mentors such as Geneva Gay, who states her perspective with working with students up front, we work hard to make a difference. Gay (2000, p. 190) writes:

> I do not believe I should use the power of my position as professor to threaten or intimidate students, or to keep the knowledge I am supposed to know shrouded in mystery. My task should be to make knowledge accessible to students and to diffuse the threat and anxiety that are often part of the learning process . . . I constantly explain the motivations behind my own actions as a scholar, theorist, researcher, and pedagogue.

In recognizing Geneva's strong commitment to students it is possible to bombard her with student problems that many of us encounter through our learning experiences; however, we must be diligent in developing our relationships and responsibilities as students seeking to be scholars for ourselves.

We must also learn to be respectful of faculty members' time and look for ways to be of assistance to them in ways they might need because we too recognize that their time is valuable as they seek to produce scholarly work that supports their intellectual and cultural development, not to mention those faculty members who are new professors with families of their own. Under these circumstances few of us begin to establish a small cultural community of our own once we understand the directions of the academy as they exist.

The recognition of being in an environment such as this is perhaps one of the most chilling and often disheartening impacts of attending a predominantly European-American institution. The effects on one's psyche, cultural practices, and academic performance can be great. Constantly, as an African-American student you find yourself defending your very existence as a qualified and critical-thinking scholar who is worthy of attending such an institution. Steele's (1997) research on decreasing what he has termed "stereotype threat" provides a substantive explanation of the causes at predominantly European-American colleges and universities. Steele (1997, p. 613) writes:

> One must surely turn first to social structure: limits on educational access that have been imposed on these groups by socioeconomic disadvantage, segregating social practices, and restrictive cultural orientations, limits of both historical and ongoing effect. By diminishing one's educational prospects, these limitations (e.g., inadequate resources, few role models, preparational disadvantages) should make it more difficult to identify with academic domains.

Steele's work seeks to make a difference for students who are challenged by these social factors. He works diligently at reducing "stereotype threat," which I believe also adds to an important connection for those seeking to develop an African center.

Participating in and learning in a Eurocentric environment has provided me with a particular experience that has created specific social and cultural contexts, which have moved me to recognize that an African center is both necessary and important to my contributions to not only myself and my people, but to others who seek to understand diverse cultural perspectives. I have found myself becoming much more resourceful with my time spent studying, learning from mentors, and working with the diversity of folk, many of whom are European American, within my community. I have found myself much more attentive to the experiences and history of my people as well as those of others with the hope of creating better venues for future students to participate in this academic world. I have recognized that I have a right and responsibility to be in the academy, which leads to a positive affirmation of an African center.

Affirmation

> What the Negro needs, therefore, of the world and civilization, he must largely teach himself; what he learns of social organization and efficiency, he must learn from his own people.
>
> —W.E.B. DuBois (1910)

The struggles that students of color face in affirming themselves and their cultures exist in having the courage to do so. For many of us who are African American, the challenge is to be bold enough and committed enough to lift up the "souls of Black folk" in the presence of our academic and social experiences. Today, growing communities are becoming much more diverse, bringing with them powerful expressions of culture, existence, and presence. And although many mainstream universities and colleges do not reflect this growing diversity, those of us who are here must begin to provide our significant contributions of intellect, critique, and culture both as individuals and as a collective body. It is using every aspect of being "expressively black" within the context and constructs of the academic world (Gay, 1987).

We can affirm each other with critical spiritual, philosophical, and thoughtful practices that support and challenge our very existence and scholarship within the academy. We can no longer stand by and accept dogmatic cultural paradigms that are static and exclusive. Collins's (1991) theoretical scholarship speaks specifically to this point of affirmation and critical challenge as she lays out a powerful example of representing the voices of many African-American women who have added and continue to add to shifting cultural ways of knowing. Collins (1991, p. xiii) writes:

> Explicitly grounding my analysis in multiple voices highlights the diversity, richness, and power of Black women's ideas as part of a longstanding African-American women's intellectual community . . . I maintain that theory and intellectual creativity are not the province of a select few but instead emanate from a range of people.

Collins's position not only affirms the presence of African-American women and their intellectual contribution but also challenges others to be more expansive in their understanding about the development of knowledge within the African-American and mainstream community. Collins's affirmation of the diversity of black women's ideas and voices is a powerful guide to follow when looking to develop an African center within the academy. Her work draws on the "everyday actions and ideas of Black women" which serves as a reminder that every voice counts (Collins, 1991, p. xiii).

I hear the words of Maria Stewart and W. E. B. DuBois echoed in Patricia Hill Collins's work. Their scholarship indicates thoughtful analysis that has maintained a powerful support and center of African-American people. They have affirmed the essence and struggle of our people through taking the time to provide descriptive, reflective, and prescriptive research and study about the existence and future of our people. Their work was accomplished in contexts where they themselves had to struggle to lift up the spirit of African descendants and yet they maintained a positive worldview about our people.

Their affirmation of African Americans is creatively captured in Margaret Goss Burroughs's poem "To Soulfolk." In the poem she provides a critical challenge to African Americans as she seeks to maintain a strong sense of humanity for our people throughout history. Here is her affirmation of our folks (Burroughs, 1981, p. 118):

Soulfolk, think a minute
It is not what is on your head
But rather what is in it.
It is not what you wear
Around your neck
But rather the head
That is on your neck.
Nor is it the cloth
that covers you
But rather the heart
That beats for you
And all of humankind.
Humanity and head and heart
Are the most important part.
Soulfolk, think on that
A minute.

Margaret Burroughs's critical affirmation should serve as a powerful example of moving toward the development of an African center within the academy. Her words instruct us to think about our existence with our minds, hearts, and sense of humanity; words that are to be reflected on daily while learning, living, and contributing to the cultural, social, and academic community. Affirming who we are and where we have come from allows us to proceed to creatively construct actions that will maintain and transform our African center within the academy.

Action

What happens to the writerly imagination of a black author who is at some level always conscious of representing one's own race to, or in spite of, a race of readers that understands itself to be "universal" or race free?

—Toni Morrison (1992)

In my closing of this article I hope to have challenged you as a reader and thinker to consider some alternative perspectives to your own existence, whether you are in the academy or not. I support one of my intellectual mentor's and friend's position that:

> When we walk through this world with understanding of our history, we are able to maintain an intellectual arsenal that not only affirms us as individuals but also allows our collective community to better defend and produce a healthy, inclusive vision for generations to come. It is now, probably more so than ever, apparent that we need to include all people of our community in the effort to empower African American children (Rochon, 2000, p. 303).

It is my goal to continue to develop an African center within the academy because of its necessity for myself, my family, colleagues, and students of all cultures that I hope to teach and learn from.

The actions that we must take toward the development of an African center will move us in directions that will allow us to be thoughtful, supportive, and equally critical of our and others' existence as we seek to bring about social justice and cultural transformations as discussed by Banks (1996, p. 84):

> Students not only must be able to interrogate and reconstruct knowledge, they must be able to produce knowledge themselves if they are to be effective citizens in the multicultural world of the twenty-first century.

In my efforts to create new knowledge that assists me and perhaps you, I want to recognize, affirm, and take action toward our journey in developing an African center within the academy. We must stay diligent in our efforts to make a difference; our future depends on it. In closing, I leave you a poem for reflection.

Listen to Each Other

Kipchoge Kirkland, 2000

When we move into the action that we need to take
we will move into the world that we need to make . . .
Think about it.
Everytime you take the time to listen, and I mean listen
with your whole body and soul
you can feel the essence of the human spirit

compelling you to engage in the deepest connection
that can only be formed through listening in this way . . .
I mean, like you know, how brothas and sistas be listenin' to each other
rappin' bout bringing social justice amongst us.
Standin' up for the people, strugglin' to make our world more equal,
instead of living in another racialized supremacist sequel
of this contemporary "Dog eat dog" world of "I got mine, now you get
    yours!"
Yeah, it's when we listen and we move to action
that maintains the humanity in our claims
for a righteous and collective existence.
Yeah, it's when we move persistently through time
delving into critical thought, conscious action, and creative expression
that is capable of unlocking the deep intricate mysteries of this racialized
    history
that continues to affect our daily interactions and lives . . .
We have got to realize that it is these socially constructed lies
which we despise and not the colorful hues and eyes and precious souls
that we seek to hold and know.
You see, we can be in this thing called life . . . Together!
We can live, breathe, sing, and dream
with culturally connected rhythms and colors,
even if some of our sistas and brothas be on another beat!
(Y'all know what I'm talkin' bout and if you don't go to the latest hip
    hop gig
and watch the kids who be on 1 & 3 instead of 2 & 4 . . . need I say
    more?)
Become rhythm in motion.
Become the rhythm in the spirit,
feel the energy of the Ancestors speaking to you . . .
Don't let their struggle be in vain . . .
So dare to make this race issue simple and plain!
Take the time to affirm each other's names!
Take the time to make intellectual and culturally connected gains
that spread through generation after generation

wrenching the hate from this nation
with an undeniable strength!
Yes . . . go the length, the distance, the course
and become the powerful force that moves us
to remember our past and embrace our future
because our survival depends on it!
Make these nonsensical issues of
institutional, individual, collective and the selective
oppression become lessons of what not to do.
Let them move you to understand that when we are together,
we have love and a world of possibilities to live through.
Recognize that there is truth in uncovering untruths.
Recognize that you will be a source of knowledge
whether it is at home or at college,
you will one day become the bearer of lost souls
and it will be your wisdom they look to to become whole.
So grab hold of your sistas and brothas
and build bridges, and families, and communities,
and both national and international unity
that is committed to stand for justice
even if it means
"lovingly and caringly breaking unjust laws"
as brother Martin Luther King once said.
Most importantly, combine your heart and your head
and create a collective artistic expression in life
that explodes all boundaries.
Find . . . NO! Make the time to listen and feel
with your senses and become living breathing
and on fire activists who are willing to affirm
the experiences of all of us
because after all, it's the 21st Century.
And let not the problem of the color line
reside in the minds of the generations to come.
Use your talents to create places were you can
eliminate the racism that seeps into our thinking and living spaces

because we all need to be free of this incredible disease.

Create a new horizon where we can converge, blend and merge

and even deflect because there is power in our collective action.

And like I said at the beginning of this piece with the flow of my
  release . . .

When we move into the action we need to take

we will move into the world that we need to make,

a world of possibilities that reaches into the past,

embraces the present and propels the fire of your passion into the future.

The power is in your spirit

I hope you are able to listen and hear it!

We are counting on you! Peace.

References

Banks, J. A. (1996). The historical reconstruction of knowledge about race: Implications for transformative teaching. In *Multicultural education transformative knowledge and action: Historical and contemporary perspectives,* J.A. Banks (Ed.), pp. 64–87. New York: Teachers College Press.

Brown v. Board of Education of Topeka, 347 US 483 (1954).

Burroughs, M. G. (1981). To soulfolk. In *Black sister: Poetry by black American women, 1746–1980* E. Stetson (Ed.), p. 118. Bloomington, IN: Indiana University Press.

Collins, P. H. (1991). *Black feminist thought: Knowledge, consciousness, and the politics of empowerment.* New York: Routledge.

DuBois, W. E. B. (1973). Education and work. In *The education of Black people: Ten critiques, 1906–1960 by W. E. B. DuBois,* H. Aptheker (Ed.), pp. 61–82. New York: Monthly Review Press.

Gay, G. (1987). Ethnic identity development and black expressiveness. In *Expressively black: The cultural basis of ethnic identity,* G. Gay & W. L. Baber (Eds.), pp.35–74. New York: Praeger Publishers.

Gay, G. (2000). *Culturally responsive teaching: Theory, research, and practice.* New York: Teachers College Press.

Morrison, T. (1992). *Playing in the dark: Whiteness and the literary imagination.* New York: Vintage Books.

Robinson, R. (2000). *The debt: What America owes to blacks.* New York: Dutton.

Rochon, R. (2000). Black success or white emulation: Who shall sit at the table to create effective solutions that empower African American children? In *Brothers of the academy: Up and coming black scholars earning our way in higher education,* L. Jones (Ed.), pp. 296–303. Sterling, VA: Stylus Publishing.

Steele, C. (1997). A threat in the air: How stereotypes shave intellectual identity and performance. *American Psychologist* 52(6):613–629.

Stewart, M.W. (1992). On African rights and liberty. In *Daughters of Africa: An international anthology of words and writings by women of African descent, from the ancient Egyptians to the present,* M. Busby (Ed.), pp. 47–52. New York: Pantheon Books.

WHEN SERVICES ARE NEEDED BUT NOT RESPECTED

Eddie Moore, Jr.

Sometimes I wonder . . .

Sometimes I wonder, are you sure this is where you want to be . . .
Is this place for me?
Sometimes I wonder, are you sure you want to stay . . .
How do you make it through each and every day?
Sometimes I wonder, are those smiles for real . . .
What's the deal? Why do I feel . . . so angry, lonely and tired, so damn
    frustrated, hated, and
under-rated?
Sometimes I wonder, how could they choose this food, this music and
    this video, this time I'll just
say nope . . .
Is there any hope?
Sometimes I wonder, do these folks even notice me standing or sitting
    here . . .
Do they really care . . . BEWARE!
Sometimes I wonder, who can relate . . .
Man, I can't wait, to leave the Corn State?
Sometimes I wonder . . .

What will it take to get more African-American faculty, staff, and administrators to work at predominantly white institutions (PWIs)? More specifically, what will it take to get more African-American professionals to work at small PWIs, located in small, isolated communities? Sometimes I wonder about my colleagues living and working in places such as South Dakota, or Minnesota. What's the attraction? Why did they go there? How do they thrive and survive there? How do they feel about their jobs, colleagues, supervisors, or surroundings? What will be their most cherished memories and experiences? How does the institution encourage and support their professional development? How can more PWIs recruit and retain more African Americans like them (us)? Sometimes I wonder. . . .

In this chapter I do two things: (1) Provide some answer to the questions using stories and research from the literature on African-American faculty, staff, and administrators at PWIs; and (2) share some of my personal experiences and suggestions for aspiring African-American administrators and the PWIs recruiting and retaining them. I want to see more African-American faculty, staff, and administrators successfully recruited and retained at PWIs.

Most importantly, "When Services Are Needed but Not Respected" is written to inspire and encourage *all* higher education professionals to continue the dialogue and conversations about the difficulties and complexities affecting the success (and failure) of PWIs in recruiting and retaining African-American faculty, staff, and administrators.[1]

Why Do They Come?

I wrote the introduction poem after a long day on the job, and it comes from my heart. I am not lying when I say, everyday I wonder why I am back in Iowa. Why did I take this job? Well, the answer is a simple one. I love this job. I love this college and the folks working here as well as the folks that got me here.[2] Cornell College saved my life and I always knew I could never show my grati-

---

1. This chapter refers to the experiences of faculty, staff, and administrators as closely related. The terms are used interchangeably. There was not a lot of research on the experiences of African Americans in higher education. The research I used for this chapter does have some similarities in the experiences of faculty, staff, and administrators. Although there are some distinct differences, for this chapter African-American professionals at PWIs will be closely related.

2. I want to thank all the Cornell folks and the people of Mt. Vernon. Many of you are still there. I owe you my life. I am happy to say that Cornell College was critical in my development as a Christian, a father, a friend, and a professional. A special thanks to Jerry Voss and Dana P. Rodgers for all you did to get me there.

tude in alumnus donations, so I came back to share my love, energy, and knowledge. That is why I am here! Sometimes I wonder if my circumstance is unique?

African-American faculty, staff, and administrators at PWIs have a variety of reasons for coming. Some come for the campus atmosphere, professional opportunities, safe communities, and solid educational environments.

According to Bennefield (1999, p. 27):

> There was a real atmosphere of inclusion, even though there was no evidence of inclusion. . . . Bowdoin would be a good place for me to mature without the concern for the pace or pressures to perform at a larger place.

Sometimes I wonder if my colleagues in Iowa, South Dakota, and Minnesota ask themselves, why am I here, is this place for me, is this where I ought to be. It has to come up every now and then. In fact I would be willing to bet these questions are not just on the minds and hearts of my African-American colleagues at PWIs. During a recent staff retreat our boss recommended we take some time each month to recover and refuel so we do not get burned out. That was awesome—a boss that understands the strains and drains for all of us working as higher education professionals. The sick and tired[3] feeling is not uncommon for all higher education faculty, staff, and administrators (especially the folks in student services).

However, I would also be willing to bet the burdens and expectations for African-American faculty, staff and administrators are a little tougher to bear. Tucker (1980, p. 311) states:

> In talking about the Black administrator in white academia—the joy, agony, expectations and opportunities—too many people expect too many things from the black administrator in higher education, particularly in white-controlled institutions. At the same time, however, not many people know very much about the men and women who are expected to be these super niggers to so many people.

According to Estella Williams Chizik, compiled by Cheryl D. Fields in the Bennefield article (1999, p. 29):

> The environment is tough because there are a lot of people who haven't seen too many African Americans. That aspect is challenging

---

3. The feelings of frustration and exhaustion after long days and nights at the college, working with the students, attending programs, attending meetings, and so forth has a tendency to wear you down.

for [Black faculty here]. The university is safe haven. But even within that environment, there are some issues that are common no matter where you go.

In an article advising African-American faculty and administrators about the importance of mentoring students of color, Cobb (2000, p. 40) points out that "African American faculty and staff are often called upon to perform a kaleidoscope of services to students of color. The roles include advocate, friend, counselor and mentor." Brother Charles H. Tucker (1980, p. 313) adds: "Black administrators must possess skills to cope with not only the normal administrative duties assigned but also the special demands placed upon them, particularly in predominantly white universities, by virtue of their blackness." The extra burdens and complexity of demands forces me to wonder more and more. Why am I here? What should be done? Am I capable of doing this job? Am I alone? According to Tucker (1980), something has to be done. There needs to be valid theoretical and practical training, education, and professional development for African-American administrators. More PWIs have to understand the demands made on African Americans and the complexities of an African-American professional's job at PWIs. It is not easy!

I can hear my white friends and colleagues challenging me now. Here is my response to them:

> Yeah, yeah, yeah, the frustration and aggravation are similar, but the feeling is different. Yeah, yeah, yeah the exhaustion is not unique, but the feeling is different. Yeah, yeah, yeah the disrespect or lack of appreciation is there for all of us, but the feeling is different. It's difficult to explain and even more difficult to understand, but it's real. I say all of that to say this to you and the college, when recruiting African-American professionals, you need to better understand the extra burdens they (we) bear.

Where Are They?
Administrators

African-American faculty, staff, and administrators are located all over America. According to the facts, the number of black administrators at U.S. colleges and universities increased by 53 percent from 1981 to 1991. In 1981 there were 7,777 black administrators (7% of all administrators). In 1989 there were 11,796 (8.6% of all administrators). In 1991 there were 11,886 (8.75% of all administrators) (The editors, 1995). We cannot be satisfied with these numbers.

Faculty

I would expect that smaller colleges and universities have a much more difficult time attracting African-American faculty, but that is not the case. Here is a quote from one article (*The Journal of Blacks in Higher Education 27*, Spring, p. 6) that examines the facts and statistics about black faculty at the nation's institutions of higher education.

> Despite the superior resources of the nation's great research universities and the fact that they tend to be located in urban areas, the nation's prestigious liberal arts colleges have a higher percentage of black faculty. This is true despite the fact that many of the liberal arts colleges are located in remote rural areas far away from black population centers.

In a survey by the *Journal of Blacks in Higher Education* (JBHE) of the 43,374 full-time faculty at the nation's highest-ranked universities (information can be found in the JBHE Report Card, Number 26, Winter 1999/2000, p. 6), 1,488 were black faculty. On the other hand, the survey shows that of the 4,534 full-time faculty at 25 of the nation's leading liberal arts colleges (typically small, with in many cases one-tenth the number of faculty that exist at the large research universities; in addition, many of these leading liberal arts colleges are located in remote rural areas far from any black population centers) there are 215 blacks, making up 4.7 percent of the total full-time faculty. This is a far larger percentage of black faculties than at the nation's leading research universities.

Why Are They Staying?

Subject Matter

According to the *Journal of Blacks in Higher Education* (2000, p.8):

> The large research universities are likely to have extensive programs in the sciences and engineering, fields that traditionally had few black academics.

The most popular majors at liberal arts colleges include education, psychology, English literature, and political science. These are fields with a larger number of black scholars.

Black Studies Programs   Despite the small size, many of these colleges have Black Studies programs and these colleges typically seek out black folks to teach them. According to the JBHE report, Black Studies are programs that fit well into the interdisciplinary programs of liberal arts colleges and universities. Hamilton (2000, p. 24) writes that "there are fewer programs than there were in the 60s and 70s. . . . The ones that have lasted are feeling much better about themselves."

Some of the faculty and staff talked about the safe environments, but also expressed concerns with the cultural isolation. Not everyone felt the environment was for him or her. The people who seem to be best suited for the job are the focused and single or those folks with families.

According to Bennefield (1999, p. 28):

> It was very cold, and they wheeled out some African American students for me to meet. . . . There are two kinds of people this environment will work for. . . . Those that are married and have families, and traditional academics who just dig in and do the work. . . . I hear a lot of isolation that African American scholars endure when they are in the boonies. But if you are transcendent [the obstacles] can be transcended.

Commitment

One common theme for both faculty and administrators at PWIs, especially during the recruitment process, is institutional commitment. A good example of this comes from an article (News and Views, 2000) about the declining number of tenured and tenure-track black faculty at Yale. The university stands at the bottom of the ivy league in its percentage of black faculty. The article includes a small but good example of institutional commitment put to the test.

The scenario went like this. Just as with every other institution of higher learning, Yale issues a public statement reaffirming its commitment to achieving a racially diverse faculty. In this case, the statement was challenged in the student newspaper, *The Yale Daily News,* soon after the president issued it. The statement was called a "weak defense" of affirmative action. There were no concrete proposals or plans in the statement. It was talk, but no walk. The Yale president should listen to a piece of advice from my colleague and role model Lee Jones, "The bottom line is results and anything else is rhetoric." Here is something else to remember.

> To maximize recruitment of faculty of color, a university should consider two things: The first and most important thing is that there is an institutional commitment to diversity from the president to the

provost to the deans to the department heads as well as the faculty. Everyone must be on the same page and not just talking about recruitment but taking affirmative steps to make it happen (Bennefield, 1999, p. 26).

A Brother's Perspective

I took my job to make a difference. I was excited about the opportunity to positively affect the lives of students. I was determined to bring positive, influential, national speakers and events to campus.[4] I was determined to encourage, inspire, and motivate students and coworkers to be advocates for peace, equity, and justice. I wanted to leave a mark because all of my life, significant events and individuals have encouraged, inspired, and motivated me. My mother was at the top of that list. Today, I am determined to be a positive, productive, caring, and critically thinking citizen. That is why I got into higher education. Cornell College was an opportunity to share my God-given talents and energy.

"Respected but not respected," is about my (and I am sure many other's) journey. It is about the efforts and struggles of African-American faculty and administrators in small and isolated PWIs settings. The folks out there working hard, studying hard, and doing all the right things but still feeling unappreciated and disrespected. As they say in my community, "I feel you." Let us not forget, my friends, our numbers are few and far between.

Why do we even take these jobs? Why do we stay in these communities and towns? Can you remember how you got there, how it all started? I can! Do you remember the initial interview process and, yes, all those smiling faces? I can! What about your first conflict with a student, a colleague, or institutional leadership. Can you recall the atmosphere afterward, the tension, and the competency doubts or questions. I can! Can you still feel the isolation and separation (the knives)? I can!

This is my (our) story. Please read it carefully and see yourself shine through. Please listen carefully to know that I feel your pain. Lastly, please embrace my survival strategies and remember you can make it. Of course we must be a little stronger, a little more effective, and a little more productive than the status quo. We must because our students of color need us at full strength, all the time. Oh, yes, of most importance, never forget the influence we have on the lives of our white brothers and sisters sitting in our classrooms and visiting our offices.

---

4. Last year the Office of Intercultural Life hosted the First Annual Conference on White Privilege. The conference included local and national speakers and was well received and attended by local schools, business folks, and community leaders.

The Smiles

During the interview process, it seems that everyone is excited about your presence. I am sure you have heard someone say this before, "Hey you know the difference between the North and South? In the South, if white folks don't want you around, they let you know. In the North, white folks will smile like they want you around, but you never know." You know where I am going with this. I was hit hard in the face with this one. Even though you know, it still stings a little bit. Here is a word of advice to my white higher education colleagues. When you are interviewing African-American professionals, be real! Do not have fake folks interviewing, escorting, or hosting folks of color. We know, and if we are fooled, it will really affect the overall atmosphere when we find out.

The Conflict

There are always going to be professional disagreements and conflicts. In fact, I would argue that disagreement and conflict can lead to growth and increased productivity. However, if they are not done with trust and respect, there can be negative consequences. Suggestions to my colleagues take some time to understand, respect, and connect. The consequences of not doing will negatively affect the social and professional atmosphere of the staff or team.

Additional Advice

Retreat and grow! Take some time to build team in a retreat atmosphere. Make sure the activities, music, food, games, and so forth are all-inclusive and inviting for everyone involved. There should not have to be a person of color there to encourage an all-inclusive retreat. Lastly, surprises are always good.

The Knives

The atmosphere and work environment following conflicts can be difficult. However, we have to remain professionals. We should respect and support staff when we praise them *and* criticize them. Unfortunately this is not always the case. Too often the results of conflicts and disagreements are negative or what I call "knives." The knives are nonverbal, isolation, or separation tactics: the silence when you enter the room; the obvious lack of attendance, feedback, support, and encouragement for your programs, events, or speakers. The lack of interest, concern, and personal or professional growth is how the team or staff deterioration begins.

The supervisors or administrators have to nip it early! You should do everything in your power to stop the conflict or heal the wound. Act quickly and mediate the situation. Keep the big picture, the staff/team mission up front. Encourage team/staff sharing or heart to hearts. Challenge folks when necessary! The sooner the better!

The Frustration

The most difficult times are after the smiles, conflicts, and knives. The situation continues to eat away at you personally, professionally, and spiritually. It becomes very difficult to be in the presence of colleagues and team members. Your presence encourages silence from folks. Some people act as if they are not sure what to say. It becomes exhausting working there. When you are making contributions to the campus there is no feedback, encouragement, or support. In fact, sometimes folks are outright rude and disrespectful.

Such times are when you need to step back and reevaluate your current situation. Talk to your supervisor. Take some time out. This is a critical point and you need to be calm and competent when making decisions and interacting with folks. My advice to supervisors and administrators: Do not take sides. Listen and validate, but do not patronize or criticize without all the evidence!

Survival

The keys to survival are friends, colleagues, students, and family.

Friends:[5] These are the people who laugh with you, cry with you, and criticize you. It is important to have folks in your life that you know are going to be there for you no matter what. You know that they are going to give you advice with your best interests in mind.

Colleagues:[6] These are the people who have advised, guided, and supported you during your professional development in higher education.

---

5. My list of friends is too long to name them all. However, I want to mention a few names that have really played an important role in my professional development: Lanese A., John P., Jesse V., Ron M., Clair O., Crystal C., Dr. Rankin, Dr. Jones, Mrs. Rodgers, Coach Voss, Brother Porter, and many, many more.

6. This list can go on forever, too. The names that stand out are Joan C., John H., Dr. Jones, Dr. Rankin, Dr. McCarthy, Dr. McNabb, Jim C., Bob B., and many, many more.

Students:[7] These are the folks who constantly remind you why the job is important. These are the folks that make the changes. They grow stronger, smarter, and more aware throughout the years.

Family:[8] Lastly, these are the folks who keep you sane. They feed you during the breaks. They remind you where you came from and not to forget it. They are your foundations, your friends, colleagues and students all together. I know I could not have made it without them. Thanks!

References

Bennefield, R. M.. (1999). Tales from the BOONDOCKS. *Black Issues in Higher Education* 16(18):26–29.

Cobb, C. (2000). Career consultants. *Black Issues in Higher Education* 17(4):40.

The Editors. Vital signs (1995). *Journal of Blacks in Higher Education* (7, Spring):51–59.

Hamilton, K. (2000). A new spectrum. *Black Issues in Higher Education* 17(7):25–28.

News and Views. Black faculty at Yale: Progress stopped 25 years ago. *Journal of Blacks in Higher Education* (27, Spring):22–30.

News and Views. A JBHE report card on the progress of African American faculty at the nation's highest ranked liberal arts colleges. *Journal of Blacks in Higher Education* (27, Spring):6.

Tucker, C. H. (1980). The cycle, dilemma, and expectations of the black administrator. *Journal of Black Studies* 10(3):311–321.

---

7. This list includes students at Loras College, Cornell College, University of Iowa, and various other places where I have given talks and presentations.

8. This list can go on forever. I want to thank Felicia, Vent, Spud, Ebony, Mejonna, Nolen, Monica, Grandma Vic, Hip, Tara, Hip2, and the many other folks from the family (extended, too) who have prayed for my well-being. I especially want to thank my mother, Marie A. Moore, and my son, Eddie Moore III. They have provided me with all the passion and desire I have needed in the times of difficulty and complexities. I love you all!

PART THREE

RETAINING AFRICAN-AMERICAN FACULTY

9

HOW TO RETAIN AFRICAN-AMERICAN FACULTY DURING TIMES OF CHALLENGE FOR HIGHER EDUCATION

André J. Branch

In the last two decades of the 20th century, some colleges and universities vowed to double the size of African-American faculty (Magner, 1994); others provided funds for new faculty lines if African Americans were hired to fill them (University of Wisconsin System, 1992). The attention-grabbing statements, incentives, and goals have been largely unsuccessful because they have focused on changing the face of the campus by hiring a few African-American faculty members without changing the climate of the campus, which would help to retain those faculty members. As colleges and universities have struggled to retain African-American faculty, they have missed opportunities to engender social climates that affirm all members of the faculty community. The revolving doors of many of the nation's more visible colleges and universities have taught us that African-American faculty members will not be satisfied to improve the look of their campuses by being one of two in their departments or part of an invisible few on the entire campus. It is reasonable to believe that the African-American members of the faculty, like faculty members of other ethnic groups, want to be full, contributing, power-sharing members of their university and college campuses.

This chapter discusses the importance of retaining African-American faculty members, as well as some of the critical institutional challenges to this goal. Bold new strategies to retain African-American faculty that are mutually beneficial to the African-American faculty community and the larger college or university community are also proposed. The goals of these strategies are: (1) to replace nonsupportive and/or discriminating campus climates that drive away African Americans, with empowering climates and supportive policies and procedures; (2) to support research that will improve the quality of life in the African-American community and enhance the status of the university or college; and (3) to reward teaching and service in all disciplines that benefit the university and the larger society.

Why Talk About Retaining African American Faculty: The State of Affairs

Although they have come far short of their goals to retain African-American faculty members, many of the institutions that have taken on this challenge have at least tried to hold the academy to one of its high ideals–that of being an agent of change. Some, however, reject this notion, believing instead that "higher education devoutly adheres to the maintenance of the status quo" (Harvey, 1994, p. 21). Whatever their motivation, the universities that have tried to recruit and retain African-American faculty members seem to understand what some higher education researchers have called a "commonly recognized need for community diversity" (Cartledge, Gardner, & Tillman, 1995). There are good reasons to retain African-American faculty members. Among them is providing a support system for students of color and African-American students in particular (Colby & Foote, 1995). Write Colby and Foote (1995, p. 4), "Minority faculty act as role models, advisors, and advocates for minority students while they expose majority students to new ideas. They are essential to a multicultural campus."

Another important reason for recruiting and retaining African-American scholars as tenure-track faculty is to increase the power of this group to change the institution in positive ways. Writes Harvey (1994, p. 22):

Small numbers of African American faculty contribute to the minimalization of their clout as a group, which reduces the degree to which they can be successful advocates for making the institutions more amenable to recruiting and retaining additional African Americans.

One or two African-American faculty members may be able to influence changes in their departments, but they are unlikely to effect significant and lasting change in all departments across the university campus. Lasting campuswide change requires campuswide efforts. Finally, African-American faculty members benefit their institutions in ways that are qualitatively and substantively different from European ethnic groups and other ethnic groups. African-American faculty members bring to the university valuable resources, perspectives, critical reasoning skills, and problem-solving abilities, research capabilities, creative teaching skills, and ways of dealing with students that are unique to them as African-American faculty.

Unless new and daring action is taken by colleges and universities to retain African-American faculty, these talented teachers and researchers are not likely to remain at the nation's colleges and universities in order to have the aforementioned positive effects on their campuses. The Executive Summary of the African-American Education DataBook reported that in 1992, only 4.9 percent of the teaching faculty at U.S. colleges and universities were African American (Frederick D. Patterson Research Institute of the College Fund/UNCF, 1997). In that same year, "The African-American faculty underrepresentation was most notable at public research universities where only 6.7% of all African-American faculty were employed, compared with 12.5% of whites" (Frederick D. Patterson Research Institute of the College Fund/UNCF, 1997, p. 19).

More recently, the *Digest of Education Statistics 1999* reported that of the 550,822 full-time faculty members employed at colleges and universities in the United States, only 26,835 of these were African American (U.S. Department of Education). At the university where I am a tenure-track African-American faculty member, the Office of Institutional Research reported that there were 830 tenure/tenure-track faculty members in fall of 1999 (San Diego State University, 2000). Only 23 of these were African American. The low numbers of African-American faculty that are employed at the nation's colleges and universities are alarming, and the challenges that mitigate against retaining faculty members present more cause for concern.

Challenges to Retaining African-American Faculty Members

There are numerous challenges to retaining African-American faculty members, among them are: (1) discriminatory or "chilly" campus climates; (2) disparity in the promotion of African-American faculty as opposed to white faculty; (3) the declining number of African-American graduate students; and (4) the overburdening of a few African-American faculty with the work that is more reasonably done by many. A chapter devoted to retaining African-American faculty members could reasonably review such formidable challenges as anti-affirmative action, budgetary debates, the attraction of lucrative job offers in other professions, and more issues that the reader can list. However, neither the identification of challenges to retention discussed here, nor the recommendations for meeting these challenges are meant to be exhaustive. This chapter is meant to highlight what are the most persistent and devastating threats to retaining African-American faculty members, and to offer bold new action that presidents, deans, and department heads can take to correct these conditions.

Discriminatory Campus Climate

Documented incidences of discriminatory or "chilly" campus climates are not new (Carter & O'Brien, 1993). A campus climate can be described as chilly if one or more of the following conditions exist: lacking a formal mentoring structure for African Americans; the perception by African-American faculty members that they are not taken seriously; a belief that African Americans have been hired not because they are the best qualified, but because their hire helps meet an affirmative action quota; not valuing differences, but expecting African Americans to "fit in" with the "white ways" of the institution (Johnson, 1997; Hayes & Colin, 1994). The responses of these campuses to the presence of African Americans suggest that African Americans and the research they do are not valued on some university and college campuses.

Concerning the scarcity of African-American faculty members on campus, Harvey and Scott-Jones (1985) more than a decade ago asked whether "we can't find any" should be interpreted to mean "we don't want any." The discrimination and lack of support that African-American faculty report (Carter & O'Brien, 1993; Hayes & Colin III, 1994; Johnson, 1997) could cause reasonable persons to answer Harvey and Scott-Jones in the affirmative. The Higher Education Research Institute reported that half of the faculty of color surveyed in 1991 identified discrimination as a stressful part of their work. The University of Wisconsin System reported that 50 percent of women of color noted a nonsupportive work environment and isolation as reasons for leaving the University of Wisconsin System.

Resistance by some faculty to university plans to recruit and retain African-American faculty (Magner, 1994) is an additional reason that fairminded people today may conclude that some universities may not want African-American faculty. Some faculty opposed to Duke University's plan to double its African-American faculty denounced it as "race-based hiring"

(Magner, 1994, p. A23). Referring to Duke's plan, another faculty member said, "My feeling is it's simply wrong. I don't think universities should be in the race-hiring business" (Magner, 1994, p. A24). To malign those who desire universities to be improved qualitatively by a culturally diverse faculty is offensive at best, and could signal to African Americans that they are unwelcome.

Disparity in the Promotion of African-American Faculty

The lower rate at which African-American and other faculty of color receive tenure (Cartledge, Gardner III, & Tilman, 1995; University of Wisconsin System, 1990) also presents a challenge to retaining African-American faculty members. Faculty of color in the University of Wisconsin System are granted tenure less often than white persons, and this, say university officials, may be the cause of faculty of color leaving the system at a rate of 7 percent per year while white faculty leave at 5 percent per year (Carter & O'Brien, 1993).

Admittedly, universities in predominantly white regions of the country may have difficulty attracting and retaining African-American faculty. However, even universities in culturally diverse geographical regions have reported similar experiences as they try to recruit and retain African-American faculty (Carter & O'Brien, 1993). The University of Maryland at College Park was confident that it could become a leader in racial and cultural diversity by the year 2000. The university committee that drafted the plan to double its African-American faculty noted that the university "is home to one of the largest, if not the largest, highly educated African-American population in the United States" (Carter & O'Brien, 1993). If demographics and geography were the only variables, this goal might have been reached. However, in the years following the initiation of the "enhancement plan" African-American faculty at the University of Maryland at College Park left the institution at a rate higher than white faculty and were promoted at a slower rate than white faculty. Write Carter and O'Brien (1993, p. 12):

> Of the 14 African-American faculty who were hired for tenure-track positions between 1982 and 1985 only one remains at UMPC (a 93 percent net loss). In three entry classes—1982, 1983, and 1984—one of 11 (9 percent) African-Americans were promoted from assistant to tenured associate professor, compared with 51 percent of white faculty.

Those familiar with the tenure process know that tenure can be a fulfilling achievement after the initial years of focused and exhausting writing, publishing, teaching, and service to the university. Academicians also know that the denial of tenure is an effective tool for removing undesirable assistant and associate professors who do not "fit in." Moreover, African-American faculty members know all too well how difficult it is to work in racially hostile university climates where the denial of tenure to others in one's group looms as an ever present threat to one's own longevity.

Declining Number of Graduate Students

Paltry numbers of African-American graduate students also contribute to an institution's inability to retain African-American faculty members. African-American faculty members benefit from having African-American graduate assistants who are likely to share their commitment to research aimed at improving the quality of life in African-American communities. African-American graduate students need African-American role models in academia that can provide nurturing preparation for professional lives as academicians. If recent and current declines in African-American graduate student enrollments at the masters and doctoral levels persist, the mutual benevolence described above is not likely to take place. Between 1976 and 1996, there was a sharp decline in the number of doctoral degrees completed by African-American students (Carter & O'Brien, 1993; Cartledge, Gardner, & Tillman, 1995; Frederick D. Patterson Research Institute of the College Fund/UNCF, 1997). In the years 1976, 1986, and 1996, the number of Ph.D.s completed by African Americans was 1,253, 1,057, and 1,636, respectively (U.S. Department of Education, 1999).

The Few Doing the Work of Many

As there are significantly fewer numbers of African Americans, as compared to their white counterparts, serving as faculty members in the nation's universities and colleges, there are obviously insufficient numbers of African-American faculty members to teach the nation's students. Similarly, there are fewer African Americans to add to the corpus of scholarship in their respective disciplines and to assist in maintaining the operation of their universities and colleges. Although excessive workload is the lament of many faculty, African American or not, the responsibilities of faculty membership are made burdensome to African-American faculty by the insufficient numbers of African-American faculty available to share the workload. Carter and O'Brien (1993, p. 2) explain the situation of many African-American faculty members as it relates to retention:

> Faculty of color are few in number and in many instances assume or are asked to assume mentoring responsibilities for students of color, in addition to fulfilling other scholarship and tenure requirements.

This additional service requirement may lead to higher levels of "burnout" and, subsequently, attrition from academe.

Put simply, institutions that expect the few African-American faculty they hire to do the work of the many more who should be hired will, in so doing, drive away the few. The few doing the work of many, like the declining numbers of African-American graduate students, the disparity in the promotion of African-American faculty members, and the discriminatory campus climates all present serious challenges to retaining African-American faculty members. Meeting the challenge to correct these conditions will require thoughtful decisive action.

A Comprehensive Approach to Retaining African-American Faculty Members

Successful strategies for retaining African-American faculty will be comprehensive, synergistic, and systematic. Institutions will retain African Americans if they make a commitment to attracting to the institution a critical mass of African Americans who work to improve the quality of life for African-American people within the university's academic community and in the community at large. Retaining African Americans will mean that this commitment is followed up by institutional support that is manifested in at least three ways: mentoring, supporting African-American faculty research agendas, and protection of workload (teaching schedule and committee assignments during probationary years before tenure). A comprehensive plan for retaining African-American faculty also includes aggressively recruiting African-American graduate students.

Attracting a Critical Mass of African-American Faculty Members

Institutions that focus on simply increasing the number of African-American faculty, without accepting the concomitant change in culture and climate of the institution, will likely see their efforts frustrated. The decades of the sixties and the seventies saw a great infusion of African-American faculty at predominantly white campuses as a result of the ethnic studies and civil rights movements. However, three decades of hiring have made little difference in the institutional culture and climate on many of these campuses (Cartledge, Gardner, & Tillman, 1995; Colin, 1994). Some writers have documented failed recruitment programs and a decline in the retention of African-American faculty (Johnson, 1997; King, 1993).

Bold and fresh will be the institutional stance that expects and encourages cultural and climatic changes to the campus when African Americans are hired onto the faculty. Significant numbers of African Americans will be drawn to universities, colleges, and departments that encourage them to have personal and/or professional research agendas that are devoted in whole or in part to improving the quality of life for African Americans in the institution and in the society at large. Harvey (1994) has conceptualized four stages of impact for African-American faculty at the community college, and they are clearly relevant for four-year institutions as well. "Presence" is the first stage, characterized by at least one African American hired onto the faculty. Harvey believes U.S. society is so conscious of race that the mere presence of one African American can bring underlying racial tensions to the forefront.

The second stage of African-American faculty impact, "Thought," is characterized by African-American faculty "introducing into the institutional environment a set of thoughts/ideas/observations that would have otherwise not been available" (Harvey, 1994, p. 23). African-American faculty can assist the faculty and university community in engendering an environment that affirms the value of cultural difference in general and African-American culture in particular. Johnson (1997) studied African-American faculty perceptions of why efforts to recruit and retain African-American faculty have failed at some colleges in Minnesota. A recurring theme in his data is that the cultural difference represented by African Americans is not valued. He writes, "The perceptions, attitudes, and actions of European-American stakeholders within the institutions characterize African Americans as outsiders who must learn to 'act white' " (Johnson, 1997, p. 119). Such characterizations are not peculiar to Minnesota (Hooks, 1989; Kellogg, 1993; Pigford, 1988; The University of Wisconsin System, 1990). Colleges and universities across the United States need African Americans and their critical observations to help these institutions change to become welcoming and affirming of African-American faculty and the differences they bring.

Universities in culturally diverse settings can fall into the trap of believing they are affirming of and benefiting from culturally diverse thought. In fact, their small numbers may intimidate the insufficient numbers of African Americans on the campus, preventing them from speaking freely about their thoughts, ideas, and observations.

Thought, in the previous stage leads to action in the next stage. At the third stage of impact African-American faculty members take concerted action concerning academic matters that are of concern to them. Accordingly, this stage is called, "Action." Harvey (1994, p. 24) explains the importance of this stage:

> It is the faculty who hold the power to modify fundamental operational aspects of their colleges, including admissions standards, curriculum offerings, and faculty hiring processes. By taking action, African American faculty challenge the community college to operationalize its stated ideals, while also modifying the existing state of affairs to make the institutional climate more receptive to attracting additional African American faculty.

When the college or university responds positively to the actions of the African Americans present on campus, the fourth stage of African-American impact has been realized. African Americans have begun to exercise power in the institution (Harvey, 1994). Harvey writes that "the most significant manifestation of that power is the increased numbers of African Americans" (p. 24). With increasing numbers of African Americans, this process is continuously repeated and the institution becomes a more empowering and affirming place for African-American faculty.

At the core of any discussion of recruiting and retaining African-American faculty, and the resultant and necessary institutional change, are issues of empowerment and power sharing. Full discussions of such issues are beyond the scope of this chapter, but those who are serious about the retention of African-American faculty members should be prepared to address empowerment and power sharing. Existing power brokers on our nation's campuses have developed clear and stationary beliefs not only about who should hold power. These traditions were well established on most college and university campuses without consulting with African Americans. The very notion of "sharing power" may be a contradiction in terms to some in academe. For some, the suggestion of sharing power may actually be heard as "losing power," as well as losing one's ability to maintain one's own power (influence, stability, place) in the academic social structure.

To be able to share power with African-American colleagues, and thereby help to retain them on campus, those with power must first admit that they have substantial power, and second, press beyond the feelings of insecurity that are evoked at the mention of sharing power. Perhaps two metaphors will be sufficient to solidify this point. Institutions that take serious action to retain African-American faculty members, inviting change and the sharing of power among all of their faculty, may be said to have taken a rattlesnake by the tail. Less than this bold action, however, affirms the status quo and amounts to rearranging the deck chairs on the *Titanic*.

Providing Support to African-American Faculty Members

Providing several kinds of support for African-American faculty members will help universities and colleges avoid frustrated efforts at retaining African-American faculty members, as well as the accompanying destruction of morale and productive working relationships. An extensive review of research found that "the lack of a supportive academic environment is an important factor in not retaining faculty of color" (Carter & O'Brien, 1993, p. 2). All of the African-American faculty in Johnson's (1997) study cited a lack of support in their responses to questions regarding the recruitment and retention of African-American faculty. These respondents, as well as deans of instruction in this same study, concurred that "being new at an institution is difficult for anyone, regardless of color or background, yet . . . starting out is even more difficult for persons of color" (Johnson, 1997, p. 115). Support can be perceived in many ways, but in the twenty-first century it will mean providing effective orientation and mentoring, valuing the African-American faculty member's research agenda, and protecting the workload of African-American faculty, including the teaching schedule and committee assignments in the probationary years before tenure.

Orientation   Johnson (1997) believes that a lack of adequate orientation and mentoring of African-American faculty engenders the chilly climate that African Americans and other people of color experience on some predominantly white campuses. When I joined the faculty of a former institution as a recent Ph.D. recipient and at the assistant professor rank, I received no formal orientation to my department, school of education, the university, the university geographical community, or the new city to which I had relocated. Fortunately, an associate dean from a different school within the university made it his business to orient me to the university. The informal introductions he made around the campus were invaluable: the director of computer technology set up my university e-mail account and provided me with the various codes for accessing the internet; the librarian gave me a tour of the library; the bookstore manager acquainted me with textbook ordering procedures; the technician in the copy center explained how I could order reading packets for my students; with the director of housekeeping I made arrangements to have repairs made to my apartment, which the university owned. The same associate dean gave me a tour of the community immediately surrounding the university grounds, including the bank, the cleaners, the grocery stores, and the restaurants where I often ate lunch. Finally, it was he who gave me directions to the site two miles from campus where I would teach all of my classes and showed me the best route to take.

The experiences I have recounted in this extended personal example are not uncommon (Johnson, 1997). Seven new faculty members joined the School of Education with me that year and none of us had a formal introduction or orientation to the campus or our departments. Four of the seven were African American; one was African. All four of these new African or African-American faculty members accepted positions at other universities after the first year. Introductions to offices and individuals essential to a faculty member's success should not be left to chance. By stark contrast, my present university provided a two-day faculty orientation that provided important information about every office and resource that new faculty members would need to be successful at the university. The Faculty Affairs office even provided directions to the Department of Motor Vehicles so that I, as a new resident in the state, could register my car. If university administrators do not provide a thorough orientation to the campus for new faculty members, especially African Americans, who are likely to feel isolated on predominantly white campuses, the revolving door phenomenon (Carter & O'Brien, 1993) is likely to continue.

Mentoring   Effective mentoring is another important supportive ingredient in a comprehensive plan to retain African-American faculty. First and foremost, an effective mentor will provide African-American faculty members with assistance throughout the promotion and tenure process. Cartledge, Gardner, and Tillman (1995) have suggested that new faculty members choose a mentor after a first year of interacting with senior and junior faculty members in a variety of professional and social events. Such selection after a year of careful consideration is reasonable since personality or research interest differences between certain junior and senior faculty who are assigned to each other may prevent successful mentoring relationships.

Circumventing or reducing the feelings of isolation that often accompanies African-American faculty on some predominantly white campuses are two other benefits to providing for mentoring relationships between African-American faculty and successful senior faculty (Cartledge, Gardner, & Tillman, 1995; Johnson, 1997). One respondent in Johnson's (1997, p. 115) study confided:

> The only mentor that I had was another African-American faculty member here on campus. He was the only person that I felt was happy to see me here and wanted me to be successful. Not having a mentor

to help figure things makes it hard to get perspective. It was hard to know what it was that people expected.

With the myriad of daily activities and responsibilities associated with the role of faculty membership, having a confidant to help one think through and understand what others may take for granted is invaluable. Having a trusted colleague review and help one reflect on manuscripts that one anticipates submitting for publication is an example. Similarly, one who knows the various institutional policies can assist with such things as choosing the best teaching schedule for one's individual needs, avoiding the university or department's unique brand of politics for as long as possible, and learning whom to see for much needed instructional supplies.

Implementation of an effective mentoring program may take the form of assigned time, or a reduced load for senior faculty members (Johnson, 1997). Senior faculty members who become mentors should be careful that they do not patronize their African-American protégés. Johnson cautions, "the mentor must not be on a mission to 'save' the African-American faculty members, but to guide them" (Johnson, 1997, p. 121). Successful mentoring relationships will be those in which mentors affirm the intellectual competence of African-American colleagues and remind them how valuable are the gifts and abilities they bring to the institution.

Valuing the African American's Research Agenda   When deans and department heads support the research agenda of African-American faculty, a clear and unequivocal message is sent to the faculty member and others in the department that the work of the faculty member is valued. Conversely, when the research interests of African-American faculty are not encouraged and supported, the message is clear that the African American's research agenda is not valued in his or her instructional unit, department, or college. African Americans, like their European-American counterparts, choose research topics that interest them. Unlike their European-American counterparts, however, the choices that African-American scholars make for study are sometimes neither recognized as "real" research, nor rewarded by the subsequent granting of promotion and tenure (Colin, 1994). What is often rewarded, according to Colin, is the adoption of an ideology inclusive of a Eurocentric worldview, value system, and ways of behaving. He writes, "The tenure and promotion of African Ameripean (sic) faculty tend to be based on the level of their commitment to the perpetuation of this ideology in the classroom and their own research" (Colin, 1994, p. 55).

The African-American brothers who have contributed to this volume, as well as other scholars (Cross, 1991; Gay & Baber, 1987; Irvine, 1990; King,

1995; Ladson-Billings,1990; Lee, 1992; Stevenson, 1998), have research agendas that are devoted in whole or in part to issues affecting the education of African-American people and improving the quality of their lives. This work is important to African-American people and all those who serve their interests in various aspects of life in the United States. Dismissing the work of these researchers, calling their scholarship "not scholarly," "not rigorous," or "not real research," is likely to drive them away from institutions that so label their work. Retaining African-American faculty will require that these scholars receive appropriate encouragement by colleagues, and institutional rewards in frequency and kind not unlike that received by their colleagues of other ethnic groups. When African Americans are not rewarded for research in areas about which they are passionate, the university risks losing them to other institutions where their work will be appreciated.

Departmental and institutional funding for African Americans' research agenda, and the inclusion of these agenda in the institution's and department's long-term goals, will go a long way toward keeping African Americans committed to institutions that provide this kind of sustained support. Similarly, institutions are likely to keep these scholars in their employ if they follow up encouragement and funding with opportunities for African Americans to report their research on campus or at professional conferences.

Protecting the Workload   It is common at some universities for new faculty members, regardless of their race or ethnicity, to have a reduced workload for the first year or two after taking a new position. At some colleges and universities, a reduction in workload does not necessarily come with a new position, but is negotiated by the astute new faculty member. Bold would be the institution of a reduced workload for African-American faculty as one strategy in a comprehensive plan for retaining these scholars and benefiting from the unique contributions that they make to the university or college. Progressive institutions will set the pace for others if they would extend such a policy throughout the probationary period and limit mandatory committee service during this time period while the new African-American faculty member is working toward tenure. Some have suggested, "a longer probationary period before tenure decisions, particularly for African Americans who join university faculties without an established publishing and research record and where collaborative opportunities are limited" (Cartledge, Gardner, & Tillman, 1995, p. 175).

Certainly, initiating or continuing work on a research agenda is difficult for any person beginning a new faculty position. However, the decline in the number of Ph.D.s awarded to African Americans (Frederick D. Patterson Research Institute of the College Fund/UNCF, 1997), the lower number of

African Americans enrolled in graduate programs (Cartledge, Gardner, & Tillman, 1995), the disproportionate number of African Americans stalled at the assistant and associate professor ranks (Frierson, 1990), the increasing revolutions of the "revolving door" for African Americans (Carter & O'Brien, 1993), and the general failure of most colleges and universities to recruit and retain African Americans warrant courageous and unprecedented action. With such action there is likely to surface unprecedented resistance. Policy makers and those leaders who implement these policies should anticipate resistance in the form of sophisticated sabotage and plan appropriate responses.

In addition to the demands that accompany taking a new faculty position, African Americans, like other people of color, must deal with discrimination and its accompanying stress on a daily basis. Carter & O'Brien (1993, p. 9) write, "This problem is difficult to get at because subtle bias exists, e.g., perceptions that women and minorities are less qualified and are hired only to meet affirmative action goals and quotas." That African Americans have the additional pressure of dealing with subtle forms of discrimination on a daily basis is another excellent reason to support them by protecting their workloads. If deans and departments heads work with African Americans to protect their workload including committee assignments, these scholars will have sufficient time for teaching, research, and service. With this support, African-American faculty members will likely have more time and emotional and physical energy to realize their research agendas, including research projects intended to improve the quality of life in African-American communities. With administrative support, writing grants to bring research dollars to the university will also be feasible. This research will in turn raise the status of the department and college or university.

Aggressive Recruitment of African-American Graduate Students

Retention of African-American faculty will also be supported by the aggressive recruitment of African-American graduate students. There are at least two advantages to aggressively recruiting African-American graduate students. First, African-American faculty members are likely to find mutual appreciation in these graduate students for the faculty member's research agenda. Energizing will be experiencing the congeniality of a shared research interest. To the benefit of the university, African-American faculty members are likely to interpret the recruitment of African-American graduate students as affirmation of their own presence at the college or university, and desire to remain in this supportive environment.

Second, it is reasonable to believe that African-American faculty members will take pride in nurturing graduate students–potential African-American faculty–into the academic pipeline. True of graduate students in general, and of African-American graduate students as well, is the fact that they are often inspired by their professors to create their own research agenda or to extend or expand the research agenda of their faculty mentors. It is not uncommon for graduate students to make the decision to become researchers and/or university faculty while in graduate programs working with a supportive faculty mentor. Cartledge, Gardner, and Tillman (1995, p. 170) say moreover, "The best preparation for university positions, however, is full-time doctoral study where students work closely with faculty to develop teaching, research, and writing skills."

Conclusions

If universities and colleges are to slow the revolutions of the metaphorical "revolving door" and retain African-American faculty members, they must think differently about their need to retain these scholars, as well as the way these educators are supported. Among the good reasons for retaining African-American faculty are the qualitative and substantive difference in critical thinking, scholarship, and meeting students' needs that they bring to their departments, colleges, and the university community. Universities and colleges that expect and encourage African-American faculty members to work on research agendas that are mutually beneficial to the faculty members' academic discipline, the university, and African-American communities are likely to retain African-American scholars.

Although some universities have been ambitious in their recruitment goals for African Americans, they have not been as courageous about changing the campus climate, a leading predictor in the retention of African-American faculty members. Changing campus climate through implementation of bold new policies regarding orientation and mentoring, protecting workload, valuing African-American faculty members' scholarship, and recruiting of African-American graduate students will have a direct impact on the retention of African-American faculty members.

References

Banks J. A. (1995). Multicultural education: Historical development, dimensions, and practice. In *Handbook of research on multicultural education*, J. A. Banks & C. A. M. Banks (Eds.), pp. 3–24. New York: Macmillan.

Carter, D. J. & O'Brien, E. O. (1993). Employment and hiring patterns for faculty of color. *American Council on Education Research Briefs* 4(6):1–16.

Cartledge, G., Gardner III, R. & Tillman, L. (1995). African-Americans in higher education special education: Issues in recruitment and retention. *Teacher Education and Special Education* 18(3):166–178.

Colby, A., & Foote, E. (1985). Creating and maintaining a diverse faculty. (ERIC Document Reproduction Service, No. ED386261.)

Colin III, S. A. (1994). Adult and continuing education graduate programs: Prescription for the future. In *New Directions for Adult and Continuing Education: Confronting Racism and Sexism,* E. Hayes & S. A. Colin III (Eds.). 61:53–62.

Cross, W. E. (1991). *Shades of black.* Philadelphia: Temple University Press.

Frederick D. Patterson Research Institute of the College Fund/UNCF (1997). *The African American education databook: Higher and adult education,* Vol. I, Executive Summary. Fairfax, VA: Frederick D. Patterson Research Institute of the College Fund/UNCF.

Frierson, H. T. (1990). The situation of black educational researchers: Continuation of a crisis. *Educational Researcher* 19(2):12–17.

Gay, G. & Baber, W. I. (1987). *Expressively black: The cultural basis of ethnic identity.* New York: Praeger.

Harvey, W. B. (1994). African American faculty in community colleges: Why they aren't there. In *New Directions for Community Colleges: Creating and Maintaining a Diverse Faculty* 22(3):19–25.

Harvey, W. B., & Scott-Jones, D. (1985). We can't find any: The illusiveness of black faculty members in American higher education. *Issues in Education* 3(1):68–76.

Hayes, E. & Colin, S. A. (1994). *Confronting racism and sexism.* San Francisco: Jossey-Bass.

Hooks, B. (1989). On being black at Yale; Education as the practice of freedom. In *Talking back: Thinking feminist, thinking black,* B. Hooks (Ed.), pp. 62–72. Boston: South End Press.

Irvine, J. J. (1990). *Black students and school failure: Policies, practices, and prescriptions.* Westport, CT: Greenwood Publishing Group.

Johnson, W. J. (1997). Minority faculty: Are we welcome on campus? *Thought & Action* 12:(2):113–124.

Kellogg, P. (1993). *Review of literature on racism of white faculty toward faculty of color.* Ph.D. diss., University of Minnesota.

King, J. E. (1995). Culture-centered knowledge: Black studies, curriculum transformation, and social action. In *Handbook of research on Multicultural education,* J. A. Banks & C. A. M. Banks (Eds.), pp. 265–290. New York: Macmillan.

King, S. H. (1993). The limited presence of African American teachers. *Review of Educational Research* 63(2):115–149.

Ladson-Billings, G. (1990). Like lightning in a bottle: Attempting to capture the pedagogical excellence of successful teachers of black students. *International Journal of Qualitative Studies in Education* 3(4):335–344.

Lee, C. D. (1992). Profile of an independent black institution: African-centered education at work. *Journal of Negro Education* 61(2):160–177.

Magner, D. K. (1994). Duke tries again. *Chronicle of Higher Education* 40(24):A23–24.

Pigford, A. B. (1988). Being a black faculty member on a white campus: My reality. *Black Issues in Higher Education* 5(18):76.

San Diego State University (1999). *Integrated post secondary education data system fall 1999 faculty survey.* San Diego: Faculty Affairs, Office of Institutional Research, San Diego State University.

Stevenson, H. C. (1998). Raising safe villages: Cultural-ecological factors that influence the emotional adjustment of adolescents. *Journal of Black Psychology* 24(1):44–59.

University of Wisconsin System (1990). *Retaining and promoting women and minority faculty members: Problems and possibilities.* Madison, WI: Office of Equal Opportunity programs and Policy Studies, The University of Wisconsin System.

U. S. Department of Education. (1999). *Digest of Education Statistics 1999.* Washington, D.C.: Office of Educational Research and Improvement, U. S. Department of Education.

10

REDEFINING AND REFINING SCHOLARSHIP FOR THE ACADEMY

STANDING ON THE SHOULDERS OF OUR
ELDERS AND GIVING CREDENCE TO
AFRICAN-AMERICAN VOICE AND AGENCY

Derrick P. Alridge

Introduction

In 1897, one of the most respected elders of black research, W. E. B. DuBois, went to Atlanta University (AU) to begin work on his legendary project, *Atlanta University Studies*. At AU, DuBois focused on creating a comprehensive and solid body of scholarship on the social, economic, and political conditions of American Negroes (DuBois, 1968). For the most part, *Atlanta University Studies* was his response to the rhetoric of Social Darwinist ideology and the Eugenics Movement of the late 1800s and early 1900s, and his desire for black institutions and scholars to take a lead in researching and disseminating accurate information on the so-called Negro-Problem[1] (Alridge, 1999).

---

1. The "Negro-Problem" was a term used by blacks and whites during the late 1800s to mid-1900s to designate the abysmal social, economic, and political conditions of American Negroes. An ongoing concern during this period was how the country should address these conditions.

DuBois and other African-American scholars of his day such as Carter G. Woodson, Anna Julia Cooper, Alain Locke, St. Claire Drake, E. Franklin Frazier, and Horace Mann Bond provide an activist and scholarly mission and vision for African-American scholars today. These elders understood the importance of doing sound scientific and meticulous research without distancing themselves, as black scholars, away from the reality of the Negro problem or from their black voices[2] in their analyses. They also understood the significance of being in the forefront of research on black people as well as disseminating such research to universities, colleges, and the public and to governmental agencies. Without such a vision and mission there can be no doubt that African Americans would still be only slightly removed from the stereotypical views and mental enslavement that they were in during the early half of the last century.

Today, some scholars of African descent assert that black researchers and scholars have been too long involved in the exercise of racial vindicationism. Reed (1997) expresses this viewpoint in describing the research agendas of many past and contemporary African-American scholars: "A general effect of the 'Negro Problem' focus on the study of Afro-American thought, however, has been to lend privilege to an approach that conceptualizes black political discourse only in its tactical dimension, as a debate over alternative styles of response to white agendas" (p. 8).

Reed's point has some merit in the sense that black scholars have found themselves often refuting racist research that purports ideas of black inferiority. I contend, however, that we have an obligation to address research that promotes racist stereotypes of black people as well as to be proactive in creating our own body of solid research on black people grounded in the black experience. Scholars such as DuBois, Woodson, and Frazier acknowledged concerns about "vindicationist" research, but they recognized more the importance of being proactive in addressing unsubstantiated racist arguments in white supremacist research from a black experiential perspective (also see Franklin & Colier-Thomas, 1996). Such vision and mission, I believe, should be revitalized among black scholars in the academy, and we need to reestab-

---

2. I refer to "black voice" as the cultural and historical perspective of black people in the United States and throughout the Diaspora. I realize that there is not a singular black voice or perspective among African-descended people. However, I speak of black voice as the collective cultural and historical experience of black people under the oppressive systems of colonialism and Jim Crow. This collective experience, I believe, yields a cultural and historical perspective that is unique to people of African descent. Therefore, as an African-descended person I am more likely to understand and identify with the black masses about black history and culture than a person who does not share many elements of black history and culture. This sharing and black perspective from which I attempt to write and speak is what I call black voice.

lish and create new collaborative research agendas and methodological approaches that capture the nuances of black racial, cultural, and historical experiences throughout the world.

The problem of silencing black voice and neglecting or downplaying black agency in scholarship remains a problem at the begining of the 21st century. Much of this, I suspect, is the result of relatively small numbers of African-American researchers and scholars within the academy, the fear of some black scholars as being perceived as doing "black stuff," which in the mind of many blacks is perceived negatively, and the reluctance of many black scholars to wait until they get tenure to do what is often perceived as "radical scholarship" within the academy. Thiong'o (1986) situates the problem of black voice or language in the historical context of colonialism in which the result has been for African-descended scholars to distance themselves from their names, languages, and cultures. He states:

> For colonialism this [domination] involved two aspects of the same process: the destruction or the deliberate undervaluing of a people's culture, their art, dances, religions, history, geography, education, orature and literature, and the conscious elevation of the language of the colonizer. The domination of a people's language by the languages of the colonizing nations was crucial to the domination of the mental universe of the colonized (p. 16).

Morris (2000) extends Thiong'o's (1986) thesis on the black experience and argues that there is an overreliance on white scholars to describe the black experience. Historian C. A. Diop also raised this issue and articulated the urgency for change:

Similarly, West (1999) echoes Morris and Thiong'o and is careful to point out that blacks need to express themselves and assert their voices even among well-meaning white researchers who study the black experience. West states:

> There is something positive and negative here. Look at the work of Eugene Genovese, a very important scholar on the subject of slavery. He is not always right, but often illuminating. He has made a great contribution, yet at the same time, one recognizes that white scholars are bringing certain baggage with them when they look at black culture, no matter how subtle and sophisticated the formulations. Therefore, we must always be on guard to bring critique to bear on the baggage that they bring, even when that baggage provides certain insights (p. 545).

Heeding Diop, West, and DuBois' call for blacks to write, speak, and research their experience with black voice and agency, this essay is a call for today's African-descended scholars to redefine and refine the study of black people, take a lead in the methodological and theoretical construction of such research, and let their voices and experiences as black people be heard in their research. Such research and scholarship must be critical, emancipatory, and proactive in addressing the continuing pathology of racism and discrimination against blacks throughout the Diaspora.

In issuing this call, I discuss four experiences surrounding the silencing of black voice and agency that I have encountered during these early stages of my career. Second, I examine examples of education and research that neglect black agency in society and in the academy. Third, I discuss exemplary studies by black scholars and researchers that utilize traditions in black voice and that promote black voice and agency.

Tales of a Black Researcher: Attempts at Silencing Black Voice and Agency

In the very short period of three years that I have taught in the academy, preceded by four years as a doctoral student, I have often struggled with the issue of situating myself in my research and of allowing my "black" voice to be heard. In graduate school, fellow graduate students and I received the socialization of most students across the country aspiring to be in the academy. Objectivity was what we were told we should strive for in our research. Placing our voices and ourselves in our research was viewed as less academic, sloppy research, "soft" research, or not research at all. In most of my classes, we were socialized to remove emotion from our writing, which for me meant removing my "blackness" from my research and writing. Students who mastered this form of "objective" writing were often awarded with research assistantships, which often are considered more prestigious because they offer greater opportunities for publication before graduation.

As objective researchers and writers, we were viewed as good writers and capable of "writing up" research for professors. Such, I believe, is the case in many social science and humanities doctoral programs across the country. The silencing of my black voice began during this period as a graduate student. The challenge thus became how to allow this voice to be heard while also trying to successfully navigate the academy.

In another experience in which I was presenting a paper on the history of black education at a conference, a professor from the audience questioned me about the "slippery slope" that I was walking up by being "a part" of my research and by trying to make comparisons between events in the past with

African-American education in the present. I was not caught off guard by this professor's questions and I understood that he was cautioning me about breaking the rules of objective research. Later, I also understood that the professor was chastising me for taking advantage of my position as a black man by using my black voice to claim authority in studying my people. As a result, such experiences, I believe, make many black scholars distance themselves from black voice in their research in their attempts to get published and to be accepted in the academy. As I discuss later in this chapter, I, too, continue to struggle with this phenomenon as I navigate the academy.

This experience had a profound effect on me as I thought and wrote about the black experience in education. I asked myself whether I should eliminate my black voice from my research and ignore similarities between the past and the current situation in black education to gain respect. In a conversation with theorist and scholar Mwalimu Shujaa, he reminded me of my cultural connection and oneness with Africans throughout the Diaspora and throughout the ages, and introduced me to the Akan concept of *Sankofa* as a methodological approach for describing my research. *Sankofa,* means "return to the past to go forward."

As a methodological construct for writing history, I am thus prompted to look at time on a circular plane in which "past" thoughts and events directly influence and can advise us in the present. On several occasions, Shujaa also encouraged me to promote my blackness rather than struggle with how to satisfy Western concerns about objectivity and voice. These concepts and ideas have stuck with me and continue to influence how I think about issues of black voice and black-centered research.

Teaching is another area of scholarship and knowledge dissemination where black scholars face the issue of the silencing of black voice. I recall a few incidents dealing with my "black" perspective and voice while teaching my first social foundations of education course at a predominately white institution. The class was about 99 percent white. In teaching the course, I relied heavily on my own worldview as a black male growing up in the American south. I also used my black voice in discussions related to our topics of educational history and policy. While I received good evaluations from the class in terms of my knowledge of the subject material and organization of the class, I was somewhat surprised at the students' response to my being "too black" or black-focused in the dissemination of the information. I later realized that no matter how objective I thought I was, many of the students still received my lectures as too black and felt that I was blaming them as individuals for the educational inequities of blacks in the United States. One student commented:

I think this class attempts at making every Anglo-American person seem racist if we don't treat African Americans like we owe them some big apology. . . . I'm sorry that slavery happened but I didn't have anything to do with it, and frankly nether [sic] did you. So get the chip off your shoulder and try to accept everyone even white folks.

Another student's comments were even more telling:

While I feel that learning about subcultures in the classroom and minorities is important to becoming effective teachers, I just feel like I'm in a black history class instead of a foundations class. I had a friend that took a foundations class at another university and she said that it was one of the most fun classes that she'd ever been in. They discussed teacher salaries, job placement, etc. While the debates in this class are thought provoking, I find myself leaving very angry and feeling almost cornered. My point being, you teach a great class but I feel that we shouldn't dwell solely on African-American history and persecution.

Ladson-Billings (1996) cogently describes this phenomenon when she taught a similar introductory education course at a small predominantly white Catholic university. Her article discusses the "silence" of her white students toward her black communication and teaching style. Her argument that white students may have felt some dissonance due to her perceived position of power as the instructor provides some understanding of why I had these experiences. Her idea of white students using their silence as resistance helped me to understand also how their silence caused me to consider silencing my own black voice in my teaching.

Last, I have also struggled with the issue of black agency as well as voice in my research and teaching. About two years ago, a young black male doctoral student solicited me and a black colleague to be interviewed about a study dealing with black male resilience in the academy. In the process of setting up this interview, my colleague and I discovered that the research project was not the study of the black graduate student who solicited us, but rather the project of a young white male doctoral student. In the end, it was revealed that the young black student was encouraged by other faculty members and his classmate, with good intentions, to solicit and interview black faculty because of the "tensions" that might come out of a white male interviewing black male professors about how they survive in a system that often presents barriers for them. In the end, I filled out and returned an interview questionnaire for the student but was not contacted for a final interview.

For some time, I wondered about whatever happened with that study and thought about how a young white man would tell the story about such a sensitive and stressful experience of the black academician. While I realized that a black researcher doing the study did not ensure an accurate portrayal of the black experience, I believed that a young black scholar would better understand the unique problems of black male scholars and would do a better job of capturing the nuances of our experiences. I also had very mixed feelings about a white male becoming the "expert" on the resilience of black males, particularly when it was not initially revealed as his research. At the same time, I felt somewhat guilty for having such feelings but realized that my feelings were normal in terms of the interviewer and interviewee relationship.

These four incidences have tremendously influenced my thinking on the purpose, vision, and mission of voice and agency in black research as a young scholar at the beginning of this new century. Historically, the academy has given black scholars and researchers the rules and guidelines for doing "respectable" research on their people and themselves. Unfortunately, many of us have at times accepted these rules as a means to tenure and for respect in the academy. The questions that we must ask ourselves is whose purpose does it serve to emotionally disconnect ourselves from the African-American experience, to write in a voice that is inaccessible to the very black folk that we are researching, and to accept methodologies that downplay our connection to the black experience.

Like many scholars of color trying to navigate the academy, while maintaining a sense of uplift to the black community, I continue to struggle with what DuBois called "double-consciousness," and "two-ness," as it pertains to my work in the academy. Social policy scholar Larry Rowley (2000) calls this contemporary phenomenon a dialectical challenge in which black scholars find themselves trying to contribute to the black uplift movement and successfully navigate a system that is often hostile to black voice and agency.

Loss of Black Voice in Historical Cinema and the Academy

The history of black scholarship dates back to the African scholars of antiquity through the period of Timbuktu and the University of Sankore to the present (Saad, 1983; Sagini, 1996). In the United States, beginning in the postbellum period, we can see this phenomenon occurring with the elders of black research who struggled with the dilemma of voice and positionality in their research but who realized the importance of situating themselves in their work in a way that promoted black agency, voice, and activism. In terms of a systematic and clear vision for contemporary research on the black experience, elder scholars such as DuBois, Woodson, Cooper, Bethune, Fanon, Diop, Clark and many others have left a legacy and road map for guiding such research.

DuBois offered perhaps the most poignant examples of integrating himself in his research and writing on the black experience. However, this was not always the case, especially in some of DuBois' very early research such as in *Suppression of the African Slave Trade*. However, DuBois expressed his black perspective and voice freely in academic studies such as *Black Reconstruction*, and in his autobiographical literature such as *The Souls of Black Folk*, as well as his novels such as *Black Flame Trilogy, Quest for the Silver Fleece*, and *Dark Princess*. The dual voices of black and white that DuBois' characters struggled with in his novels reflected his own experiences as a scholar and academic in America. His novels and literature allowed him to express his black voice while also contributing to black research and the intellectual climate of his time (see Stewart, 1983).

It needs to be made clear, however, that while such black voice and perspectives have typically espoused the black perspective of the researcher it may also draw from perspectives that are nonblack in origin. For instance, DuBois even noted that he often drew from the philosophical perspective of James' pragmatism and from Albert Bushnell Hart's historical methods, but his research and voice usually remained grounded in the black experience. In *Philadelphia Negro* (1899) and *Atlanta University Studies*, DuBois conducted studies of the black condition in using both black epistemology and European-based worldviews. However, as Stewart and I have pointed out elsewhere, DuBois continued to anchor his thinking in the black condition in which he lived (Alridge, 1999; Stewart, 1984).

Black agency in the research of black people is very important as we redefine and refine our mission in the academy as black scholars in the academy and as public intellectuals in the popular culture. As an example, the agency of black people is ignored in the media. Chennault (1997) has done some important work on the media and the cinema in particular, and points out that these sites of popular culture are forms of education and scholarship about black people paraded before its audiences as truth. A very simple example of the loss of black agency can be easily seen in Hollywood's portrayals of African-American history. In the 1997 film *Amistad*, black voice and agency is lost once John Quincy Adams, played by Anthony Hopkins, enters the film to defend Cinque and the other enslaved Africans by using his wit and love of the American constitution to free the enslaved Africans.

Although it is true that Adams did in fact defend Cinque and the other Africans, one can feel the loss of black agency of the Africans in their own struggle for freedom. Such master narratives and silencing have often been played out in many educative and historical films. Many such historically inspired films deny black agency and turn to a white hero to bring freedom or to save the day for black people (see Gresson, 1995). I could not help but think of the narrative this film would have taken had it been directed by Spike Lee.

In academic research, one can examine studies of the African-American experience to see the lack of depth such research can have in understanding the black condition. In 1965, professor Daniel Patrick Moynihan conducted a study of the black family entitled *The Negro Family: The Case for National Action,* in which he concluded that a major problem of black youth was the demise of the black family and the absence of two-parent homes in lower-class black communities. The problem, however, with Moniyhan's report was that he chose to examine the black family using the white family structure as a point of reference.

Moynihan's view that single-parent female-headed families contributed to high levels of black pathology is ahistorical. He does not adequately explain the historical reasons why black women have often been single parents or heads of the household. From a historical perspective, one might attribute such high levels of black female-headed families to high unemployment among black males and the legacies of Jim Crow (Kershaw, 1990).

Today much of Moynihan's work is questioned by black scholars for not recognizing the reconstruction or adaptability of black families under nontraditional western modalities, the resilience of existent Africanisms in black society, or the agency of the black community to sustain black people at the impressive levels given the harsh social conditions of American apartheid. As one can observe, West's (1999) idea of baggage that the white researcher, discussed earlier, brings to the study of the black experience resonates loudly when examining Moynihan's report.

Situating Self, Agency, and Voice in Black Research: Exemplars of Four Studies

Contemporary research on the black social, historical, and educational experience by scholars such as Dyson (1999), Siddle Walker (1996), Hill-Collins (2000), and Woods (1998) carry on the vision and tradition of systematic black-centered research. The concerns of these and other scholars is that blacks need to continue to develop theories and methods that transcend the limits of the dominant traditional European-based worldview and that stresses a black cultural and historical perspective of the black experience (Anderson, 1990).

In her groundbreaking study and book *Black Feminist Thought*, Hill-Collins (2000) makes no apologies for using her experiences as a black woman in examining the black woman and man's situation in society. In fact, it is her methodology of situating herself as a black woman within her research that brings the story to life in a way that is compelling, action-oriented, and no doubt academically rigorous. She also reflects on the risks one may feel in expressing his or her voice in the academy:

> By identifying my position as a participant in and observer of Black women's communities, I run the risk of being discredited as being too subjective and hence less scholarly. But by being an advocate for my material, I validate epistemological tenets that I claim are fundamental for Black Feminist thought. . . . To me, the suppression of Black women's intellectual traditions has made this process of feeling one's way an unavoidable epistemological stance for Black women intellectuals (p. 19).

Siddle Walker (1996) also makes a bold statement on black-centered research and agency in her important historical ethnography of a black school and community, titled *Their Highest Potential: An African American School Community in the Segregated South*. Until Siddle Walker's book, few historical studies on education placed the black researcher within the context of the history of black people. Siddle Walker makes it clear that she was a student at the Caswell County Training School in Caswell County, North Carolina—the school that she studied in and to which her own history is intimately tied. Her work provides an excellent example of giving credence to black voice by allowing the voices of former teachers and students of the school to be heard through the many interviews of that community.

The oral interviews also give much credit to black agency through Siddle Walker's portrayals of blacks operating an excellent school in the midst of oppressive Jim Crow conditions. Her reliance on black voice and agency through her oral interviews in no way invalidates the study, but rather strengthens it because of her keen attention to accurately bringing the stories of black people to life rather than relying merely on secondary accounts of events at the school.

In Dyson's recent historical analysis and interpretation of the life of Martin Luther King, Jr., *I May Not Get There With You: The True Martin Luther King Jr.*, he provides a richly contextualized picture of King and the period in which he lived and cogently connects King to the contemporary African-American struggles of poverty and lack of strong leadership in the black community. Dyson, himself a Baptist minister, places the tradition of black religious voice and the cries of Black youth at the center stage in the essays in the book (Dyson, 2000).

Dyson's technique of using black voice reaches out to an audience that may not have been born when King was alive. It is Dyson's understanding of the nuances of black hip hop culture and the black religious tradition that allows him to reach multiple generations of black folk that so-called objective and scholarly works on King have not managed to do. Dyson's methodological approach does not silence his black voice or downplay his experiences as a black minister and former black youth, but rather utilizes his experiences and voice to connect with a wider audience.

Like Dyson and Siddle Walker's research on the black experience, social scientist and policy analyst Clyde Woods uses black voice and interpretation, as well as black southern lyrical forms to examine black poverty, oppression, and social policy in the Mississippi Delta during the 20th century. Titled *Development Arrested: Race, Power, and the Blues in the Mississippi Delta,* Woods' interdisciplinary study draws from the disciplines of anthropology, rural studies, musicology, history, political economy, and developmental studies to offer black rural and urban critique of black poverty and social policy. In fact, it is the use of the black southern vernacular that illuminates the poverty and conditions of black people that can only be alive through the use of such black voice. Wood's work also demonstrates the agency of blacks in his presentation of the blues as a form of resistance as well as a coping mechanism for blacks to deal with the harsh conditions of Jim Crow society. While the aforementioned studies are only a few of the emergent works infusing black interpretation and voice into their analysis, they are few and far between.

Conclusion: Toward a Vision for Researching, Writing, and Rewriting the Black Experience

A mission for black researchers and scholars in this new century should be to extend the work and voices of elders of black research by producing a solid body of research on the black experience. This research must be well theorized, analyzed, interpreted, and reflect, as much as possible, the multiplicity of black experiences in society. Such research will not occur in one study nor will it take place over only a few years. Instead, it must be a calculated and well-planned endeavor in which black researchers collaborate and bring together disparate research agendas, resources, and methodologies. In order to do this, it will be imperative that black researchers transcend their respective disciplines and engage in interdisciplinary research projects that examine the black experience.

Because society continues to purport notions of black racial inferiority and black hopelessness in society, some of the research that I am advocating for black scholars will inevitably be called "vindicationist" in nature. However, we must not allow such labels to deter us but we must instead stand on the shoulders of the elders and continue to do solid and meticulous research on the black experience. The nature of the type of black agency and perspective that I am advocating must move beyond being reactionary and must be proactive in addressing the social, economic, and political conditions of black people.

I also need to make it perfectly clear that I do not believe that only scholars of African descent can and should do research on the black experience. To do so would dismiss the many scholars who have made significant contributions to studies on the black experience. However, we must be in the forefront of researching our people and telling our own stories in this new century.

Nearly a century ago, DuBois suggested a model for black voice and agency in research in which he proposed that research on the black experience occur in 10-year cycles over a 100-year period. Each year and each cycle, DuBois hypothesized, would yield better research methods and theories, and the research vision would sharpen in subsequent years. The time is ripe again for such an ambitious black research agenda. In this tradition of DuBois and other black elders, this chapter is a call for reclamation of black voice and agency and a invitation for black scholars to refine and redefine ourselves in the academy in the 21st century.

References

Alridge, D. P. (1999). Conceptualizing a DuBoisian philosophy of education: Toward a model for African-American education. *Educational Theory* 49(3):359–379.

Anderson, T. (1990). Black studies: Overview and theoretical perspectives. In *Black Studies: Theories, method, and cultural perspectives,* T. Anderson (Ed.), pp. 2–10. Pullman, WA: Washington State University Press.

Bond, H. M. (1972). *Black American scholars: A study of their beginnings.* Detroit: Balamp.

Chennault, R. (1997). Race, Reagan, education, and cinema: Hollywood films about schools in the 1980s and 1990s. Ph.D. diss. The Pennsylvania State University.

DuBois, W. E. B. (1968). *The autobiography of W. E. B. DuBois: A soliloquy on viewing my life from the last decade of its first century.* New York: International Publishers.

DuBois, W. E. B. (1989). *The souls of black folk*. New York: Bantam Books. First published in 1903.

Dyson, M. E. (2000). *I may not get there with you: The true Martin Luther King, Jr.* New York: Free Press.

Franklin, V. P., & Collier-Thomas, B. (1996). Biography, race vindication, and African-American intellectuals: Introductory essay. *Journal of Negro History* 81(1–4):1–16.

Gresson, A. D. (1995). *The recovery of race in America*. Minneapolis: University of Minnesota Press.

Hill-Collins, P. (2000). *Black feminist thought: Knowledge, consciousness, and the politics of empowerment*. New York: Routledge.

Kershaw, T (1990). The emerging paradigm in Black studies. In *Black Studies: Theories, method, and cultural perspectives*, T. Anderson (Ed.), pp. 16–24. Pullman, WA: Washington State University Press.

Ladson-Billings, G. (1996). Silences as weapons: Challenges of a black professor teaching white students. *Theory into Practice* 35(2):79–85.

Morris, J. E. (2000). *Race, social science, and school desegregation research: African American scholars' challenges to traditional interpretations*. Paper presented at the American Education Research Association (AERA). AERA in 2000 under the title Embracing an Ethic of Scholar Activism.

Reed Jr., A. L. (1997). *W. E. B. DuBois and American political thought: Fabianism and the color line*. New York: Oxford University Press.

Rowley, L. L. (2000). African American men in higher education: Historical, cultural, and social reflections for mastering the dialectical challenges. In *Brothers of the academy: Up and coming black scholars earning their way in higher education*, L. Jones (Ed.), pp. 83–99. Sterling, VA: Stylus Publishing.

Saad, E. N. (1983). *Social history of Timbuktu: The role of Muslim scholars and notables, 1400–1900*. New York: Cambridge University Press.

Sagini, M. M. (1996). *The African and African American university: A historical and sociological analysis*. Lanham, MD: University Press of America.

Siddle Walker, V. (1996). *Their highest potential: An African American school community in the segregated South*. Chapel Hill: University of North Carolina Press.

Stewart, J. B. (1983). Psychic duality of Afro-Americans in the novels of W. E. B. DuBois. *Phylon* 44(2):93–108.

Thiong'o, N. W. (1986). *Decolonizing the African mind: The politics of language in African literature*. London: James Curry.

West, C. (1999). Conversation with bell hooks. In *The Cornel West Reader*, C. West (Ed.), pp. 541–548. New York: Basic Civitas Books.

Woods, C. (1998). *Development arrested: Race, power, and the blues in the Mississippi Delta*. New York: Verso.

11

IDENTITY, PURPOSE, AND IMPACT

Bebop Innovators as Intellectuals and Models for African-American Academic Success

Shuaib Meacham

Perhaps, the most prominent metaphor associated with African-American intellectual and academic practice is that of "crisis." While the prominence of this metaphor is due in part to the shadow cast by the landmark work of Cruse (1967), *Crisis of the Negro Intellectual,* the theme has also been taken up by a number of other writers and scholars. Emphasis on the retention of African-American faculty in the academy suggests that the crisis is one of number. Intellectuals such as Cruse (1967), West (1991) and Sivanandan (1976), however, who have documented and described this crisis, claim that the crisis is not of number but of identity, purpose, and impact. Cruse in the late 1960s and West in the early 1990s questioned the significance of African-American intellectual production. They claimed that African-American intellectual ideas had exerted little influence on the prevailing conceptions and political forces that shape our world. Cruse went so far as to claim that the "Negro (sic) intellectual does not rate as a serious thinker in the intellectual establishment" (Cruse, 1967, p. 459).

Interpreters of the Black World for the White

In contrast to the work of African-American literate intellectuals, the musical ideas of African-American musicians have had a profound impact on U.S. society (West, 1991). One of the most intellectually influential movements in African-American music was that jazz idiom known as Bebop. Bebop musically identified vital social changes of the postwar era—changes hidden beneath layers of antiquated social norms and assumptions. Artists, scholars, and writers throughout the world were profoundly impacted by its ideas. Albeit musically articulated, Bebop's broad intellectual influence begs the questions that form the content of this chapter: (1) What were the intellectual factors that contributed to the relevance and impact of Bebop? and (2) What might we learn from those factors as we look to construct a faculty climate that not only fosters African-American faculty retention, but new levels of academic relevance and excellence?

This chapter examines the issue of academic culture conducive to African-American faculty retention through the metaphor of crisis, and the possibilities for overcoming this crisis implicit within the intellectual ethos of Bebop. The first section of this chapter examines structural factors contributing to African-American intellectual and academic crisis. The second portion of this chapter provides a detailed account of Bebop, as an intellectual practice, and the manner in which Bebop musicians cultivated the developed ideas. The final section of this chapter examines the implications of the Bebop ethos for African-American academic practice, concluding with recommendations, not only for retention, but for the cultivation of broader traditions of academic excellence.

African-American Academics and Intellectuals: The Parameters of the Crisis

As alluded to earlier, Cruse (1967) conducted the seminal work on African-American intellectual practice, identifying limitations and shortcomings in the late 1960s that continue to be prominent today. Speaking then of primarily nonacademic intellectuals, Cruse described a fundamental disconnect between intellectuals and African-American communities and a general confusion regarding their social roles and identities. Specifically, Cruse pointed to the absence of a coherent framework within which to define their necessarily dual affiliations with the mainstream establishment and the African-American community. Without a guiding framework of relationships and goals around which to organize, Cruse described African-American intellectuals as "a root-less class of displaced persons" (1967, p. 454). Without a truly functional role, African-American intellectuals serve the community primarily as symbols of having "made it" and the mainstream establishment as spokespersons for African Americans.

Writing almost 25 years later, West (1991) discussed what he referred to as the "tragedy" of African-American intellectual practice. The tragic nature of this practice, according to West, stems from the failure of African-American intellectuals to construct a collective ethos through which to cultivate organically derived procedures and standards. These collectively developed standards, as West conceives, would enable African-American scholars to speak to complex issues in a manner that reflects the unique insights historically encountered in African-American experiences. Both Cruse and West portray African-American intellectuals as out of step with African-American communities and thereby lacking cultural grounding. This cultural disconnect has affected African-American scholars' ability to not only speak to African-American issues with accuracy and insight but precludes their drawing from the epistemological strengths within African-American communities to effectively speak to broader issues. This double failure, both local and global, comprises the parameters of the African-American intellectual crisis.

Structural Factors Underlying the Crisis

Far from being an unintended condition, Ahmad (1999) and Baker (1993) suggest that the cultural discontinuities described by Cruse and West reflect broad sociopolitical strategies on the part of those who resisted African-American social liberation. Both Ahmad and Baker emphasize the key role that African-American entrance into the academy played in these strategies. Prior to the unprecedented influx of people of color into major U.S. universities in the early 1970s, African-American intellectual energy had been devoted primarily to liberation from political, economic, and cultural oppression. In fact, it is difficult to identify prominent African-American thinkers and scholars of this era who were not to some extent directly involved in political action. Even a physicist such as Earl Shaw entered the academy following involvement with the Black Panthers (Russell, 1998). This ethos of political engagement reflected a dominant cultural tenor of African-American people and their collective yearning for an end to oppression (Harding, 1981).

Ahmad (1999) suggests that the unprecedented recruitment and admission of African-Americans students into the academy constituted a strategy by which to deflect energy away from resistance and toward immersion into mainstream consumer culture. Those students who entered the academy would eventually, in the course of their professional careers, come to constitute a privileged class of African Americans. This new racialized privileged class would be in need of goods and services that would appeal to their unique mix of cultural and economic consumer tastes. This opened up a host of corporate opportunities for educated African Americans to meet the needs of this burgeoning African-American privileged class. George (1998, p. 2) refers to this racially profiled corporate consumer niche as "special markets." Special markets, while enhancing the economic and social profile of those who worked in this portion of the corporate world, retained the residue of subordination and second-class status. George captures this combination of factors for African Americans who worked in the sector in the following passage:

> They walked through the doors cracked open by dog bitten marchers in the South and radical nationalists in the North . . . For the first wave of black corporate employees, special markets were often a trap that guaranteed its employees the perks of mainstream American life (suburban living, credit cards, ski weekends) yet kept them segregated from their businesses' major profit centers and from any real shot at company-wide power (George, 1998 p. 2).

These same structural factors have shaped the experiences of African-American faculty who have entered into the academy. The large increase in the numbers of African-American students created a consumer demand for more academic services tailored to the needs of this unique group. Consequently, a broad range of institutional and administrative accommodations, such as "minority" student services, "minority" student affairs, and "minority" cultural centers were established to meet the needs of the coming generations. African-American faculty within this framework functioned in a manner analogous to the corporate executives who serve "special markets." In this case, however, the "special market" consisted of a market for courses with subject matter reflective of the cultural inclinations of African-American students and a growing general interest in African-American issues.

Given this need to speak to categorically defined special-market interests, African-American faculty have been channeled into the role historically allocated to African-American intellectuals, that of "spokesman" (sic) (Baker, 1993; Ross, 1999). The role of spokesman involves interpreting the ways of black people for white people (Cruse, 1967) and helping the establishment to identify and address the question regarding "What does the [Negro] want?" (Ross, 1999, p. 25). In many institutions, the majority of not only African-American faculty, but all faculty of color in general are found in ethnic studies-related disciplines. In other disciplines, African-American faculty research frequently looks at cultural diversity issues within those disciplines. This places African-American faculty in the precarious, "special market" position of claiming expertise confined to issues that the academy has historically conceived of as academically second class (DuBois, 1990; Stanfield, 1994).

Already marginal within prevailing academic frameworks, African-American faculty, far more than African-American students, become susceptible to the conservative foundational ideologies on which the academy is based. Whereas the prevailing cultural ethos among African Americans has historically been one ot engagement, resistance, and liberation, the underlying ethos of the academy has been one of "ivory tower" distance and isolation. Thus, the natural tendency to accommodate institutional standards toward professional survival takes African-American scholars and intellectuals further from engagement with the community and deeper into the conservative norms and expectations of the academy. While African-American scholarly work may speak to or about issues of African-American community, it rarely speaks from the community, particularly in a manner that brings insight to larger sociopolitical issues. African-American academic teaching and scholarship becomes confined to the narrow parameters of the special academic market, existing exclusively in a world populated by privileged classes. Ahmad (1999, p. 11) describes this crisis of black academic practice in the following manner:

> Radicalism came to be identified almost exclusively with rhetoric, in the classical sense of the art of persuasion; lectures in the classroom and books issued from university presses . . . a whole intellectual faction arose which made for itself the largest radical, even revolutionary, claims but which had no affiliation, past or present, with political parties, trade unions . . . working class neighborhoods, or insurgent struggles of the poor outside the academic arena.

Instead of strategies for "retention" narrowly defined by which to retain African-American faculty within this prevailing ethos, the above-described conditions call for a reenvisioning of African-American academic possibility. Toward that end, the following section examines the intellectual ethos of Bebop intellectuals for potential insight into the challenges faced by African-American academics.

Bebop: Turning Rhythm into New Language

Prior to examining the intellectual ethos of Bebop, it is important to identify just what kind of intellectual impact Bebop exerted on the larger nonmusical society and among literacy-based intellectuals in particular. Bebop musical innovations existed primarily in the areas of rhythm and harmony. Prior to Bebop, popular music in general and jazz in particular, consisted of danceable rhythms and major key harmonies that served as a pleasant soundtrack to enjoyment and entertainment. Bebop, however, disrupted these musical expectations by accelerating the speed and length of musical improvisation and confounding listener expectations with dissonance. The intellectual power of this music stems from the fact that these rhythms and sounds musically articulated social currents, fears, and processes buried deep beneath the surface of the national consciousness. The intellectual quality of Bebop's diversion from musical norms emerged not only in the changes from the expected sounds of African-American music, but in the manner in which the musicians related to audiences and regarded their role as musicians:

> Bebop was as much a listener's music as anything heard at Carnegie Hall. Bebop differed from swing and rhythm and blues not just musically, but in the players' attitude toward their audience. Cool, self assured, and . . . often dignified in appearance . . . Gillespie, Parker, Monk and others took this music seriously and considered it art as high minded and elitist as . . . Western classical music (George, 1988, pp. 24, 42).

This change in sound and professional comportment comprised a symbolic political and intellectual statement, altering the manner in which to consider African-American music. It was not only to be regarded as a soundtrack for entertainment, but as a vehicle for ideas.

The accuracy and insight of Bebop's musical ideas may be evidenced in the extremes of response that Bebop generated among both musicians and intellectuals. As one might expect, such a sharp disruption of musical and performance norms elicited harsh, even violent reactions on the part of some listeners. Musicians and critics committed to "Swing" regularly equated Bebop with noise, even "violence." White as well as African-American critics and musicians castigated Bebop musicians for what they perceived to be the destruction of the jazz tradition (Blesh, 1946).

While Bebop elicited extreme negative reactions, it also generated profound levels of allegiance, particularly in the literary and artistic communities of the time. Allegiance within these communities extended to the point where one's identity within these communities depended on one's stance with respect to Bebop. In the following passage, novelist John Clellon Holmes describes the impact of Charlie Parker on his artistic identity as well as the identities of his peers:

One of the key conversion experiences of that time involved Bop, which was not merely expressive of the discords and complexities we were feeling, but specifically separated us from the times just passed. . . . When you "went over" to Bird, when you "heard" him all of a sudden, you were acknowledging that you had become a different sort of person. . . . If a person dug Bop, we know something about his sex life, his kick in literature and the arts . . . and the very process of awareness (Holmes, 1988, pp. 52–53).

It must be emphasized that Bebop's intellectual influence extended far beyond the temporal domain of postwar America. As Bebop's intellectual credibility increased over the years, academics began to employ Bebop figures and personalities within scholarly work as a means of symbolizing, not just Bebop itself, but artistic and intellectual excellence. In his historical account of postwar U.S. culture and the deeper social processes rarely acknowledged by postwar historians, Jezer (1982) spoke of the intellectual insight of Charlie Parker. Describing the V-Day victory celebration at the end of the war, Jezer wonders how Parker and the Bebop idiom captured the qualities of confusion and despair that were to follow the U.S. victory:

Who, on that most wonderful of summer nights would have imagined that this black bopster genius (and not the celebrants dancing, cheering, singing, kissing, hugging, and winding their way through tons of confetti . . . was attuned to the future? (Jezer, 1982, p. x).

Echoing the question posed by Jezer, the remainder of this section looks at the processes that enabled Bebop musicians and innovators to so accurately assess the times in which they were imbedded. In analyzing the intellectual ethos that informed Bebop practice, three factors shape this practice most significantly: the orientation of speaking from African-American communities; the primacy of motion and incorporation; and the quality of collective language cultivation. The following sections examine these qualities in further detail.

From the Community

One of the aforementioned characteristics of African-American intellectual practice was the fundamental disconnect from African-American community traditions, perspectives, and epistemologies. This disconnect has lead to an intellectual orientation where African-American academics primarily speak from the academy about African-American communities, rarely drawing from their community connections. Thus, the impact of academic research rarely travels to the communities on which it concentrates its focus. By contrast, Bebop musicians cultivated an ethos wherein they spoke from African-American communities about a broad range of phenomena. While the specifics of Bebop's musical commentary are explored in the following section, this section looks at the cultural basis from which this commentary emerged.

Bebop and the Tradition of the "Crossroads"   In saying that Bebop musicians spoke from the African-American community, I am speaking of a pattern wherein Bebop intellectual dispositions are best explained by processes found in African-American culture. Discussing the impact of rhythm on the life and work of writer James Baldwin, Kun (1999) emphasized the primacy of "the beat" in particular and rhythm in general on African-American cultural identity. Specifically, Kun describes the beat as integral to the African-American imperative of "confront[ing] and transform[ing] realities imposed from above" (Kun, 1999, p.313). An ethos of rhythm and sound versus one informed primarily by the written word fosters a more fluid conception of text. In contrast to singular and formalistic conceptions of text that dominated both musical and literary critical work, rhythmic and sonic texts are more variable, able to more easily adapt to contextual factors. Gates (1988 p. 25) refers to this quality of text as "texts in motion":

> The text, in other words, is not fixed in any determinate sense; in one sense it consists of the dynamic and indeterminate relationship. . . . Interpretation . . . even—or especially of the same text . . . is a continuous project . . . life is a form of reading texts in motion, constantly variable.

Writing on possible cultural precedents for African-American language practice within an African-American theory of text, Gates (1988) looked to the Yoruba West African Cosmological tradition. Gates found therein an ethos of textual interpretation informed by the contingencies of "the crossroads" (p. 25). Also a foundational metaphor in the blues tradition, the crossroads symbolizes the basic life experience of crisis in the disruption of one's singular path with intervening roads of uncertainty. Thompson (1984, p. 88) describes the crossroads according to the following spatial parameters:

> A fork in the road (or even a forked branch) . . . [a] crucially important symbol of passage and communication between worlds . . . the point of intersection between the ancestors and the living.

The crossroads, as Thompson suggests, is that space where worlds come together, that point where differences intersect, and often it is this intersection of different worlds, territories, and boundaries that precipitates crisis. Within the context of crisis, the Yoruba turn to a clergy called Babalaawo, who interpret the crisis and offer recommendations. These interpretations and recommendations, however, are not direct statements of advice, but codes rendered in an abstract language that require a change in the thinking of the petitioner in order to understand. In many ways, the change of thinking not only leads to the answer but is itself the answer. The following passage delineates the specifics of this connection between language and illumination:

> [The crossroads process] destroys normal communication to bring men (sic) to speak a new word and to disclose a deeper grammar to them and then to restore them to a conversation that speaks more accurately to Yoruba life. At this moment, the language of the Yoruba is enlarged to name and to humanize an otherwise unintelligible and therefore unassimilable event (Gates, 1988, p. 41).

As the passage suggests, insight within the Yoruba tradition involves the destruction of the conceptual blinders found in "normal" communication, so that "new" more insightful and intellectually accurate words might be spoken. These new words enable the Yoruba to incorporate that which was formally perceived to be fundamentally outside of their personal and cultural landscapes.

Bebop musicians, particularly primary innovators such as Charlie Parker, Dizzy Gillespie, and Thelonious Monk, carried out a similar interpretive or intellectual function. Within this framework, Bebop innovators constructed a "rhetoric," a language that spoke new words of intellectual insight in response to the crisis encountered in their engagement of postwar U.S. society. As Jezer (1982) emphasizes in his postwar account, the United States and in fact the whole world was in the midst of unprecedented social and geopolitical tumult. The Cold War, challenges to prevailing race relations, the global uprising of Third World states, and the beginnings of the corporate global economy all lay before Charlie Parker as he blew his disturbing, dissonant, high-speed interpretations through his horn while others celebrated. His insight and power resided, not in mimicry of literate intellectuals, but through immersion in the perfection of craft and a collective ethos that emphasized integration of multiple influences. In other words, African-American cultural practices such collective orientation of musicians served as an intellectual resource. The primary context for this immersion was found in the context of the Big Bands. The following section looks at the Big Bands and their role in augmenting the Bebop primacy of motion and the integration of multiple influences.

The Primacy of Motion and Integration

As stated earlier, Bebop's sound within the context of the 1940s was that of chaos and dissonance. Tonal harmony requires structural organization around a central key around which all elements of a composition are related. By contrast, dissonance or atonality involves the abandonment of any central point of reference. In atonal structures, "Wherever you are at at the moment is the key you're in. . . . Such space is not uniform, but rather multidimensional" (MacLuhan & MacLuhan, 1988, p. 52). The MacLuhans also refer to this atonal construct as "multilocationalism" (p. 238). Bebop innovators' primary experience of multilocationalism occurred within the context of their participation in Big Bands. Big Bands and the Big Band jazz of "Swing" were the prevailing jazz contexts and the prevailing jazz idioms prior to Bebop. While commercially and conceptually designed to conform to the tastes of the popular entertainment audiences, Big Bands supported a collective ethos within which musicians could cultivate ideas. The economic contingencies of Big Bands also required musicians to travel extensively throughout the country, performing in venues ranging from small rural towns to major urban centers. Thus, Bebop musicians were not only conceptually inclined through crossroads processes, but physically positioned to observe and musically comment on the emerging postwar society. This section examines the constant crossroads motion experienced by Bebop musicians and its impact on the development of the Bebop sound.

Texts in Motion   The metaphor of the crossroads implies that life itself is a process of constant motion, perpetual change, and transition. Due to the travel required of the Big Bands, Bebop musicians, with few exceptions, both literally and figuratively lived lives of constant crossroads motion. In Baker's (1987) discussion of the crossroads, he describes musicians as not only travelers engaged in passive, distant contemplation, but active interpreters, literally embodying the energy of the forces they encounter:

> At the junctures, the intersections of experience where roads cross and diverge, the blues singer and his performance serve as codifiers, absorbing and transforming discontinuous experience into formal expressive instances, refusing to be pinned down to any final dualistic significance (Baker, 1987, p. 8).

This quality of embodiment is critical because this form of data collection, if you will, distinguishes the Bebop intellectual engagement from that of the academic. A revealing example of this occurs in Clifford's (1988) discussion of

Stanislav Malinowski's anthropological diary collected during fieldwork in the Trobriand Islands. In contrast to the orderly, academic, and "objective" quality of Malinowski's inquiry methods, his diary reveals that in the context of his fieldwork, he experienced a "crisis of an identity" (Clifford, 1988, p. 98). This identity crisis was brought on by his excursion into a "cacaphonous [jungle] filled with too many voices" (p. 102). Specifically, Malinowski's grasp of the singular norms of Western structural thought weakened as, literally in the jungle, he confronted a multitude of forces pushing at him from without. Malinowski's response to this struggle with multiple sounds and voices was to maintain a tonal center and impose a "personal coherence . . . [a] unified personality" (Clifford, 1988, p. 103) over this threat of chaos and multidimensionality.

Bebop innovators, as Baker's conceptions suggest, welcomed the sounds, the voices of multiple places and experiences, and literally absorbed them into their musical expressions. Musicians spoke in terms of hearing new sounds and incorporating them into their performances. Not exclusive to Bebop, what Murray refers to as the entire "blues idiom" (1970) emphasizes the integration of sound and experience.

Speaking of the ideas that contributed to his composition "Chinoiserie," Duke Ellington captured the manner in which Jazz innovators integrated new sounds and experiences into their musical ideas:

> The title was inspired by a statement made by Marshall McLuhan [which said] that the whole world is going oriental and that no one will be able to retain his or her identity. . . . And of course we travel around the world a lot and in the last five or six years, we too, have noticed this thing to be true. So as a result, we have done a sort of thing.

In the context of the postwar United States, where multivocal, multidimensional changes were taking place, Bebop musicians were able to draw on their crossroads' ethos to accept the harsh atonal sounds of impending change. Instead of responding to crisis with an imposition of a singular norm, as was the dominant practice of the time, they accepted the sounds and rhythms and incorporated them into their intellectual conceptions and musical performances. During the constant travel required by the musical marketplace, musicians cultivated these sounds in furtive spaces and isolated domains away from the marketplace. In short, they cultivated a language within which to collectively reinforce and express the ideas and sounds they encountered. The following section describes this cultivation of language and the practices of community that reinforced its development.

Bebop and the Collective Cultivation of Language

As alluded to earlier, the constant motion of the Big Bands was complemented by a collective ethos in which musicians regularly exchanged ideas and musical insights. This collective functioned as a form of "alternative culture" from which African Americans have historically resisted externally imposed structures and norms (Sidran, 1971, p. 73). Reflecting West's (1991) recommendations for literacy-based intellectuals, these alternative cultural spaces comprised the sites wherein Bebop innovators collectively derived standards and procedures for the new idiom.

In truth, the Big Band experience comprised only one site of these collective activities; the other sites consisted of the homes of native New York musicians, and most famously, the after hours establishment known for late night jam sessions named Minton's Playhouse. The following paragraphs delineate this collective process, paying special attention to both the implicit and the explicit intellectual practices.

Furtive Spaces and Bebop Apprenticeship in the Big Bands

Berliner (1994), in his study of the pedagogy that contributed to the development of jazz improvisational expertise, emphasized the primacy of informal spaces for the learning of key improvisational. The Big Bands adhered to an ethos of interpersonal exchange through which important information was shared and disseminated. Thus, in contrast to many academic settings, jazz musicians passed down information through social mechanisms. In fact, several jazz figures specifically contrasted the Bebop ethos with academic modes of learning as a means of illustrating the importance of the interpersonal. Writer Ralph Ellison (1964, p. 208) makes this contrast when he said, "it is more meaningful to speak, not of courses of study, of grades and degrees, but of apprenticeships, ordeals, initiation ceremonies, of rebirth."

Although the Big Bands played a key role in Bebop's development, the commercial pressures on Big Band music and musicians to entertain meant that much of the talk of music innovation had to be confined to the private realm. Some bandleaders such as Cab Calloway were openly hostile to new music, particularly when musicians performed Bebop ideas in conjunction with the Big Band performance. Thus many of the musicians emphasized the secret, nearly hidden spaces in which their learning and development took place. On rooftops, in the back of theaters, at the foot of drum-kits represent just a few of the places in which musicians learned or shared seminal ideas. In the following passage, bassist Milt Hinton shares the manner in which he exchanged Bebop insights with Dizzy Gillespie in secret spaces (Deveaux, 1997, p. 183):

While Dizzy was with the band and when we were playing at the College Club . . . Dizzy and I would go up on the roof between shows, I'd get my bass and climb those spiral steps, going round and round, and we would blow right over Broadway. Dizzy would show me the new tunes and his substitution changes, so I could play with him the next time he took a solo.

Minton's and the 24-Hour Intellectual Process   Bebop's initial sounds occurred within the Big Bands wherein its key innovators shared time as they met their economic obligations through the playing of "swing." The real core of the music, however, developed in New York where many of the musicians either lived or gathered between tours with the Big Bands. In New York City, Bebop musicians engaged in a nearly 24-hour process of study, performance, and information exchange. It was through this process, supplemented by the stability and social discourse found at Minton's Playhouse, that Bebop developed into the idiomatic musical tongue that achieved such insight into the postwar times.

In contrast to the Big Band ethos of surreptitious communication and compromise with commercial constraints, the New York musical nightclub economy, also problematic in many respects, supported the small group ethos of Bebop and allowed Bebop musicians to cultivate and develop their ideas.

According to Miles Davis, Bebop musicians were able to spend time with one another all through the day and night when on the scene in New York. "Dizzy Gillespie's apartment at 2040 Seventh Avenue in Harlem was the gathering place for many musicians in the daytime" (Davis & Troupe, 1989, p. 64). The daytime exchange of ideas fed into the extensive series of jam sessions and performances that took place in the night. In the following passage, Miles Davis provides a description of this process of constant information exchange and practice:

> We'd play downtown on 52nd Street until about twelve or one in the morning. Then, after we finished playing there, we'd go uptown to Minton's, Small's Paradise, or the Heatwave and play until they closed around four, five, or even six in the morning. After we'd be up all night at jam sessions . . . [we] would sit up even longer talking about music and music theory about approaches to the trumpet. . . . Then after classes, me and Freddie would sit around and talk more music. I hardly slept (Davis & Troupe, 1989, p. 63).

The key in the circuit of Bebop experiences described by Davis was Minton's Playhouse, where a sense of community reinforced the language and intellectual insight. For many, Minton's was considered the "home" of Bebop. Minton's was the sight of the literal crossroads of comings and goings of the musicians as they passed through New York, that worldwide crossroads of transition and immigration. Whenever musicians came to Minton's, there were the jam sessions, and the constant presence of Thelonious Monk, submitting ideas for musical consideration, but there were also sounds and social validation of home. Musical innovation was supplemented by food and a sense of temporary stability through which to renew their spiritual resources and continue the struggle to express their idiom. Speaking of the importance of Minton's, Ralph Ellison emphasized this idea of home when he referred to Minton's as "the rediscovered community of the feasts, evocative of home" (Ellison, 1964, p. 200). While not immediately obvious, this sense of home was integrally related to the maintenance of intellectual growth. The ability to speak new words, to survive the consequences of disrupting norms, requires a stabilizing force to sustain one as the world turns away and conflicts ensue. West (1991, p. 77) captures this requirement when he describes the perennial question of the insurgent intellectual as:

> Where can I find a sense of home? That sense of home can only be found in our construction of communities of resistance. . . . Renewal comes through our participation in community. . . . In community we can feel that we are moving forward, that struggle can be maintained.

The Lessons of Bebop for African-American Academics and the Academy

Based on the Bebop intellectual processes described above, Bebop's intellectual impact can be attributed to the following characteristics: (1) a sense of belonging at the vanguard of the ideas and cultural influence and the intellectual power of the African-American legacy; (2) the ability to roam the world of ideas and incorporate multiple voices into their intellectual expressions; and (3) the ability to gather collectively to share insights and support one another at the level of human, interpersonal need. The final section of this chapter discusses each of the above-mentioned factors and the implications that each holds for the academic climate and the retention of African-American faculty.

The Cultural Vanguard and the African-American Legacy

In discussions of faculty retention, a great deal of emphasis has been placed on accommodations required of the academy to create a climate appropriately hospitable to culturally diverse faculty. It is my contention, however, that there is little that the academy can do if African-American faculty do not have a sense of purpose and mission regarding their role and intellectual legacy.

The intellectual example of Bebop musicians, while undeniably informed by the genius of its innovators, reflects the power of a sense of belonging at the cultural vanguard and a confidence in their musical heritage and legacy. While much has been made of the jazz musicians jealousy regarding the cultural status of the classical musician (George, 1988), there had been few attempts to imitate classical musicians as a way of raising the stature of jazz. Bebop innovators in particular realized that their own traditions were as relevant as any and deserved the respect and consideration due to a sophisticated art form. Toward that end, Bebop musicians drew from the best of whatever they encountered, including the classical music tradition, but integrated the classical into their musical priorities. This enabled Bebop musicians to grow and expand intellectually, while retaining their identity and style.

African-American academics have to begin to cultivate a sense of tradition and epistemology. Many African-American academic organizations celebrate African-American accomplishment without reinforcing the particular insights and which African-American ways of knowing have contributed. Particularly in a profession of knowledge, it is vitally important to know the multiple factors underlying knowledge representation so that one may make effective strategic decisions regarding how to situate oneself at the forefront of relevant thought. African Americans have to examine their structural position as a "special market" and make appropriate modifications to disrupt the expectations that coincide with that role. A knowledge of epistemological heritage enables scholars to draw from African-American epistemological dispositions to make broader statements that disrupt the "spokesperson" paradigm.

The Ability to Roam the World of Ideas

As West (1993) has noted, African-American academics face multiple pitfalls in cultivating an academic identity. Specifically, African Americans frequently foster an alternative "black" canonical structure that replicates the dynamics of the mainstream canon, albeit in black form and thus limits the ultimate possibilities for intellectual development. African-American intellectual practice has to purposefully move through the world of ideas, integrating the best into our own framework. Confident in their idiom, the Bebop musicians did not fear losing themselves in the "jungle" of ideas, but relished the multiple sounds and novel possibilities. Bebop musicians embodied the music and created new interpretations that enabled new ideas to emerge. African-American academics need to foster intellectual encounters and novel interpretations that can provide commentary regarding the most vital issues of our day. As discussed earlier, African-American epistemological constructs enable its users to engage a myriad of ideas and intellectual traditions and interpretations and provide fresh insight and commentary, revising and updating our own identities and perceptions as we integrate the multiple conceptions we encounter.

A Collective Ethos Integrating the Informal and the Social

The final area of implication bears the most on faculty climate and accommodations that can be made at the academic level. The academy, by ideology and tradition, can be an intensely individualistic and isolated profession. Advancement often depends on single-authored publications and service is far subordinate to the pursuit of making one's individual name. Whereas, constructed through scholarship and the media in terms of individual reputation and achievement, Bebop intellectual development involved a collective process of idea exchange and social discourse. These characteristics, while openly embraced by Bebop musicians, also function, albeit more informally, within the academy. Frequently, in contrast to the stated ideology of individual achievement, academic growth itself depends on a mentoring quality of relationships where vital information is exchanged interpersonally. To retain and enhance the excellence of African-American faculty, the academy must augment both the number and quality of occasions for collective consideration of issues. Beyond the mere lecture or symposium, these occasions should be linked to a larger sense of purpose regarding what might be accomplished in the way of social and intellectual impact. Especially when bringing in new faculty, a collective ethos may be encouraged through events that involve newer and experienced faculty taking in artistic events over time, to foster a sense of trust and communication through which more significant issues may be taken up.

Finally African-American faculty must be encouraged and supported for participation in African-American academic organizations. Participation in these organizations provides the motion and then collective experience that can also support intellectual development and provide needed support and sustenance as African-American faculty engage the rigors and pitfalls of the academic profession.

In conclusion, it must be kept in mind that given the qualities that contributed to the success of the Bebop idiom, African Americans face a difficult task in our effort to take on these qualities. As discussed earlier, multiple structural factors work specifically against the kinds of meaningful relationships that support and sustain culturally valid intellectual development. However, these barriers constitute both the cross and the crossroads faced by the "many thousands" before us. In the same manner as African-American musical, spiritual, and academic intellectuals of the past have overcome, we must accept the difficulty, move improvisationally, and celebrate the insights gained from seemingly small but ultimately significant day-by-day victories. We would not be in the academy without such miracles.

References

Ahmad, A. (1999). Out of the dust of idols. *Race & Class* 41(1 & 2):1–23.

Baker, H. A. (1987). *Blues, ideology and Afro-American literature*. Chicago: University of Chicago Press.

Baker, H. A. (1993). *Black studies rap and the academy*. Chicago: University of Chicago Press.

Berliner, P. F. (1994). *Thinking in jazz: The infinite art of improvisation*. Chicago: University of Chicago Press.

Blesh, R. (1946). *Shining trumpets: A history of jazz*. New York: Alfred A. Knopf.

Clifford, J. (1988) *The predicament of culture: Twentieth century ethnography, literature and art*. Cambridge: Harvard University Press.

Cruse, H. (1967). *The crisis of the Negro intellectual: From its origins to the present*. New York: William Morrow.

Davis, M., & Troupe, Q. (1989). *Miles Davis: The autobiography*. New York: Simon & Schuster.

Deveaux, S. (1997). *The birth of bebop: A social and musical history*. Berkeley: University of California Press.

DuBois, W. E. B. (1990). *The souls of black folks*. New York: Vintage Press.

Ellison, R. W. (1964). *Shadow and act*. New York: New American Library.

Gates, H. L. (1988). *The signifying monkey: A theory of African American literary criticism*. New York: Cambridge University Press.

George, N. (1988). *The death of rhythm and blues*. New York: Pantheon Books.

George, N. (1998). *Hip hop and America*. New York: Penguin Books.

Harding, V. R. (1981). *There is a river: The black struggle for freedom in America*. New York: Harcourt Brace.

Holmes, J. C. (1988) *The horn*. New York: Doubleday.

Jezer, M. (1982). *The dark ages: Life in the United States 1945–1960*. Boston: South End Press.

Kun, J. (1999). Life according to the beat: James Baldwin, Bessie Smith, and the perilous sounds of love. In *James Baldwin now*, D. A. McBride (Ed.), pp. 307–330. New York: New York University Press.

McLuhan, E., & McLuhan, M. (1988). *Laws of media: The new science*. Toronto: University of Toronto Press.

Murray, A.(1970). *The omni Americans: Some alternatives to the folklore of white supremacy.* New York: Vintage Books.

Ross, M. B. (1999). White fantasies of desire: Baldwin and the racial indentities of sexuality. In *James Baldwin now,* D. A. McBride (Ed.), pp. 13–55. New York: New York University Press.

Russell, D. (1998) *Black genius and the American experience.* New York: Carroll and Graff.

Savinandan, A. (1976). Race, class and the state: The black experience in Britain. *Race and Class* 17(4):101–131.

Sidran, B. (1971). *Black talk.* New York: Holt, Rinehart and Winston.

Stanfield, J. H. (1994). Ethnic modeling in qualitative research. In *The handbook of qualitative research,* N. K. Denzin & Y. N. Lincoln (Eds.), pp. 92–105. Thousand Oaks: Sage Press.

Thompson, R. F. (1984). *Flash of the spirit: African & Afro American art and philosophy.* New York: Random House.

West, C. (1991) Tragedy of the black intellectual. In *Breaking bread: Insurgent black intellectual life,* B. Hooks & C. West (Eds.), pp. 120–157. Boston: South End Press.

West, C. (1993). *Keeping faith: Philosophy and race in America.* New York: Routledge.

12

RETHINKING
W. E. B. DUBOIS'
"DOUBLE CONSCIOUSNESS"

IMPLICATIONS FOR RETENTION AND
SELF-PRESERVATION IN THE ACADEMY

Leon D. Caldwell and James B. Stewart

Lessons from DuBois: "Double Consciousness" and Psychic Liberation

The concept of double consciousness and psychic duality reflects the perception that the collective psyche of peoples of African descent has been bifurcated, that is, torn between competing cultural dictates as a result of its encounter with European culture. DuBois' perspectives on identity dynamics are captured in this paragraph:

> It is a peculiar sensation, this double-consciousness, this sense of always looking at one's self through the eyes of others, of measuring one's soul by the tape of a world that looks on in amused contempt and pity. One ever feels his two-ness—An American, a Negro; two souls, two thoughts; two unreconciled strivings; two warring ideals in one dark body, whose dogged strength alone keeps it from being torn asunder (DuBois, 1897, pp. 194-195).

DuBois' novels are the greatest source of information regarding his perspectives on identity dynamics and introduce the concepts of double consciousness and psychic liberation. DuBois' perspective on identity dynamics is illustrated in an unpublished novel, *A Fellow of Harvard* (ca. 1892). In this novel, a loosely veiled autobiographical treatise, the protagonist finds temporary salvation in a historically black institution following bad experiences at Harvard University. DuBois' belief at that time about the psychological turmoil emanating from psychological duality manifests itself in the protagonist's eventual loss of sanity. For a more in-depth discussion of DuBois' perspectives on identity dynamics see Stewart (1984). However, summary observations can be offered. For DuBois the problem of psychic duality emerges principally when individuals develop an uncritical commitment to western values, and in particular overestimate the efficacy of formal education (higher education) before acquiring knowledge about and an appreciation of black culture, that is, alienation from the common experiences of peoples of African descent distorts the process of identity development. Participation in predominantly white universities and even those that function as black in namesake only provides an incubator for identity distortion. DuBois offers a process of "psychic liberation," as a remedy; wholesome psychological functioning is to be achieved.

For African Americans participating in a system of formal higher education that promotes the uncritical adoption of western values and negates a black cultural knowledge base (Akbar, 1998; Caldwell, 2000), the issue of identity dynamics is particularly noteworthy. We must understand the university as an institution for what it is worth. How come African Americans continue to fight for access and equity on college campuses? How come there are more black males in the penal system than in the educational system? The masses of African Americans have only occupied the halls of "ivy towers" for a relatively short period considering that many universities have celebrated their centennial anniversaries. Black students, faculty, and administrators dupe only themselves by uncritically accepting university goals without reviewing university history. It is with a certain benign naivete or negligence that our community sends our students to enter higher education with no sense of a historical context to protect them against the inherent psychic duality presented by the university. Therefore, students, faculty, and administrators who enter the university with no historical references are prone to the types of psychological dilemmas DuBois foretold.

Without historical references providing elementary preparation for the cultural challenges of the institution, the unsuspecting will perish (culturally)—in anger or aloofness. They may graduate or be tenured or promoted but at the cost of their soul. However, there is an alternative. The process of "psychic liberation," as described by DuBois, is imperative for successful navigation and negotiation of systems dominated by an alien European cultural thrust. Students, faculty, and administrators of non-European descent or cultural worldview are at risk for developing a distorted identity.

Those who enter institutions of higher education searching for validation, seeking approval, or expecting appreciation from their institutions are setting themselves up for an internal conflict caused by double consciousness. Students, faculty, and administrators stymie the psychic liberation process by accepting a foreign cultural standard that will always render them deficient and remedial. Standards of excellence and success should be predicated if one resolves the internal conflicts of "double consciousness and achieves psychic liberation." In DuBois' view psychic liberation would not require the eradication of the European elements of the psyche, but rather its subordination to the African core personality.

Thus, the purpose of this chapter is to assert that the issue of identity dynamics is integral to any discourse about retention in higher education. We propose that psychic liberation in higher education is not merely the process of neutralizing dysfunctional Eurocentric interpretations, of social dynamics, educational pedagogy, and organizational structure, but rather the reclamation of an African personality core and worldview. In this chapter we provide the reader with implications of identity dynamics for retention, a developmental model of psychic liberation, and an adoption of psychic liberation as a method of self-preservation in the academy.

Identity Dynamics and Retention in the Academy

DuBois' perspectives on identity dynamics offer a useful theoretical frame in which to propose innovative retention strategies. The concepts of double consciousness and psychic liberation have profound implications on the retention and self-preservation of African Americans, in specific, non-European-American students, faculty, and staff, in general. The ability to negotiate and navigate institutions of higher education is a skill often spoken of but rarely explained. The requisite psychological energies, exerted both explicitly and implicitly, required for navigational skill development can manifest themselves in ways that detract from matriculation and even cause physical health problems. Students who enter the university searching for validation from white culture or, even more detrimental, unclear as to where their validation comes from, are prone to become attrition statistics. Social alienation, a lack of academic direction, and purposeless pursuit of a credential makes student, faculty, and administrators susceptible to double consciousness. For example, the students who commonly report "being lost," "finding themselves," or questioning the need for the "white man's degree" but are sporadically enrolled and on the edge of academic probation each semester are the students who are trapped by the psychological dilemma caused by double consciousness.

For faculty, the implications of double consciousness are less obvious. Faculty suffering from psychological distortions can hide their distress in the name of scholarly production. Double conscious faculty members find themselves disengaged from the university community under the guise of chasing the tenure and promotion clock. They only participate in activities that pad the "T & P" document. Double conscious faculty members are so disengaged that they become socially awkward and sometimes hostile and angry toward students or colleagues for tacit reasons. These faculty members are prone to health complications (e.g., heart complications, headaches). Faculty members in this dilemma could even teach in African and African-American studies departments as a way of appearing connected to black culture; however, they are held captive by the conundrum caused by "two thoughts, two unreconciled strivings, two warring ideals in one dark body" (DuBois, 1897, pp. 194–195). They may teach black studies but their identity predicament precludes them to connect Africa to African-Americans thus their cultural analysis begins with the American slave experience. Their refusal to subordinate European training to their African core personality leaves them at risk for developing a dysfunctional academic identity. Although the identity dynamics for faculty are less publicly pronounced, they are just as critical to the retention process as they are for undergraduates. Faculty in the bind of double consciousness may begin to experience psychical and mental health problems in addition to social alienation from black and liberated faculty members. The sustaining power of self-preservation becomes jeopardized because they lack access to cultural rituals of renewal (e.g., Bid Wists, Spades, black community involvement, etc.).

A similar dilemma arises for administrators who have yet to achieve psychic liberation. Like faculty members administrators are at higher risk of health complications because they are constantly confronted with double consciousness. Both perceived and real power create greater scrutiny and always the possibility of race-based second guessing (or the invitation to ask "would they ask the same questions if I were someone else?"). Retention is compromised as a result of experiencing social isolation, black faculty and student perceptions of supporting black interests, limited university support for decisions, and limited resources for self-preservation as a result of double consciousness. For administrators, psychic liberation is integral to retention because of the public and tenuous nature of their administrative positions.

DuBois' concepts of double consciousness and psychic liberation provide an alternative to popular hypotheses that claim institutional climate and academic unpreparedness, among others, as the core issues of understanding retention. In proposing an alternative theoretical postulation, we assert that, given the historical resiliency of people of African descent, aforementioned popular rationales only help to validate what we should know and expect from institutions that were never intended for our education and upward mobility (Caldwell, 2000).

The link between identity dynamics, retention, and self-preservation in higher education is often overlooked. Attrition can be a manifestation of psychological conflicts as a result of students', faculty's, and administrators' inability to focus undiluted energy to the cause of psychic liberation due to contradictory cultural/political loyalties. Internal conflicts as a result of double consciousness catalyze the development of certain dysfunctional psychological profiles that at best cause one to leave the university and at worst deteriorate one's natural tendency for self-preservation, thereby creating a cadre of cultural disengaged, self-serving, deracinated academic elitists colloquially known as "Uncle Tom's," "sell outs," or "player haters." We suggest that retention and self-preservation of black students, faculty, and administrators is achieved through the development process of psychic liberation as outlined in the next section.

The Process of Psychic Liberation

DuBois' strategy was to use double consciousness (psychic duality) as the vehicle to promote psychic liberation (Stewart, 1998). Assuming that one is first conscious of the inherent tension caused by their presence at the university, the process of merging a "double self into a better and truer self" can begin (DuBois, 1903; p. 17). (Note the qualitative conclusion.) There is no doubt that the success (in this case retention and self-preservation) of African Americans in higher education hinges on a sort of integration (in the true sense of the word) where there is synergy between self, culture, and environment. In essence, if one is to be bicultural, then he or she willfully chooses which cultural worldview will serve as the predominant frame of reference. But again, we must realize that the systems of higher indoctrination are not predicated on cultural options. Therefore, the acquisition of psychic liberation must be an active process with a developmental quality.

Psychic liberation does yield a "better and truer" student, faculty, and administrator. Yet the majority of those on college campuses never bring up the subject because most have their energies consumed by double consciousness or assimilation. The achievement of psychic liberation for faculty and administrators depends on how deeply entrenched in academic dogma they are when they emerge from education and if they have resolved the internal conflicts as a result of previous contact with an institution. The chances are that if you are a protege of a liberated mentor, you will already be engaged in continuous cultural self-preservation and will have adopted a repertoire of behavioral responses and values that are accessible when the oppressive pressure of academic assimilation threatens your liberation.

A Developmental Model of Psychic Liberation

Borrowing language from Cross' (1971, 1994) racial identity model, we propose a psychic liberation process model. The following example demonstrates the process for a faculty member.

Pre-encounter   Pre-encounter black faculty members believe that they are under the same microscope as all faculty in the university. In their minds being a faculty member is a result of their hard work, excellent grades, and ability to get along with the majority culture. These faculty members may see no correlation between their position, the civil rights movement, equal opportunity policies, or affirmative action legislation. In fact, they subscribe to the notion of rugged individualism, the "boot strap theory," and that the tenure and promotion system is egalitarian and meritorious. Therefore they create a chasm between themselves, the campus, and local communities in hot pursuit of tenure because involvement would detract from tenure and promotion obligations. Frequently, these faculty members find themselves at university functions, hosted by the administration, reintroducing themselves to other faculty of color. In addition, they may only publish in mainstream journals, focus on race issues in their scholarship, and attend only dominant culture-sponsored conferences. They may even pejoratively refer to nonmajority journals as second-tier or nonscholarly.

Catalyst   Then an event confronts the belief that academic loyalty equals academic security. It could be an unwarranted critical midtenure review or a racially inflammatory remark by a departmental colleague. The flabbergasted pre-encounter faculty member is propelled to reluctantly reevaluate his or her previously held loyalties, purpose, and aim. This experience causes the pre-encounter faculty member to question all previously held notions about the academy.

Transition and Transformation   The next phase of development toward psychic liberation is a pivotal phase because it involves deep emotional energy (usually anger). In this phase black faculty members, in response to frustration and disappointment of their previous academic posture, become vigilant in the reclamation of a black culture frame of reference. They immerse themselves in black professional organizations to commiserate with others who have been duped. They might change their names or hair to proclaim themselves as African centered. Yet they lack serious thought, purpose, or consideration for cultural deep-structure (Nobles, 1984; Kambon, 1998) knowledge. It becomes an "I'm Blacker than you" struggle with everyone else.

At this phase faculty members decide to spend the latter half of their pretenure time making up for lost ground. Their anger results in an overextension in service activities or obsession with conspiracy theories, or engaged in other counterproductive activities. These faculty members may take out their frustrations on students and colleagues. Ultimately, they self-sabotage the tenure process as a recognition of having misallocated their previous energies as a faculty member. Faculty in this position would much rather start all over in a new position than sit in the incubator of their psychological conflict. The result is an emotional response that could lead to drastic superficial changes in a brief period of time or a deep sense of disappointment and isolation that could lead to seclusion.

With the help of liberated faculty members this phase could be one of transition and transformation. In some cases the internally conflicted and wounded junior faculty seeks solace from a liberated senior faculty member. In other cases, a compassionate liberated senior faculty member recognizes the struggles of double consciousness and initiates a mentoring relationship. The liberated mentor serves as a model, an earpiece, a strategist, an informal teacher, a protector, and a catalyst for cultural "deep structure" transformation. The liberated mentor can help normalize the experience of double consciousness; create opportunities for exposure to cultural scholarship; promote continuous engagement with an African-core worldview; and protect the junior faculty member from injurious university politics. Only a liberated faculty member can initiate the liberation process and expose the transitioning faculty member to the community of the liberated.

The confluence of consciousness, mentoring, and cultural knowledge mitigates internal conflicts, thereby creating an environment to support ascension toward psychic liberation. Once enveloped by the potential of psychic liberation, the transitioning faculty member confronts the institution with a renewed sense of purpose that is passionate and energetic (but not recklessly emotional). The neophyte to psychic liberation has learned how to reconcile the demands of the university culture while preserving and advancing his or her cultural and scholarly goals. These faculty members become well respected in the community because of their cultural clarity, consistency, scholarly knowledge base, and self-presence. They actually seem physically bigger than they are.

The mentor has demonstrated that liberated faculty members are not dependent on the tenure and promotion process for validation of worth or even job security. Tenure becomes a means to an end that ultimately affirms and advances black culture, specifically, and humanity in general. Liberated faculty members, within institutions of higher education, create self-sustaining institutions for cultural and scholarly preservation. Their life work becomes the gathering and usurping of resources—resources that will be used to create institutions where liberation does not come at the cost of years and where there is a reduction in those lost to double consciousness or unconsciousness. The mission of cultural work in the academy requires maintenance—preservation.

Psychic Liberation and Self-Preservation

The concepts of double consciousness and psychic liberation are appropriate to discuss not only retention but also how one must survive after being retained—self-preservation. The process of psychic liberation does not have a dimension that would support "recycling" (Parham, 1989); it is dynamic and must be preserved to sustain its mission. Self-preservation is the process of continuous engagement in cultural activities to regenerate and reproduce other liberated people of African descent. We suggest the following self-preservation activities for the liberated:

1. Recognize the inherent psychological dilemma caused by double consciousness. This acknowledgement will be the first step into consciousness and toward psychic liberation.

2. Remember that your purpose, aim, and potential is much deeper than your credentials or position. Your presence rests on ancestors seen and unseen.

3. Continuously engage in deep structure (epistemology, cosmology, and ontology) cultural knowledge from a non-European perspective. Ground yourself in your own cultural concepts and tradition, then find similarities within other cultural worldviews.

4. Measure your success with culturally relevant criteria not "by the tape of a world that looks on in amused contempt and pity" (DuBois, 1903, 194–195). Assess your progress with the black community "tape." The university provides a performance evaluation not a quality-of-life measure. The true measuring rod of your success is scholarship and service that contribute to the uplifting of humanity.

5. Engage in integrated learning, teaching, service, and research that emerges from your own cultural paradigm and promotes culturally synergetic practices. Remember that tenure and promotion criteria, in an African worldview, are circular. Predicated on cultural advancement, creative strategies for integrating teaching, service, and research can produce applied scholarship that our communities desperately need.

6. Stop looking for validation from the unliberated.

7. Come-correct! There is nothing worse than an educated fool, because they actually think they know something. Take your scholarship and potential seriously. Remember the old advice that says we need to read from two sets of books—one for the class and the other for learning. Buy books, tapes, videos, and so forth by a variety black scholars. Study archives, the blues, autobiographies, and essays from different eras. Remember that people of African descent are continental, not national. There are ancient, diasporic, regional and national genres of cultural intellectualism, tradition, ethics, and good old common sense. These are our classics.

8. Study abroad. Not just internationally, but nationally. It is surprising how many college students never leave their home state or region.

9. Learn the skill of code-switching. DuBois thought that the experience of multidimensional psychic structure was an advantage over adversaries in the ongoing struggle for liberation. He stated that "the Negro is a sort of seventh son, born with a veil, and gifted with second sight in this American world" (DuBois, 1903, p. 16).

10. Remember: In the absence of psychic liberation is insanity!

The Final Analysis (for Now)

Retention efforts in higher education are often limited to external expectations in the quest for equity. The campus climate, curriculum, and organizational structures were never intended to be inclusive or accommodating—tolerant as of recent. Therefore, a majority of the attempts aimed at reducing dispropor-tionate attrition statistics of students, faculty, and administrators of color have been cyclical. They miss the mark in addressing a core retention issue—for what? Social contradictions, discrepant pay scales, racism, sexism, discrimina-tion, and harassment remain a part of the American economic and political system. Why should one stay in any institution that teaches short-term coping skills rather than long-term changing skills? Students need more of a buy in than a booming economy. Retention of African-American students, faculty, and administrators should not be synonymous with accommodation; however, it should be consistent with the task of bringing forth one's African core personality and life purpose through spiritual illumination (Akbar, 1998). DuBois' perspective on identity dynamics warrants further elaboration as not only an intellectual pursuit, but as a theoretical frame in which to develop intervention strategies for preserving the pool of students, faculty, and administrators who have achieved psychic liberation.

References

Akbar, N. (1998). *Man know thyself.* Tallahassee, FL: Mind Productions.

Caldwell, L. D. (2000). The psychology of black men. In *Brothers of the academy,* Lee Jones (Ed.), pp. 131–140. Sterling, VA: Stylus Publishing.

Cross, W. (1971, July). The Negro-to-black conversion experience. *Black World* 20(9):3–27.

Cross, W. (1994). *Shades of black: Diversity in African-American identity.* Philadelphia: Temple University Press.

DuBois, W. E. B. (ca. 1892). *A fellow of Harvard,* unpublished manuscript contained in *The Papers of W. E. B. DuBois* (Microfilming Corporation of America, 1981), Reel 87.

DuBois, W. E. B. (1897, August). Striving of the Negro people. *Atlantic Monthly* 70:194–198.

DuBois, W. E. B. (1903). *The souls of black folk: Essays and sketches.* Chicago: A. C. McClurg.

Kambon, K. K. K. (1998). *African/black psychology in the American context: An African-centered approach.* Tallahassee, FL: Nubian Nation.

Nobles, W. W. (1986). *African psychology: Toward its reclamation, reascension, and revitalization.* Oakland, CA: Black Family Institute.

Parham, T. A. (1989). Cycles of psychological nigrescence. *The Counseling Psychologist* 17(2):187–226.

Stewart, J. (1983, June). Psychic duality of Afro-Americans in the novels of W. E. B. DuBois, *Phylon* XLIV(2):93–108.

Stewart, J. (1984). The legacy of W. E. B. DuBois for contemporary black studies. *Journal of Negro Education* 53:296–311.

Stewart, J. B. (1998). *Toward a synthesis of radical, reformist, recovery, and African womanist approaches to understanding black identity dynamics.* State College, PA: Pennsylvania State University.

13

THE POLITICS OF TENURE AND PROMOTION OF AFRICAN-AMERICAN FACULTY

Lemuel W. Watson

Introduction

Since I am an American of African descent, this essay is influenced by what I have seen and heard with regard to my colleagues, especially black colleagues, about tenure and promotion. Hence, I bring some understanding of what it is like to be of the academic guild but also of a subgroup that is losing ground— the black scholar (Cross, 1994). What do I mean by the black scholar? I mean those who are visibly black or choose to publicly identify themselves as black. This notion is important in part because of how I see the world and therefore the tenure process. However, it also influences what I think is important to teach, research, and devote my energies toward. Therefore, race and self are inseparable due to one's development in a historical sociopolitical context such as the United States, where race is a determining factor for access and opportunity.

Therefore, race makes a difference, although it should not; the results of the tenure decision are up to your colleagues and the institution. Regardless of how mainstream and optimistic you might be, racism, classism, sexism, and elitism continue to be present in mainstream academy, in spite of major changes in students, faculty, or curriculum in most colleges and universities

(McKay, 1988). How do you manage the day-to-day task of your faculty appointment toward tenure and promotion and not get weighed down with the politics? How do you stay focused on what you need to do to enhance your chances of getting tenure in spite of the politics?

Due to the diversity that exists among institutions of higher education, I attempt to present a general and global perspective on the tenure process. This chapter cannot provide a cookbook approach to tenure; however, it will enlighten you to the processes of tenure and other important concerns you might consider on your journey. By the questions I pose, the examples I use, and the personal insight I offer, you should feel more empowered to engage in your quest to get tenure or at least to better understand the process.

Blacks and the Professorate

How does one begin the journey to the professorate? Why does one choose to proceed on a journey that so many have called a long, hard path? I have heard many stories by faculty members about their trials and tribulations to obtain the Golden Fleece of tenure. Black graduate students and junior faculty need to know the reason why they have chosen the route of the professorate and must have a vision of what they would like to accomplish from the beginning to be successful in today's academy.

Knowing what is expected of a tenure-track faculty member in institutions of higher education is vital for success. This knowledge is important because time is of the essence in the tenure process. For those who have not been socialized through graduate training at research institutions about the demands of the professorate, the tenure process might seem brutal.

Even some black students who attend major research institutions to obtain their doctorate find that, due to lack of mentoring, they are still baffled at the lack of understanding for what is required to be successful in the tenure process. Some professors are calling for mentors for female and minority professors to enhance their chances of obtaining tenure (Willdorf, 2000). Mickelson and Oliver (1991) revealed some insight about the route that black students take to faculty positions from a study conducted by the National Study of Black College Students. What they discovered was that qualified Ph.D. students are found not only in premier institutions, but in a variety of graduate programs across multiple institutional types, which indicates that their backgrounds and training are not typical of the traditional middle-class white male route.

The life of junior faculty members, especially black faculty members, is complex and stressful. Complex because of the dynamic environment in which they have become engaged through teaching, research, and service. Stressful because no one seems to be able to assist them in making meaning out of the environment in which they must become engaged (Blackwin & Blackburn, 1981; Boice, 1991; Olsen, 1993; Ragland-Sullivan & Barlow, 1981; Whitt, 1991). I have served on committees that evaluated faculty and have had to cast judgment on my fellow colleagues with regard to tenure and promotion. I must say, serving on such committees is never an easy task. Therefore, the issues of preparedness for the professorship are added challenges for black junior faculty.

In an essay by John H. Franklin, he gives us a historical insight into his experiences and those of his colleague as "first black" faculty members in higher education. He summed up the experience nicely by stating:

> The Negro who aspired to be a scholar in the closing years of the nineteenth century and the opening years of this century must have experienced the shattering and disturbing sensations as he looked about him in an attempt to discover one indication of confidence, one expression of faith in him and his abilities. If he doubted himself, it would be understandable, for he had been brainwashed, completely and almost irrevocably, by assertions of Caucasian superiority, endorsements of social Darwinism, with its justifications for the degradation of the Negro, and political and legal maneuverings that lowered the Negro still further on the social and intellectual scale. But the aspiring Negro scholar did not doubt himself, and he turned on his detractors with all the resources he could summon in the effort to refute those who claimed he was inferior" (Franklin, 1989, p. 298).

Black faculty have unique ways of viewing the world and unique ways of addressing current problems. Their contributions need to be inserted wherever possible in keeping with the definition of true university. Consider the definition of a university as used by Newman (1910, p. 31):

> If I were asked to describe as briefly and popularly as I could, what a University was, I should draw my answer from its ancient designation of a Studium Generale, or "School of Universal Learning." This description implies the assemblage of strangers from all parts in one spot;—from all parts; else, how will you find professors and students for every department of knowledge? And in one spot; else how can there be any school at all? Accordingly, in its simple and rudimental form, it is a school of knowledge of every kind, consisting of teachers and learners from every quarter. Many things are requisite to

complete and satisfy the idea embodied in this description; but such as this a University seems to be in its essence, a place for the communication and circulation of thought, by means of personal intercourse, through a wide extent of country.

In simple terms, Newman believes that a university needs people from every walk of life to be engaged in the pursuit of knowledge and to disseminate that knowledge in order to share experiences and give the pupil the most dynamic and global learning process possible. Hence, that would include the perspective of black faculty or would demand the presence of black faculty among the ranks in our colleges and universities.

It is worth noting that the black faculty status in white institutions continues to be likened to that of the dawn of a new day. Considering the number of years that we have had to become engaged, black faculty at white institutions is still a new phenomenon. Hence, most black faculty continue to experiences higher stress levels due to lower rank and untenured status. Table 13.1 shows the percentage by race and ethnicity with regard to tenure status. Eighteen percent (22,486) of the 122,516 tenure candidates are minority faculty. The remaining 82 percent (100,030) are white. Black faculty represent approximately 5 percent.

One's responsibility as a black scholar and intellectual is a lifestyle, not a position or job. The doctorate certainly, in my opinion, is a degree that calls one to duty to contribute to the literature, to enhance the practices, and to create new policies and question old policies for all organizations in our society.

Table 13.1   Tenure Status by Race and Ethnicity (by percentage)

Race/Ethnicity	Tenure	Tenure Track	Other*	Faculty by Ethnicity
White	54.3	19.4	26.3	86.4
Asian	44.0	26.3	29.7	3.0
Black	42.8	27.3	29.9	5.0
Hispanic	43.7	32.5	23.8	2.6
American Indian	42.3	25.5	32.2	0.05
Average	52.8	20.6	26.6	

Source: Adapted from National Education Association (September, 1995). *Tenure.* NEA Higher Education Research Center Update.
* This category includes faculty not on tenure track, faculty with positions that do not offer tenure, and faculty employed by institutions with no tenure process.

Again, Franklin gives us an example and warning with regard to the stress associated with the responsibilities of a faculty position:

> It must have been a most unrewarding experience for the Negro scholar to answer those who said that he was inferior by declaring: "I am indeed not inferior." For such a dialogue left little or no time for the pursuit of knowledge as one really desired to pursue it. Imagine, if you can, what it meant to a competent Negro student of Greek literature, W. H. Crogman, to desert his chosen field and write a book entitled *The Progress of a Race*. Think of the frustration of the distinguished Negro physician C. V. Roman, who abandoned his medical research practice, temporarily at least, to write *The Negro in American Civilization*. . . . How much poorer is the field of the biological sciences because an extremely able and well-trained Negro scientist, Julian Lewis, felt compelled to spend years of his productive life writing a book entitled *The Biology of the Negro* (Franklin, 1989, p. 299).

Franklin's statement is a tremendous testimony to the energies and focus of black faculty members' natural way of focusing their scholarship and other efforts. One is affected in a powerful way by race in his or her quest to shed new light on the literature, pedagogy, and policy regarding the operations of institutions of higher education. The need is simply obvious for black faculty to bring into the light a new perspective that must be revealed to the world.

The Meaning of Tenure

What is tenure? Rovosky (1990, p. 178) gives a general definition and description of tenure but warns that such definitions can be difficult.

> In 94 percent of colleges and universities in the Unites States, some professors hold their jobs for life—i.e., until the stipulated retirement age—and in general, cannot be removed by the administration except for gross neglect of duty, physical or mental incapacity, a serious moral lapse, or grave institutional financial stringency. There is the additional requirement that the discharge of a tenured professor, a rare event, entails some form of due process.

Academic tenure is a privilege of the professorate to choose the path of intellectual development and inquiry.

In reality, given current court cases regarding tenure, there is no "realistic uniformity" for tenure because it all depends on the institution and participants. Yet, there appears to be some agreement in terms of a contractual relationship between a professor and an institution in general for lifetime employment (Hutcheson, 1997). As a junior faculty member, you will question the decision you have made about the institution that employs you. In addition, members of the department's academic guild will be asking of themselves whether they have made the most appropriate choice in giving you the opportunity to fulfill your promise as a potential colleague. If you survive the three-year review with positive evaluations, you may continue onward at the institution or try the process elsewhere. However, at the end of six years, the faculty guild will decide to invite or not to invite you to spend a lifetime in their midst.

Therefore, the black faculty member needs to discover and have a clear understanding of the department's and institution's expectations of him or her with dates to accompany. Such information includes knowing exactly the nature of the review and the value of each review in the total process. One hopes that during one's interview and before accepting the job, the role that teaching versus scholarship plays in promotion and or tenure would have been well defined. Any information should be shared in writing from the department chair, unit coordinator, or dean. Always ask for a personal appointment to go over your evaluations and to discuss them in detail so that you will have a clearer understanding of how your faculty evaluates you. In return, this request informs your colleagues of your seriousness about your responsibilities.

The Process
The First Level: Department or Faculty Unit
There are two basic questions that the department will be concerned with for your tenure. First, how will this person add to the quality of our department over his or her life span? Second, is this person a team player who will consider his or her colleagues regarding workload and responsibility of advising, curriculum development, teaching, committee work, and other necessary duties?

Your department has the responsibility of collecting your dossier (curriculum vitae, copies of publications, student evaluations, statement of research agenda, philosophical statement of teaching, course syllabi, and other appropriate items). A committee of several department members, the department senior faculty members, and/or an elected group of faculty members from your college will read the materials and/or request a list of peers suggested by you and/or themselves to review your work; this is known as an external review. This committee will be the first group to prepare a recommendation regarding your tenure, and your first-level committee's recommendation will be the one to rally your case to the next level for review.

The Second Level: The Faculty University Review Committee

The faculty university review committee is made up of faculty from multiple disciplines. Like the first-level review committee, this committee is primarily concerned with three basic issues. First, did the departmental-level committee do a fair and just appraisal of the candidate for tenure or promotion. The second-level committee will make sure that the guidelines and standards were followed for the department's decision to support or deny your case for tenure. "The committee's task is to protect both the institution and the candidate; it should provide detachment and a level of objectivity comparable to that sought for in our larger society in the civil courts" (Goodwin, 1988, p. 104).

Second, this committee will use comparison data from the candidate's peer group from comparable institutions to assist them in their decision making and assessment of your dossier and qualifications. The third concern of the committee will be to assess whether the individual candidate has come of age in the probationary period as a faculty member.

This committee will, more than likely, be looking for a clear research agenda that has developed based on your interests and specialty without the heavy assistance of others. Establishing a research agenda and a teaching philosophy that supports your interests and the interests of the institution is a major concern for this committee. "The institution-wide review is complicated particularly if the institution is attempting at the moment to improve itself and to identify sources of strength and weakness" (Goodwin, 1988, p. 104). Remember, at this level your dossier must stand on its own. There may not be anyone on this committee who has heard of you or your work. Summaries from the first-level review and your ability to articulate who you are as a faculty member (teacher, researcher, team player, program builder, etc.) are extremely important during this level of review.

The Third Level: The Administration

After the first two levels of review, you must get the final and third review from the administration of the institution. Most of the time the senior academic officer will be the person to render the final results of your tenure decision. However, because each institution is uniquely different, this officer might be called the vice chancellor of faculty, the dean of faculty, the provost, or the vice president of academic affairs. This level of review does not necessarily excuse the president, board of trustees, or coordinating boards.

At this third level, the concerns will be regarding a more global perspective about the viability of the department, the college, and the individual and how they will add to the value of the institution. For example, "the administrators may come to the conclusion coincidentally with tenure consideration that either your department, or the school of which it is a part, has become weak, lacking vigor, and unable even to operate its own processes" (Goodwin, 1988, p. 107).

However, in most cases the administration will support the recommendations of the two previous committees. If there is a conflict in recommendation between the department and university committees, the administrators will want to know why with a detailed explanation. It is also possible that a tenure decision may have less to do with the individual compared to the conditions and needs of the institution. "One's tenure will be denied based on the circumstances of a larger remedial action toward the department or school. Finally, the administration has the authority to deny your tenure on the grounds of financial exigency: they find suddenly that they cannot see ahead the means to guarantee your salary to retirement without imperiling earlier commitments to already tenured faculty" (Goodwin, 1988, p. 107).

Final Thoughts

Planning from the beginning of your doctorate degree would be of benefit to you as a future black faculty member, with the understanding that there are only six short years to build a case to prove your promise to the institution that you are worth the investment. However, never forget that, at the same time, the institution may need to prove to you that they are also worthy of your investment. The match needs to be a good one for all parties involved. Given these considerations you should develop a plan that would propel you toward a successful journey toward tenure. You must conduct research that is respected by peers and provide articles, chapters, and/or books within the time frame provided. You also need to conduct yourself in a respectable and responsible manner within the academic, professional, and general community. Beyond all else, you need to demonstrate that you know what to do and how to do it as an independent faculty member while being empathetic to colleagues and remaining to be seen as a team player.

McKay (1988, p. 51) shares that black faculty should always be aware of the day-to-day challenges of the academy when it comes to the tenure process, which may include:

(a) Overt hostility on the part of individuals or groups of mainstream faculty members and students toward minority group faculty members and or minority studies or minority groups students.

(b) Subtle and less easily detected expressions of prejudices or biases that occur in (a), on the same issues.

(c) Unconscious racism, classism, and elitism toward minority group faculty colleagues or minority studies or students by otherwise well-intentioned mainstream faculty members.

McKay reminds us that we must always be in control of our emotions regardless of what ignorance may appear. We should never jeopardize self-respect in dealing with colleagues. As black faculty, "we fare best when our dignity appears untouched; otherwise among colleagues, we are typed as overly sensitive, without a sense of humor, or uncollegial. Try to remain outwardly calm" (McKay, 1988, p.51). In such incidents, you must remember your reasons for choosing the professorate. However, I am not advocating that black faculty become doormats, yet I do recommend choosing your battles carefully. Always ask Does it really matter? Will my insight truly change another's opinion?

Next, accept as many invitations to socialize with your faculty colleagues as possible because such communications give you the chance to discover each individual as a human being with greater issues beyond the institution. However, do not engage in gossip. Listen but never be drawn into the negative downtrodding of individuals in the department or university. Always remain open and receptive to the diversity of people in a new college or university without appearing emotionally needy and without giving the impression of a prima donna.

Third, it is acceptable to say "no" to those assignments that take you completely away from your agenda. Nevertheless, you should do so with grace. For example, "I would love to accept this assignment, but I have several other assignments this semester and this one would really not serve me well." Always use the department chair as a resource in your selection of committee work. "Be protective of your time, especially if someone wants you to spend it in ways that will not have beneficial results for you. There is a thin line between selfishness and survival on this score" (McKay, 1988, p. 55).

In the classroom, black faculty are probably challenged in ways that white faculty are not. Semester after semester, black colleagues often talk to me about their expectations and the white students who challenge them. Therefore, black faculty should be well organized and demonstrate a firm but fair policy in the classroom.

Black faculty must remember that they must be businesslike in giving attention to those concerns that make a difference in their short- and long-term appointment. You must always address and pay careful attention to:

- Terms of the initial contracts for appointment and reappointment
- Conditions of each faculty evaluation (Do not sign anything until an understanding is reached and the terminology is understood.)

- The step-by-step process of the tenure timetable and requirements

- Departmental dynamics and how other departments view your colleagues, school, and discipline

- Colleagues' opinions of your actions (Remain a neutral and independent soul when there is a department dispute. You are always operating in a "stream of history" and should not speak or act until you understand the conditions of events.)

- Professional involvement and connections. They should, at all cost, be developed and maintained. Your colleagues in the professions are the ones to keep you sane and motivated. For black faculty, professional involvement is one of the most important and best investments you can be engaged in. Regardless of cost, as a novice faculty member you must see yourself as cosmopolitan (concerns beyond the institution) when it comes to your survival and your tenure process.

Given the context of the academy, black faculty, in addition to surviving in a stressful environment like their counterparts, must also deal with other concerns while trying to secure tenure and promotion. You must understand from the onset that the academy can be an isolated and lonely place for most black faculty. Hence, you must accept the responsibility to be both an intellectual to the academy and your field of study and also to the community and the world in order to enhance the process of enlightenment.

Regardless of the stress and pressures that surround the faculty position in institutions of higher education, compared to many other positions that I have had, I am far happier and content as an individual. I also believe that I have found my purpose in life and nothing will hinder me from achieving what I must achieve as a scholar and black intellectual during my lifetime, with or without tenure. For those who feel they are called to become a faculty member or black intellectual, there is no better place or greater reward than life in the academy.

References

Blackwin, R. G., & Blackburn, R. T. (1981). The academic career as a developmental process: Implications for higher education. *Journal of Higher Education* 52(6):598–614.

Boice, R. (1991). New faculty as teachers. *Journal of Higher Education* 62(2):150–73.

Cross, T. (1994). Black faculty at Harvard: Does the pipeline defense hold water? *Journal of Blacks in Higher Education* 4:42–46.

Franklin, J. H. (1989). *Race and history: Selected essays 1938–1988*. Baton Rouge, LA: Louisiana State University.

Goodwin, C. D. (1988). Some tips on getting tenure. In *The academic's handbook*, A. L. Deneff, C. D. Goodwin, & E. S. Mccrate (Eds.), pp. 101–109. Durham, NC: Duke University Press.

Hutcheson, P. (1997). The corrosion of tenure: A bibliography. *Thought and Action* 13(2):89–106.

McKay, N. Y. (1988). Minority faculty in [mainstream white] academia. In *The academic's handbook*, A. L. Deneff, C. D. Goodwin, & E. S. Mccrate (Eds.), pp. 46–60. Durham, NC: Duke University Press.

Mickelson, R. A. & Oliver, M. L. (1991). Making the short list: Black candidates and the faculty recruitment process. In *The racial crisis in American higher education*, P. G. Altbach & K. Lomotey (Eds.), pp. 149–166. Albany, NY: SUNY Press.

Newman, J. H. (1901). The idea of a university. In *The Harvard classics: Essays—English and American*, C. W. Eliot (Ed.), pp. 31–62. New York: Collier & Son.

Olsen, D. (1993). Work satisfaction and stress in the first and third year of the academic appointment. *Journal of Higher Education* 64(4):453–471.

Ragland-Sullivan, E. & Barlow, P. (1981). Job loss: Psychological response of university faculty. *Journal of Higher Education* 52(1):45–66.

Rovosky, H. (1990). *The university: An owner's manual*. New York: Norton & Company.

Whitt, E. J. (1991). Hit the ground running: Experiences of new faculty in the school of education. *Review of Higher Education* 12(2):177–197.

Willdorf, N. (2000, January 21). Female and minority law professors said to need mentors. The *Chronicle of Higher Education*, p. A18.

CONCLUSION

14

ORGANIZING THE STRUCTURE OF THE UNIVERSITY TO ACHIEVE SUCCESS IN RECRUITING AND RETAINING AFRICAN AMERICANS IN HIGHER EDUCATION

Lee Jones

As noted from previous chapters in this book, with the dramatic increase in multicultural learners, it has become increasingly important for universities to reaffirm their commitment to provide a quality education for all students. At many institutions it has become necessary to develop a university-wide strategy specifically for African-American students. Recognizing the considerable task a university has to attract, recruit, and retain African Americans, all colleges, campuses, and departments can profit from a concerted effort to share programs and resources.

To assist universities in providing ongoing retention initiatives to retain and ultimately graduate large numbers of multicultural students, it is important for them to develop a comprehensive retention plan that will guide them and all of their units in developing and maintaining a climate that is conducive and reflective of the type of students enrolling at institutions of higher education. The strategy I propose is not intended to provide all the answers to what is noted to be a very complex issue. Rather, the intent of the university's development of a retention strategy is to provide a document that is a *work in progress*. That is, although a retention strategy should be developed to cover a minimum of five years, it is beneficial to make yearly revisions to its specific objectives and strategies. Ideally, the president and senior vice presidents need to work with the multicultural task force to ensure that appropriate accountability structures are in place that will ensure responsible and timely implementation of this important initiative. In short, this retention strategy will be a living document for the university.

Getting Started

Given the multidimensional character of minority retention problems for most predominately white institutions, the retention strategy will need to use several different approaches. Four major objectives help define the tasks for developing this retention strategy: (1) The first objective is to review actual retention and graduation data of the university and compare this with selected peer institutions; (2) the second objective is to assess the various aspects of the university environment to determine factors that may lead to the attrition of multicultural students; (3) the third objective is to ascertain what specific multicultural retention initiatives are available; and (4) the fourth objective is to develop a specific retention plan and time lines with built-in accountability structures designed to increase the retention and ultimate graduation of multicultural students.

While the retention strategy will not necessarily identify cause-and-effect relationships between variables, it should offer a view of the latest retention literature, a statement of the problem, national recruitment, retention and graduation data by ethnic group, and operational definitions. When adopting a retention plan, it will also be necessary to include an extensive audit of retention initiatives occurring throughout the university, a synopsis of the university's recruitment history, retention graduation data; the university's athletic retention and graduation data, retention and graduation data of selected peer institutions, and so forth.

Finally, a comprehensive retention strategy, by definition, must focus on the complete student (e.g., intellectual, social, spiritual, physical, and cultural). While some strategies are generalizable to all underrepresented groups, it is important to recognize that the strategies that follow are meant to look at each underrepresented group as a separate entity.

Definition of Terms

An unavoidable dilemma when dealing with multicultural issues is that of the terminology used to conceptualize them. It is evident that there is no consensus in the use of terms, particularly in the area of labels for specific groups. In the development of your university's retention strategy, as is the case throughout the literature, there are bound to be some inconsistencies in the way some people use terminology. To assist the readers and users of this writing, some terms are defined for the purpose of this document. Other definitions are also included in an attempt to make the reader aware of the diversity that exists within specific racial/ethnic groups.

Common questions that exemplify the complexity of these situations include inquiries such as who are multicultural students, students of color, minority students? Who are Asian-Pacific Americans, Native Americans, African Americans, Chicano/Latino, Hispanic, and Mexican Americans? Development of the definitions was perhaps the most difficult part of planning a campuswide retention strategy.

Terms defined for the purpose of this document:

- **Culture:** The ideations, symbols, behaviors, values, customs, and beliefs that are shared by a human group. Culture is transmitted through language, material objects, ritual institutions, and is passed on from one generation to the next.

- **Diversity:** Recognition and acknowledgment of differences that are unique to each group that is part of the multicultural community.

- **Multicultural Students:** The four underrepresented racial/ethnic groups: African American, Asian-Pacific American, Chicano/Latino, and Native American.

- **Race:** A socially and historically defined human grouping hereditarily assigned but not biologically defined. Refers to very large human groups comprised of diverse populations and ethnic groups.

- **Recruitment:** The process of identifying and informing African-American, Asian-Pacific-American, Chicano/Latino, and Native-American populations in order to provide them with support systems that will facilitate improved and enhanced access to the university with the expectation of increasing enrollment of multicultural students.

- **Retention:** The continuous process to create, maintain, and support ongoing strategies for meeting the personal, academic, social, and financial needs of multicultural students to ensure academic success and graduation.

- **The University:** The main campus of the home institution and any branches that may comprise a multicampus system.

Five-Year Multicultural Student Retention Plan

Once the data have been collected and compared with your university's sister institutions and national retention data, frequently used terms have been operationally defined for your campus, and a review of the retention literature has been obtained, it is then time to begin with the most important part of the retention plan: the Strategy. Below is an outline of a Five-Year Multicultural Retention Strategy. While I do not purport that this retention strategy has all the answers, it is one that could provide a good start for those institutions that are serious about institutionalizing efforts to retain underrepresented students.

Vision

The university seeks to develop a universitywide approach to increase the retention and graduation rates of multicultural students. The ultimate goal is to increase the retention and graduation rates of these students so that they equal or exceed that of the majority of students at the university.

Statement of Values

In the process of developing and implementing a strategy that aims at increasing the retention and graduation rates of multicultural students, the following principles must permeate all actions taken. First, an institutional commitment that communicates respect, inclusion, trust, a challenge for growth, and understanding of and positive regard for multicultural students is imperative. Second, students must be made aware of the importance of individual responsibility, the freedom to grow, self-confidence, and a sense of their own authorship of their destiny. Third, in order to meet multicultural students' needs holistically, student services and support will be based on a spirit of collaboration and cooperation across the university community.

Mission Statement

The university is committed to developing, implementing, and assessing a five-year plan to improve the retention and graduation rates of multicultural students.

Goals, Objectives, and Strategies

I. To create an inclusive university climate that supports the well-being and enhances the total educational experience and ultimate graduation of multicultural students

A. To increase awareness and appreciation of multiculturalism across the academic community.

  1. Survey multicultural students to assess their needs, their concerns, and their recommendations for improving the campus climate.

  2. Offer diversity education workshops to every advisor, faculty, and staff member and ensure that their efforts for diversity are included in performance evaluations.

  3. Encourage student participation in multicultural/diversity training.

  4. Develop and promote events that recognize diverse cultural heritage.

  5. Project a positive multicultural image through publications related to the university.

  6. Hold an annual multicultural convocation and reception.

  7. Support and collaborate with a curricular diversity committee in its efforts to increase the number of courses that address multiculturalism and diversity.

  8. Include a presentation on the university's diversity and its enrollment management recruitment and retention plans for multicultural students during orientation sessions for new faculty, staff, and administrators.

  9. Continue partnerships that will ensure the successful transition for students transferring from other colleges and universities.

  10. Continue and develop new working relationships with other minority offices, agencies, and organizations that provide support services for students.

B. To increase incrementally each year the number of faculty and staff of color.

  1. The president will meet each year with deans and heads of major units to personally reaffirm multicultural hiring goals, with special emphasis on tenure-track faculty.

  2. Identify staff and financial assistance at the university level to provide incentives for departments and units to hire a more diverse staff.

  3. Produce an annual report documenting the number of faculty and staff of color employed by the university.

C. To integrate the campuses and surrounding communities to improve the local racial climate.

   1. Expand special living community opportunities to better support multicultural student populations.

   2. Host teleconference presentations on campus that address racial issues that would include the university and the surrounding community.

   3. Participate in city council meetings.

D. To provide opportunities for faculty and staff of color to interact with multicultural students as the students adjust to the campus environment.

   1. Implement a biannual reception for faculty, staff, and students.

   2. Implement activities celebrating cultural heritage that comprise faculty, staff, and students.

E. To provide opportunities for all faculty and staff to interact with multicultural students as the students adjust to the campus environment.

   1. Establish a professional mentor program for multicultural students.

F. To provide multicultural students with a permanent space that they can call their own and where they can see an immediate reflection of their cultural heritage.

   1. Allocate spaces for a multicultural student services office on all campuses.

   2. Provide more artwork across campuses.

II. To provide an academic environment and support structure that is aimed at improving the retention and graduation rates of multicultural students

A. To coordinate academic retention programs to maximize their effectiveness.

   1. Have each college and branch campus appoint a person to coordinate its retention initiatives, monitor the implementation of these initiatives at the college level, and serve as an active member of a council on retention.

   2. Provide this representative with the resources and authority to oversee services to multicultural students in the areas of advising, mentoring, and participation in academic clubs and activities.

B. To systematically assess the effectiveness of retention programs and use the results to improve them.

   1. Provide an accurate database to track *all* undergraduate students.

   2. Perform annual evaluations of existing retention programs by departments, offices, and majors.

   3. Analyze the multicultural student demographic report in regard to retention data to identify trends.

   4. Survey nonreturning multicultural students to identify the reasons why they leave the university.

C. To provide all incoming multicultural students with a precollege experience.

   1. Continue to provide on- and off-campus programs targeting multicultural students in which they are introduced to the history of higher education, how the system works, and the demands and expectations of college life.

D. To develop culturally responsive classrooms that actively engage students in learning.

   1. Assess pedagogical needs of the faculty members.

   2. Encourage faculty members to utilize campus educational centers for the review of curriculum and teaching style for multicultural inclusiveness.

   3. Facilitate cross-disciplinary collaboration among faculty, administrators, and students in the development of culturally sensitive classrooms.

E. To assist multicultural students with their social, academic, and cultural adjustment to college.

   1. Assess the academic needs of multicultural students and how those needs are being met by the university.

   2. Monitor multicultural student academic progress.

   3. Establish a comprehensive university mentoring program to assist multicultural students in adjusting to and maximizing the university experience.

   4. Highlight and recognize multicultural students' academic achievement and scholarship.

F. To provide the ongoing information and guidance necessary to facilitate connecting multicultural students to educational and career programs that meet their needs.

1. Assist multicultural students to inventory their existing education skills and help focus their interest in selecting a degree program.

2. Provide multicultural students with sensitive and appropriate academic advising.

3. Assist multicultural students in accessing academic support services as their need for these services arises.

4. Promote multicultural student enrollment in a four-year degree agreement.

5. Provide options and information on postgraduate education and assist with preparation for the application process.

6. Publicize the academic support structure available to multicultural students.

7. Collaborate with student groups and other units across campus working in existing and future multicultural retention efforts to apply principles of career development and success to educational experiences.

8. Provide a multicultural perspective that enhances career development, employability, and preparation for graduate studies.

9. Provide opportunities for students to link their education with their cultural communities through service learning, observation of service delivery, internships, cooperative education, and research.

III. To assist multicultural students in securing adequate financial aid

A. To assist students and their parents in understanding and utilizing the financial-aid process and eligibility.

1. Include financial aid information in all publications and mailings to prospective students.

2. Include presentations on all types of financial aid as a regular of component of recruitment events and new student orientation.

3. Conduct workshops that assist students in filling out financial aid applications.

4. Continue to assist students in the aid-distribution process.

B. To assist students and parents in identifying suitable scholarships and grants.

   1. Include scholarship and grant information in all publications and mailings to prospective students.

   2. Include scholarship and grant information as a regular component of recruitment events and new student orientation.

   3. Conduct workshops to assist students in filling out scholarship applications.

C. Increase scholarships available to multicultural students.

   1. Create a multicultural scholarship endowment fund.

   2. Increase allocations for multicultural scholarship support from ongoing fund-raising efforts.

D. Inform students and parents on loan eligibility and how to apply for guaranteed student loans.

E. Inform students and parents on work-study eligibility and how to qualify and apply for work study.

F. To obtain resources for an emergency loan program.

   1. Provide interim financial support for students whose aid is delayed.

   2. Provide emergency money for students not eligible for financial aid.

IV. To monitor the implementation of the university's five-year multicultural student retention plan

A. Provide an accurate database for all students.

B. Maintain periodic meetings to discuss the implementation of the plan, receive and provide feedback to various departments, and redirect efforts as needed.

C. Provide the various departments with a format for the evaluation of their particular efforts regarding the implementation of the retention plan.

D. Make council members available as consultants to the campus in the development, implementation, and evaluation of specific retention plans.

E. Generate an annual report showing the overall impact of the plan and providing recommendations for improvement as needed.

The multicultural retention strategy is designed to provide structure to the retention strategy. Further, in recognizing the university's strong commitment to recruiting multicultural students, it is imperative that each academic department and academic support unit play a significant and ongoing role in formulating, implementing, and maintaining coordinated retention strategies and plans. The next section deals with providing an organizational structure that will be at the center for implementing the day to day activities of a university's multicultural office.

Reorganization of Your Multicultural Office

Planning for the campus reorganization can be a very painful process. Although change is inevitable for many people participating in the development of a campus retention strategy, there will be some who would prefer to cling to the way things are. There must be clear and strong leadership from the president and provost of the institution. Another important feature of reorganizing your campus office of multicultural affairs is to ensure that the university has invested financially to the structural changes. Figure 14.1 highlights an example of a midsize university multicultural affairs structure before the reorganization.

Phase I included the appointment of a university-wide Council for Multicultural Student Retention and Council for Multicultural Student Recruitment, both of which were designed to provide a strategic approach to how we recruit and retain students of color at Washington State University. Since the evolution of the Phase I reorganization, we have made a few modifications that reflect the feedback from the Multicultural Student Services staff, students, and other supporters of our office.

Finally, the goal of this retention strategy is simply to provide a blueprint from which universities may operate as they begin to retain multicul-

The first phase of the reorganization was to review the department's mission and current structure. The director, in consultation with senior administration, presented five functional areas for the department: (1) Recruitment and Community Relations, (2) Counseling Services, (3) Retention Services, (4) Strategic Planning and New Program Initiatives, Operations, and (5) Evaluation and Assessment.

FIGURE 14.1 Example of a midsize university multicultural affairs structure before reorganization.

tural students. It is not in any way intended to provide the total solution for very complex problems many universities have in retaining minority students. As most of the retention literature denotes, there will be a dramatic shift in the demographic makeup of society as a whole. We have to assume that as the demographic shift occurs, universities will experience some of the change. If we are to live in a true ethnically diverse society, we must begin to look at and proactively address university structure and institutional values.

Appendix: Job Descriptions
Associate Director of the Office of Multicultural Student Services

The associate director of Multicultural Student Services serves as one of the senior administrators for the department. This person functions in the absence of the director and assumes full responsibilities for the strategic planning and new program initiatives unit within the department.

> Reports to the director of the Office of Multicultural Student Services
> Serves as a member of the senior management team for the department
> Assists with managing the strategic planning and new program initiatives
> Coordinates all functions for the graduate and professional school
>   preparation program (Saturday academy)
> Coordinates the Multicultural Parent Association
> Coordinates the multicultural single-parent initiatives
> Serves as the liaison between the department and the branch campuses
> Assists the director and the Division of Human Relations and Resources
>   with multicultural faculty and staff recruitment and retention
> Assists the director and the senior management team with the strategic
>   planning for the department
> Assists the department with writing grant proposals
> Serves as the liaison between the department and the external
>   community (i.e., religious, civic, social organizations, etc.)
> Supervises and coordinates all internal committees of the department
> Assists with the supervision of the staff
> Serves on university-wide committees for the department
> Develops training schedules and outlines for the department
> Performs all other duties as assigned

Associate Director of Recruitment and Community Relations for the Office of Multicultural Student Services

The associate director of recruitment and community relations supervises all precollegiate and community college initiatives for the department. The associate director supervises the staff and is responsible for the budget and strategic planning for the unit. The associate director serves in the absence of the director and also serves on the senior management team for the department.

> Reports to the director of the Office of Multicultural Student Services
> Supervises and oversees all precollegiate, transfer, and high school activities for the department
> Serves as a member of the senior management team for the department
> Assists the director and the senior management team with the strategic planning for the department
> Manages the budget for the recruitment and community relations area
> Serves as the chair of the Council for Multicultural Student Recruitment
> Is responsible for the planning, organizing, and implementing of all recruitment initiatives for the department (i.e., College Knowledge for the Mind, Cougar Monday(s), Student Phone-a-thon, high school visits, etc.)
> Serves as the liaison between the department and the state's multicultural communities regarding recruitment initiatives
> Serves in the absence of the director
> Assists with writing grant proposals for the department
> Represents the department on university-wide committees
> Serves on the department's internal committees
> Conducts annual performance appraisals for all personnel in the recruitment area
> Performs all other duties as assigned

Assistant Director of Multicultural Counseling Services for the Office of Multicultural Student Services

The assistant director of multicultural counseling services is responsible for the day-to-day supervision of the four ethnic centers. The assistant director also manages communications between the four centers and all other units within the department. The assistant director serves on the senior management team.

> Reports to the director of the Office of Multicultural Student Services
> Supervises all counselors and the operation of four ethnic centers

Provides annual reports on all student centers
Conducts annual performance appraisals for all counselors
Serves as a member of the senior management team for the department
Serves on internal committees for the department
Serves as chair of the marketing and development committee for the
    department
Serves as department liaison between Alumni Alliances of Color
Serves on university-wide committees
Assists with the development of the department's strategic planning
Works cooperatively with the retention services staff
Serves as liaison between other academic support programs on campus
Works closely with the evaluation and assessment component of the
    department
Assists with the planning of the university's annual Rev. Dr. Martin
    Luther King, Jr. celebration
Co-advises multicultural student organizations
Conducts annual performance appraisals for all counselors
Serves as the department's liaison for the Office of Counseling Services
Performs all other duties as assigned

Assistant Director of Retention Services for the Office of Multicultural Student Services

The assistant director of retention services manages the day-to-day cross-functional retention initiatives and programs for the department. The assistant director also works very closely with the four ethnic centers and the central administration office. The assistant director serves on the senior management team for the department.

Reports to the director of the Office of Multicultural Student Services
Serves as a members of the senior management team for the department
Supervises the retention services staff
Supervises and oversees all functions of the retention services component
    for the department:
    University mentoring program
    Career, orientation, and internship programs
    Structured group leadership development
    Academic enrichment
Assists the director with coordinating the Council on Multicultural
    Student Retention
Represents the department on university-wide committees

Serves as the department's liaison between the Bridge Program and the
Student Advising and Learning Center

Assists the department with writing grant proposals

Assists the assistant director of multicultural counseling services with the
coordination of the long-range programming calendar for the
department

Assists with the training of all staff within the retention area

Oversees the budget for the retention services unit

Provides annual reports on all cross-functional retention areas

Serves as liaison between the department and the Office of Career
Services

Advises the Council on Multicultural Student Presidents

Provides annual performance appraisals of staff within the retention
services unit

All other duties assigned by the director

Counselor for the Chicano/Latino Student Center for the Office of Multicultural Student Services

The counselor for the Chicano/Latino Student Center is responsible for the
day-to-day management of the center, supervision of staff, planning and implementing programs, and so forth. This is a full-time nontenure-track position.

Reports to the assistant director of multicultural counseling services

Is responsible for the day-to-day management of the Chicano/Latino
Student Center

Assists with co-advising Chicano/Latino student organizations

Plans and implements student leadership retreats for student groups
associated with the Chicano/Latino Student Center

Assists with the planning of the university's annual Dr. Martin Luther
King, Jr. celebration

Assists with the planning the annual *Semana de la Raza* activities

Counsels Chicano/Latino and multicultural students as required

Organizes, plans, and implements programs for the center

Supervises work-study students and peer mentors

Provides formal and informal academic advising to multicultural
students

Represents the department on university-wide committees

Participates on interdepartmental committees

Serves as liaison with other academic support programs on the
campus

Works with the evaluation and assessment component to provide
requested data for students associated with the Asian-Pacific-
American Student Center
Performs all other duties as assigned

Senior Recruiter/Coordinator for the Office of Multicultural Student Services

African-American Student Emphasis   The senior multicultural recruitment coordinator has responsibility for increasing ethnic enrollment at Washington State University, particularly African-American undergraduate and
graduate students. This position is a full-time, nontenure-track, permanent
position.

Reports to the associate director of recruitment and community relations
Assists the associate director in developing, implementing, and enforcing
office policies and procedures
Supervises undergraduate students
Under the direction of the associate director, develops and implements
training programs and materials for new staff
Takes leadership in coordinating one or more of the office's major
recruitment programs (i.e., Cougar Monday, Horizon Air, Adopt-a-
School, Phone-a-thon, etc.)
Takes leadership in working with recruitment staff to ensure travel and
other paperwork is initiated and processed in a timely fashion
Assists the associate director in writing fiscal reports
Identifies working relationships with African-American communities
across the state of Washington
Works closely with the manager for community relations
Serves on interdepartmental committees
Serves on university-wide committees
Works closely with multicultural students as they transition to
Washington State University
Assists the department with the evaluation of African-American and
other multicultural student applicants
Assists other departmental staff with implementing retention initiatives
Works closely with the counselor for the African-American Student
Center
Performs all other duties as assigned

Recruitment Coordinator for the Office of Multicultural Student Services

Chicano/Latino Emphasis   The multicultural recruitment coordinator has the responsibility for increasing ethnic enrollment at Washington State University, particularly Chicano/Latino undergraduate and graduate students. The position is a full-time, nontenure-track, permanent position.

Reports to the associate director of recruitment and community relations

Develops, implements, and evaluates strategies for recruiting Chicano/Latino undergraduate and graduate students. This includes recruiting students from high schools, middle schools, community colleges, and so forth.

Assists the associate director in planning and organizing early outreach activities for the department

Participates in the preparation and implementation of all recruitment activities within the department

Identifies working relationships within Chicano/Latino communities and organizations within the state of Washington

Assists with the coordination of recruitment efforts with the Office of Admissions, Office of Student Financial Aid, Residence Life, Scholarship Services and Academic Support departments on campus

Serves on interdepartmental committees

Works closely with the manager for community relations

Serves on university-wide committees

Actively participates in ethnic communities across the state

Works closely with ethnic students as they transition to Washington State University

Assists the department in securing necessary financial support by working with various university departments

Assists with the evaluation of Asian-Pacific Americans and other multicultural student applicants for admissions

Assists other departmental staff with implementing retention initiatives

Performs all other duties as assigned

Program Assistant for the Office of Multicultural Student Services

Reports to the assistant to the director

Is responsible for providing support for all cross-functional retention initiatives for the department

Provides administrative support to the assistant director of retention
   services

Is responsible for the layout and follow-up logistics of the departmental
   newsletter

Assists with the development of a tracking system for mentors, academic
   achievement students, student leaders, interns for the department

Assists the counselors with the development of forms, reports,
   evaluations, and other documents that relate to cross-functional
   programming

Assists with the development of computer programs that meet the needs
   of the retention areas

Maintains files, weekly logs, semester reports, and so forth for retention
   initiatives

Attends interdepartmental meetings

Assists with maintaining inventory for the department

Assists with the development of training of student staff

Serves as the office manager for the multicultural center

Processes all internal fiscal request forms as submitted by the retention
   staff and other staff within the department

Maintains key inventory for all ethnic centers and the Heritage House

Is responsible for maintaining office equipment and property inventory
   for all ethnic centers and the Heritage House

Performs all other duties as assigned

Assistant to the Director of the Office of Multicultural Student Services

Reports to the director of the Office of Multicultural Student Services

Is responsible for the day-to-day management of the operations
   component of the department

Assists the director with the management of the budget

Assists with establishing annual financial goals and target dates

Serves as liaison between the department and assigned university
   committees and councils

Coordinates the activities of all work-study students for the department

Supervises all support staff for the department

Coordinates special projects as assigned by the director

Is responsible for the coordination of the department's computer network

Assists with the development of the department's strategic planning

Serves as a member of the senior management team for the department

Composes and transmits confidential and sensitive information
regarding department's business

Cochairs the departmental grants and development committee

Performs all other duties as assigned

Program Assistant for the Office of Multicultural Student Services

Reports to the assistant to the director

Rotates from the multicultural center and Wilson Hall for the purpose of
providing equitable clerical and programmatic support to the
counselors and the assistant director of multicultural counseling
services

Assists with the planning, organizing, and implementation of major
programming initiatives sponsored by the ethnic centers (i.e., Rev.
Dr. Martin Luther King, Jr. Day, Asian-Pacific-American Awareness
Week, *Semana de la Raza,* Pow Wow, etc.)

Assists students and other customers who have business with the
department

Serves as the primary support staff person while working for and around
the ethnic centers

Composes correspondence, printed material, and/or news releases related
to program policies, procedures, operations, and so forth

Compiles and distributes information relative to program activities

Confers with other departments on campus and external constituencies

Coordinates arrangements for departmental programs

Establishes and maintains records and files

Performs complex word-processing tasks (i.e., merging, sorting,
integrating text with graphics, etc.)

Is responsible for fiscal paperwork relating to programming through the
four ethnic centers

Performs all other duties as assigned

Office Assistant III for the Office of Multicultural Student Services

Reports to the assistant to the director

Provides primary support to the central administrative team and the
recruitment and community relations staff

Answers the telephone, resolves problems, responds to inquiries
regarding departmental procedures and services, receives and refers
visitors to appropriate office, and so forth

Create departmental forms

Assists in the development of departmental reports

Assists with the preparation, compilation, and coordination of reports
and records

Composes routine office correspondence

Assists the recruitment and community relations area with the
development of reports and evaluations

Screens and distributes mail to departments

Performs electronic mail functions

Assists with the supervision of work-study students

Operates office equipment

Relays messages to departmental staff

Attends departmental meetings

Proofreads material and makes corrections

Maintains office filing system

Assists the recruitment and community relations area with travel
arrangements and travel fiscal paperwork

Performs all other duties as assigned

Manager of Community Relations for the Office of Multicultural Student Services

Reporting to the associate director of recruitment and community relations for
the Office of Multicultural Student Services, the manager for community relations is responsible for the day-to-day management of the College Knowledge
for the Mind programs throughout the state of Washington.

Reports to the associate director of recruitment and community relations

Is responsible for the statewide College Knowledge for the Mind
programs

Assists with writing grants for recruitment and retention programs

Assists with the strategic planning for the department

Assists the department with developing and implementing a
comprehensive alumni development program

Provides leadership in developing community-college relations

Assesses and evaluates recruitment initiatives for the department

Serves as liaison with cooperative extension offices across the state

Actively participates in ethnic communities across the state

Assists the associate director in planning early outreach activities across
the state

Serves on interdepartmental and university committees as assigned

Assists the department in securing external funds

Works as liaison between the recruitment and retention units within the department

Develops, implements, and evaluates strategies for recruiting multicultural graduate and undergraduate students to Washington State University

Supervises graduate staff

Performs all other duties as assigned

INDEX

ABOUT THE CONTRIBUTORS

Derrick P. Alridge is assistant professor in the Department of Social Foundations of Education at the University of Georgia. He completed a Ph. D. in educational theory and policy with specializations in the history and philosophy of education at the Pennsylvania State University in 1997. Today, Professor Alridge writes and teaches in the field of African-American and American educational history and philosophy with interests in the educational thought of W. E. B. DuBois, intellectual history, and historical policy analysis. His most recent publication includes an article on W. E. B. DuBois in *Educational Theory* and forthcoming articles in *Journal of Negro Education* and *Journal of Human Behavior in the Social Environment*. His most recent research project is work on a civil rights documentary examining the desegregation of the University of Georgia.

Eugene L. Anderson is currently a doctoral candidate in the Department of Educational Policy Studies at the University of Virginia. He holds a bachelor of arts in African-American studies from the University of Pennsylvania, and a master of urban planning from the University of Virginia. His areas of interest are higher education policy, intercollegiate athletics, and urban planning.

Eugene is a doctoral fellow of the National Science Foundation and has received scholarships from the American Planning Association both as an undergraduate and graduate student. He has presented at national conferences for the Association for the Study of Higher Education, the Comparative and International Education Society, the American Planning Association, as well as international conferences in England and Spain.

He has worked with numerous community development organizations in both Philadelphia, Pennsylvania, and Charlottesville, Virginia. He also has interned with the Department of Housing and Urban Development and the

American Council on Education. Since his arrival in Virginia, Eugene has mentored student-athletes at the University of Virginia and at a local high school.

André J. Branch is assistant professor in the School of Teacher Education at San Diego State University. He teaches multicultural education and ethnic identity development courses. His research interests include multicultural curriculum development, teacher-facilitated ethnic identity development, and the recruitment and retention of African-American faculty members in higher education, as well as teachers of color in K-12 schools. With a colleague, he recently published, *Creating Effective Urban Schools: The Impact of School Climate.* Branch earned the Ph.D. in curriculum and instruction at the University of Washington, Seattle, Washington. Dr. Branch is a former principal of Cultural Diversity Associates, a consulting firm that provided workshops in cultural diversity to educators in K-12 public schools, colleges and universities, and businesses in the public and private sectors.

Leon D. Caldwell is currently an assistant professor of Educational Psychology at the University of Nebraska, Lincoln (UNL). He is a native of West Philadelphia, Pennsylvania and the oldest of three from a female-headed household. He received the Ph.D. in counseling psychology in December of 1998 from Pennsylvania State University where he specialized in multicultural counseling. He earned a bachelor's degree in economics, while playing Division I basketball, and a master's degree in secondary school counseling, from Lehigh University, in Bethlehem, Pennsylvania. At UNL he teaches in the counseling psychology program and supervises doctoral and master's degree level students. Since joining the faculty at UNL he has become active in the Lincoln and Omaha communities. He will teach an African and African-American psychology course at UNL during the summer term.

Leon's goal is to continue to advance the reascension and revitalization of black psychology in the tradition of our great African-centered scholars for the next century. Building the next cadre of community servants is Dr. Caldwell's purpose. In addition to the academic life, Dr. Caldwell is a fanatic student of African drum (Djembe) and dance. Currently he advises the Afrikan People's Union, an undergraduate student organization, and serves on the advisory board for community organizations. Dr. Caldwell is interested in research related to career development, mental health service delivery, school counseling, and counseling issues for underserved populations.

He is married to the beautiful Celika Caldwell.

Jason De Sousa, a native of New York City, is vice president for student affairs at Savannah State University. Previously, he served as assistant vice president for student affairs for enrollment management at Morgan State University and assistant vice president for student affairs at Alabama State University. A recipient of the National Association of Student Affairs Professionals' Benjamin L. Perry Award, he also served as director of the Career Development Center at Tuskegee University. He receved the B.A. degree in sports administration from Morgan State University; the M.A. degree in college student personnel from Bowling Green State University; and the Ed.D. degree in higher education administration from Indiana University.

He is a distinguished member of Kappa Alpha Psi Fraternity and is involved in several civic, academic, and professional associations.

Paul E. Green is assistant professor of Urban Politics, Policy and the Law at the University of California. He has taught at secondary schools in the Orleans Parish Public Schools and St. Louis Public Schools, and has held the position of principal in a secondary alternative high school in Dayton, Ohio. He earned a bachelor of arts in Spanish education from Dillard University and a master of education degree from the University of New Orleans, as well as a doctorate of philosophy in educational policy and politics from the University of Virginia. His research awards and fellowships include the Walter E. Campbell Scholarship, Nathan E. Johnson Scholarship, California Regents Faculty Fellowship, the Center for Ideas and Society Fellowship, among others. Professor Green's areas of expertise include the politics, policies, and practices of governmental, institutional, and judicial decision making; social justice; racial and ethnic inequality in lower and postsecondary institutions; and organized resistance at the federal, state, and local levels.

Raphael M. Guillory is currently a doctoral student in higher education administration at Washington State University. He holds a master of education degree from Washington State University and a bachelor of arts degree in sociology from Eastern Washington University. He currently serves as the graduate support coordinator for the Office of Grant and Research Development at Washington State University and currently serves on the Research and Arts Committee that directly advises the vice provost for research at Washington State University. He is also a Gates Millennium Scholar.

Raphael hails from the Nez Perce Indian Reservation in Lapwai, Idaho. He and his wife, Gloria, a Nez Perce Indian, have two daughters, Imani and Sophia. Devout Christians, he and his family enjoy traveling to church revivals throughout the Pacific Northwest. He aspires to become a college professor and serve as an advocate for minority students in higher education.

Jerlando F. L. Jackson is a visiting assistant professor of Higher and Postsecondary Education in the Department of Educational Administration at the University of Wisconsin-Madison and a research associate with the Center for the Study of Academic Leadership (University Council for Educational

Administration). Prior to his current position, Dr. Jackson served as the assistant to the dean in the College of Education at Iowa State University.

He holds a bachelor of music education from the University of Southern Mississippi. He has a master of education degree in higher education administration from Auburn University. He also received a Certificate of Public Management and the Ph.D. in higher education from Iowa State University.

Dr. Jackson has made presentations at numerous conferences and universities throughout the United States. He has several publications to his credit. Among the publications he has authored are *Scholars of Color: Are Universities Derailing Their Scholarship* (1999), and *NPHC/IFC/CPH Relations: A Product of the Greek System Structure* (1998).

In addition to his many academic and professional associations, Dr. Jackson is a distinguished member of Kappa Alpha Psi Fraternity.

Lee Jones serves as the associate dean for academic affairs and instruction in the College of Education and associate professor in Educational Leadership at Florida State University. He is a member of the dean's administrative team. Dr. Jones is responsible for coordinating many functions within the College of Education, including the offices of Clinical Education, Academic Services, and Student Access, Recruitment, and Retention. In addition to his academic and administrative responsibilities, Dr. Jones produces and hosts a television talk show, which reaches over one million viewers throughout the state of Florida and parts of southern Alabama and Georgia.

Dr. Jones has received over 175 awards and citations including the Alumnus of the Year Award from Delaware State University, and the Graduate School Leadership Award from Ohio State University. He holds a bachelor of arts degree from Delaware State University, in drama, speech, communication, and theater. While at DSU he was elected president of the student body. He has a master of arts degree in higher education administration, a master of arts degree in business administration, and a Ph.D. in organizational development from Ohio State University. Dr. Jones completed his high school education at Newark, New Jersey's Barringer High School, the third oldest high school in the country. He is editor of the book, *Brothers of the Academy*, and is completing two additional books, *Black in America: When a Ph.D Is Still Not Enough*, and a motivational book, *You Must Give Yourself Permission*.

Known as a prolific orator, Dr. Jones has been in great demand as a speaker throughout the country. He has also been invited to speak in England, Canada, and Puerto Rico. His speeches have received rave reviews, and he is consistently requested to appear for repeat visits at numerous engagements. He is a member of Kappa Alpha Psi Fraternity, National Association for Equal

Opportunity, American Association for the Study of Higher Education, American Association for Higher Education, Academy of Human Resource Development, American Association for Quality Control, and a host of other civic and professional organizations. His motto is "the bottom line is results, and anything else is rhetoric!"

Kipchoge N. Kirkland is a doctoral student attending the University of Washington on the Seattle campus. He is studying in the area of curriculum and instruction with a specialization in the field of multicultural education. He also serves in the community as a high school volunteer social studies and biology teacher.

Kipchoge holds a bachelor of science degree in microbiology from Washington State University as well as a master of education degree in the area of teaching and learning from the same institution. After receiving the master of education degree, Kipchoge worked one year as a full-time high school biology teacher at a private high school located in Seattle, Washington. Following his teaching experience, he decided to pursue a doctorate in education.

Kipchoge is a creative and active student who enjoys reading, studying, writing, and delivering spoken-word poetry at the university and within the local community. His research interests include addressing historical and contemporary practices of consciousness raising among ethnic groups of color within the United States. His primary focus is centered on how African-American high school students begin to develop a critical cultural consciousness with poetry as a pedagogical tool for reflection and analysis. Focusing on the school experiences of students of color, his work also explores the possibilities of blending the arts with multicultural theory for the development of school curriculum, pedagogy, and classroom culture. Kipchoge aspires to be a creative and culturally conscious professor within the academic community

Shuaib Meacham is assistant professor of Literacy Instruction in the School of Education at the University of Delaware. His research aims to apply insights from African-American culture and epistemology into educational challenges broadly conceived toward the development of a multicultural sense of mainstream. He is also a spoken-word poet who has worked with community poets to introduce teachers to the writing processes implicit within spoken-word poetry. He works with cultural centers and other poetry venues to host "Young Poet's Nights" for middle-school students. Shuaib Meacham also works to integrate teacher education programs with community-based educational organizations, working with teachers, community leaders, and university faculty to construct teacher education experiences. He presently lives in Wilmington, Delaware, with his wife Karen, and his daughters Aisha (12) and Karis (1).

Eddie Moore, Jr. currently serves as assistant dean of students and director of intercultural life at Cornell College in Mount Vernon, Iowa. Prior to his current position, Mr. Moore was a teaching assistant and adjunct instructor. Mr. Moore has also served as a motivational speaker, camp counselor, and coach for the Loras College All-Sport Camp for four summers. During the 1996-1997 school year, Mr. Moore served as hall director and supervised a staff of seven resident assistants at Loras College. Mr. Moore also served as an assistant football coach for the Loras Duhawks during the seasons of 1993, 1994, and 1995.

In 1996 Mr. Moore developed and maintains a growing diversity consulting and research team: *America & Moore.* The team, which consists of several on-call presenters in addition to Mr. Moore, has given interactive and motivating presentations/workshops to students from kindergarten through post-secondary levels. Presentations/workshops have also been given to parents, community members and organizations, and city and state government employees across the nation. The presentations/workshops focus on issues of cultural competency, race relations, community, and self-esteem.

Mr. Moore holds a B.A. in political science from Cornell College. He received the M.A. in educational administration from Loras College in Dubuque, Iowa. He is currently preparing for doctoral comprehensive exams in education (educational leadership) at the University of Iowa in Iowa City.

Mr. Moore has been actively involved in community work along with his academic responsibilities. He worked at the Broadway Neighborhood Center in Iowa City, Iowa. He conducted a parent discussion group for a Headstart Program in Dubuque, Iowa, and Mr. Moore has also worked with adolescent students attending an after-school program funded by Substance Abuse Services Center.

Mr. Moore has given numerous academic presentations, including FINE: First in the Nation in Education, Iowa's Educational Research Foundation, AERA in Montreal in 1999, AESA, Philadelphia in 1998, and as keynote for MLK day in Fort Madison, Iowa, in 1999 and in Dubuque, Iowa, in 1997. During the school year of 1995-1996, Mr. Moore organized and facilitated a series of forums/panel discussions for Loras College and the surrounding community, discussing views about affirmative action, interracial dating, flag burning, women and minorities in higher education, religion/segregation and race relations.

Recognized for his ability to challenge, educate, and motivate students and adults into advocates for peace, equity, and justice, Mr. Moore continually strives to provide opportunities and hope to children across America by being an effective, intelligent, and consistent educator. Mr. Moore maintains an energetic, positive and caring attitude professionally and spiritually. "God has blessed me with the ability to affect and inspire folks."

James L. Moore III is assistant professor in counselor education at the University of South Carolina. He received the B.A. in English education from Delaware State University, a small, historically black land-grant university in Dover, Delaware. He earned an M.A.Ed. in counselor education and is currently completing the final requirements for a Ph.D. in counselor education at Virginia Tech. He is writing his doctoral dissertation on *The Persistence of African-American Males in the College of Engineering at Virginia Tech.*

Mr. Moore is listed in *Outstanding Young Men in America* (1998 edition) and is a member of numerous professional and honor societies, including Alpha Kappa Mu, Phi Kappa Phi, Phi Delta Kappa, Kappa Delta Pi, and Chi Sigma Iota. The Delaware Association of Teachers of English recognized him for his exceptional contribution to English education with its Outstanding Achievement in English/Language Arts Award (1995). Perhaps more dear to him than any of his accolades, he was the recipient for Delaware State University's Class of 1995 Outstanding Service Award. Also, while he was at Delaware State University, James was a scholarship college football player for five years. He received many accolades and honors as a student-athlete and was team captain during his last year of eligibility (1994).

Over the years, Mr. Moore has actively presented at several state and national conferences. Many of his presentations and papers have been directly or indirectly related to black males. As a result, James has landed many speaking engagements and potential consulting opportunities related to such topics. In addition to his presentations, papers, and dissertation, Mr. Moore is currently working on several publications and projects. His research areas of interest include but are not limited to multicultural issues, counseling student-athletes, counseling adolescents, black male issues, counseling college students, counseling at-risk youth, mentoring, and community approaches to psychosocial issues.

James B. Stewart is professor of Labor Studies and Industrial Relations and African and African-American Studies at Pennsylvania State University. He formerly served as vice provost for educational equity and director of black studies and is now the senior faculty mentor, providing support to untenured faculty of color. In 1997 Dr. Stewart taught at the University of the Western Cape in South Africa. He has authored/co-authored/edited/coedited six monographs, including *Black Families: Interdisciplinary Perspectives; The Housing Status of Black Americans; Research on the African-American Family: A*

Holistic Perspective; Blacks in Rural America; W. E. B. DuBois on Race and Culture: Philosophy, Politics and Poetics; and African-Americans and Post-Industrial Labor Markets. Dr. Stewart has published over 40 journal articles and is a former editor of *The Review of Black Political Economy.* He is currently president of the National Council for Black Studies and is a past president of the National Economic Association.

Lemuel W. Watson is associate professor of Higher Education, with a B.S. in business from the University of South Carolina, an M.A. from Ball State University, and a doctorate of education from Indiana University. He is a certified training consultant and certified systems engineer. His career spans various divisions in higher education, faculty, and administration, and he has numerous experiences in all types of institutions, including two-year colleges and four-year institutions, public and private. His research agenda surrounds issues of educational outcomes and the environments that enhance or hinder; faculty development issues; social and political issues that affect schools, community, and families with regard to advancement in a capitalist society. He has recently been asked to conduct research on the South Carolina Reading Recovery program outcomes. He is also senior research fellow for the Charles Hamilton Houston Center at Clemson University. In addition, he is co-coordinator for Clemson's Ph.D. program over the web. He has written articles, chapters, and edited monographs on a variety of issues.

J. W. Wiley is the director of the Center for Diversity, Pluralism, and Inclusion at State University of New York-Plattsburgh and adjunct professor of Philosophy. He has taught at both Cerritos and Citrus colleges. Prior to that he served as assistant dean of academic affairs and director of both recruitment and the McNair Scholars Program at Claremont Graduate University.

Mr. Wiley is finishing an interfield Ph.D. in philosophy and cultural studies at Claremont Graduate University. He has a master of arts degree from Claremont Graduate School and a bachelor of arts degree from California State University, Long Beach, both in philosophy. Prior to his academic career, J. W. worked for three *Fortune 100* companies. He is a member of Alpha Phi Alpha Fraternity. He was featured in the October 28, 1999 issue of *Black Issues in Higher Education* and was a contributing author to the book, *Brothers of the Academy.*

J. W. sees tennis and exercise as both the secrets of his sanity and his fountain of youth. He believes if a good tennis workout will not get him past life's frustrations, a poem will put them in perspective. J. W.'s motto is: Perspective is the objective.

J. W. Wiley is married to Adrienne Boyd-Wiley of East Palo Alto. They have a four-year-old son named Justin Xavier Wiley and a ten-month-old daughter named Autumn Blake Wiley.